W9-CDO-836

Praise for *Money Magnet*

"Every ambitious private business owner should understand the role of investors and how to attract them. *Money Magnet* is an indispensible guide to the process."

—*Austen Beutel, Chairman and CEO,
Oakwest Corporation Ltd.*

"*Money Magnet* begins with a startling proposition: some businesses succeed more than others simply because they know how to raise money. By sharing these processes, tools and secrets, Jacoline Loewen is daring Canadian entrepreneurs to dream bigger than they've ever dreamed before."

—*Rick Spence, Entrepreneurship Columnist for
the* National Post *and* PROFIT Magazine

"Don't put another nickel into your business until you have read this book. *Money Magnet* is Financing 101 for entrepreneurs and owners who want to grow their business. How to get the money you need at the price and terms you deserve in eleven easy chapters filled with war stories from the success stories and train wrecks of financing history and those who lived them."

—*Greig Clark, Entrepreneur (College Pro Painters
and ARxx Building Products) and Venture
Capitalist (Horatio Enterprise Fund)*

"Business owners attracted to *Money Magnet* will be treated to a wise, comprehensive and readable book. Jacoline Loewen's dandy advice-filled guide shows you how to bring in the money you need to build your business."
—*Michael de Pencier, Founder and Former Publisher,* Toronto Life; *Chairman, Investeco Private Equity Fund*

"Knowing how much you need to start a business is one thing; knowing where and how to look for those funds is quite another. There are many books on 'how much' but *Money Magnet* shines in its straightforward, honest advice on 'where to find it.' It's the 'rainbow' that can lead you to your 'pot of gold.'"
—*Ken Wong, Business and Marketing Strategy, Queen's School of Business*

MONEY

MAGNET

MONEY
MAGNET

HOW TO
ATTRACT INVESTORS
TO YOUR BUSINESS

J.B. LOEWEN

WILEY

John Wiley & Sons Canada, Ltd.

Library and Archives Canada Cataloguing in Publication Data

Loewen, Jacoline, 1960–
    Money magnet : how to attract investors to your business / Jacoline Loewen.

Includes index.
ISBN 978-0-470-15575-2

    1. Small business—Canada—Finance. 2. Private equity—Canada.
I. Title.

HG4027.7.L64 2008   658.15'224   C2008-902204-1

Production Credits
Cover design: Jason Vandenberg
Interior text design: Tegan Wallace
Typesetting: Thomson Digital
Printer: Quebecor–Fairfield
All figures sourced from Jacoline Loewen, unless otherwise noted.

John Wiley & Sons Canada, Ltd.
6045 Freemont Blvd.
Mississauga, Ontario
L5R 4J3

Printed in the United States of America

1 2 3 4 5 QW 12 11 10 09 08

To my loving sons, Ross and Craig

TABLE OF CONTENTS

Acknowledgements   xi

Part I: Why Your Company Needs Private Equity   **1**
Chapter 1: What You Should Know about Attracting
                Money   3
Chapter 2: The Big Difference: Other People's Money   25
Chapter 3: Taking on a Private Equity Partner: How
                It Works   41

Part II: Building Blocks of Money Magnet   **65**
Chapter 4: The Food Chain: Match Your Business with the
                Right Investors   67
Chapter 5: What Angels and Seed Funds Need   91
Chapter 6: What You Should Know about Venture
                Capitalists   105
Chapter 7: The Valuation: Create the Framework for
                Fund Managers   127

Part III: Getting "Investor Ready"   **141**
Chapter 8: Four Brutal Questions and Why You Need to
                Answer Them   143
Chapter 9: Creating Plans That Get You Funded   163

Chapter 10: The Smart Presentation: Raising Capital
        Face to Face   189

Chapter 11: The Win/Win Deal   219

**Appendix: Selected Web Links to Government-Funded
Programs**   237

Glossary of Commonly Used Terms   243

Index   249

ACKNOWLEDGEMENTS

M*oney Magnet* is rooted in a journey through the world of private equity and the conversations with a network of top investors about which entrepreneurs succeed in raising money and why. First and foremost, thank you to all of those experts quoted throughout the book who took the time to share their philosophy on business and their best experiences as investment partners. The most rewarding part of this book is meeting the people behind the money who do deserve respect for the enormous risks they take. This book is also to help their public relations in the marketplace. Many of these experts donated their time to participate in our workshops and CEO roundtables to open up their business knowledge to business owners.

Thank you to Karen Milner for her enthusiasm and editing skills as well as the impressive team at Wiley. Since this is my third book, I often get asked about how a publishing company can assist. Many comment that surely it would be better to self publish or go with an e-book on the Internet. Simply put, Wiley is firmly rooted in the wired 21st century with a hard-working team to get *Money Magnet* out to the readership that will benefit from its contents.

How could I not thank the hard working, cheerful team at Loewen & Partners: Anastassia Kobeleva, Phil Loewen, Chuck Loewen, Theva Naidoo, Jeffrey Watson, and Jacky Xie. You all carried the ball forward when most needed.

Finally, there are a few personal acknowledgements. I would like to thank my mother, Alainnah Robertson, who always fires up my entrepreneurial spirit and encourages me.

Thank you to life-long friends Susanna Nankivell, Angela Fairbank, Amy Cross, Ingrid Mida, and Tom Deans who gave support and good cheer. Finally, thank you, John, for putting up with all the time spent on my book and to my two sons who gave their unconditional support.

PART I

WHY YOUR COMPANY NEEDS PRIVATE EQUITY

CHAPTER 1

WHAT YOU SHOULD KNOW ABOUT ATTRACTING MONEY

You see things; and you say, "Why?"
But I dream things that never were; and I say, "Why not?"

George Bernard Shaw

It's a strange phenomenon that people who have the courage to run a business often do not realize that they also have the power to attract a whole range of financial options. And I don't mean the soul-crushing bank loans from yesteryear.

If you are the owner or CEO of a business, congratulations. I am thrilled to have your attention. Using the information in this book will guide you to the money you deserve for having the gumption (some might say craziness) to take your kernel of an idea and grow it. Perhaps right now your business is a little sapling or maybe you've got yourself a fine, mature oak. However large or small the plant, wouldn't you agree that it needs a reassuringly continuous flow of water to survive? Every business, similarly, needs a continuous flow of cash to keep growing. Did you know that today attracting investors is astonishingly within reach of all but a few businesses?

My own interest in the subject of private equity came with the surprising realization that some businesses grow simply because they know

where to get money—not because they have a better strategy, more motivated staff, or leaner business processes. It comes down to knowing
how and where to get capital.

My parents did a most extraordinary thing in their mid-fifties; they
started up a business in typesetting, a field they knew nothing about.
Even more astonishing, they kept it going for fifteen years, making a
nice living. They did a lot of things well and had an ambitious vision
to deal with changing technology and where they wanted to go. They
lacked in one area, however—understanding money. They failed to
see that there were different ways to finance their enterprise and that
many investors would have given their eye teeth to partner with them.
They had the most attractive type of business too as it had expensive
machinery—a creditor's dream as these can be sold to recoup their
investment.

The bank recognized a good thing. It offered heaping helpings of
money, along with repayment schedules, but it brought almost no strategic support to the table. Despite their inexperience, my parents wanted
to take their business beyond supporting their lifestyle and they could
have if they'd had more financial muscle and insight into the boardroom.

Outsiders with Talent

With their dread of facing the money head on, my parents did not buy
the necessary equipment, make strategic acquisitions, or invest in new
product lines. Despite steady cash flows and enviable customer contracts, they did not think anyone would be interested in investing as a
partner—this was an alien concept to them. My parents did not discover
private equity and how their bigger view of trends and competition
would have helped them. They did not read or attend any conferences,
not because they did not have the time, but because they just did not
know finance was available from other groups. They thought financing
began with the bank and ended with the stock market—nothing else.
When it came to selling the business at the end of a long, emotional
road, the next owner was the one to exploit the opportunities and reap
the benefits of my parents' hard work.

After spending the past decade and a half advising smart and energetic business people on strategy, I could see that my parents' good ideas needed outside capital to make them go. Like my parents, I also thought that banks and issuing stock on the public market were the sole sources of the green stuff. I now know that this is not the case and have written this book for all business owners, whether you are early-stage, aiming achieving an initial public offering (IPO), wanting to get some cash out of the business, or looking to sell outright. What is interesting is that it does not matter if you are making $30,000 in revenue, $5M, or $50M: it's all part of the journey and when you know the steps ahead, it can make the going a little faster.

There are millions of private equity dollars out there looking for good businesses and smart owners. Even if you think your operation is not up to snuff—perhaps it's not large enough, making too little profit, or employing too few people—you may be surprised how highly others value it. I can say this because in my experience, I have often been astonished at which businesses are liked and coveted by investors—yes, even those that are not currently profitable.

McGregor Socks, a long-serving Canadian company is such a case. After struggling to adapt to the quickly changing global market, McGregor knew it needed to add China as a destination for knitting Canadian-designed creations. It was a private equity fund that put up the money since they already had experience doing business in China. Bringing in partners is a difficult transition, but with supportive investors, an excellent Canadian brand continues to fill store shelves (look for a pair of McGregor's the next time you need socks).

What Is Private Equity?

One way to describe private equity is, simply put, privately-held money invested into privately-owned companies that are not listed on the stock market. Investments could be your Uncle Jim's $1M he put into your brother's video gaming company. This is private; it is not listed on the public market where the shares can be bought and sold by anyone. This definition, however, omits the key difference that sets private equity far apart from alternate capital.

One of the leading private equity players, David Rubenstein of The Carlyle Group, gets to the nub. "Private equity is the *effort* made by individuals with a stake in a business."[1] These individuals will put capital in, try to improve the business, make it grow, and, ultimately, sell their stake.

You can split private equity further into:

- the What,
- the How, and
- the Result.

The What

Private equity is money that buys some ownership into a business and gives a longer time frame than the traditional bank loan to use the cash to grow. The most popular way to describe private equity is to list the dollar value of capital put into the business. Your stage of business development will determine how much is invested and the type of private equity investor you would approach. For example, a business requiring over 2 million dollars is usually invested in by what is called a "venture capitalist." In other words, the range of private equity investors and their size of capital investment (illustrated in Figure 1.1) is determined by the stage of maturity of your company.

Rick Nathan, of Kensington Capital and president of the Canadian Venture Capital Association (CVCA), agrees that it is difficult to settle on a definition shared by all stakeholders in the finance industry, as some think private equity is for companies making $50M and more, while others believe it begins with seed-stage financing or "angels," the name for investors putting in amounts under $1M. Nathan says, "The label of private equity can cover the full gamut—from the top end private equity buyouts through to institutional funds, venture capital, angels, and the start-up seed funds. Essentially, it's all privately-held money and this capital is invested into companies that need financing."

---

[1] Rubenstein's definition: www.bigthink.com/business-economics/6380.

Figure 1.1: Types of Private Equity Investment

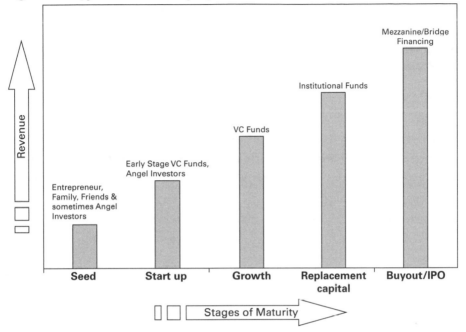

The How

Think of the private equity investor as a skilled sports coach: you are encouraged to pitch and catch at a far higher standard than achieved before but with support and help from the coach. The "how" of private equity investment is unique, for each deal has its own negotiation process to hammer out terms of the deal including board involvement and how the communication and decision process will work. Typically, but not always, a private equity investor will take an equity interest in the company. This comes with varying degrees of Board participation and decision making. The private equity investor becomes a partner and shares in the risk and reward, which keeps a high level of motivation to help the company do well.

Once the deal is signed and cheques deposited, just like the sports coach, the private equity investor will seek to improve efficiencies in the business as well as encourage, in more established companies, transformation, taking a more active, dynamic role in management. You, the founder or entrepreneur, will discover there is significant help to improve the business substantially with a strong growth, expansion, or revitalization strategy.

The End Result

Finally, the third piece of the definition of private equity is the big zinger. You get capital for a stretch of time, perhaps three to six years, which is why private equity is called "patient capital" and, thanks to your part-ners and their collaboration with your team, you can go further in the big leagues than you believed possible. The end part of the definition of private equity is that the investors are driven to improve your company because they are not merely lending cash with a fixed rate of return. They will want to sell out after five years—either back to you, your team, a larger company, or by taking the company to the public stock market. This is your decision and, in fact, the investor will want to know what you dare to dream five years from now.

For simplicity, we will place the startup stage of angel capital ($100,000 to $1M), venture capital ($1M to $10M), and private equity ($10M and up) all under the same umbrella of "private equity" and leave out "buy-out." The darlings of business journalists are these massive buyouts of Hertz from Ford, for example, which take companies off the publically held stock market and into the hands of private money. Domino's was a publicly held company sold to a private equity team led by Bain Capital for $1B, which is the size of private equity beyond the scope of this book; however, we will look at their winning ways.

Private equity investors, as you can see, also go by many titles ac-cording to the size of their investment. Instead of referring to angels, venture capitalists (also tagged VCs), and the more corporate title of institutional fund manager, for simplicity's sake, we will scoop all of these under the title of "fund manager" or "the investor," as all of these potential partners are managing funds and investing in your company. However, each of the stakeholders will be dealt with separately because, despite the search for investments being similar enough for this book, there is a world of difference between venture capital and private equity investors' *raison d'être*.

DO YOU HAVE A BUSINESS THAT APPEALS TO PRIVATE EQUITY?

1. Are you passionate about what you do?
2. Are you ambitious for your business to grow—with or without you at the helm?
3. Do you have a track record?
4. Do you do something tangible? Can your business have patents or be knowledge-based (e.g., health care, medical devices, sophisticated technology)?
5. Is it family owned, a mature business with steady clients?
6. Could your business model be expanded?

Chances are you have heard of Research in Motion (RIM), Open Text, Sleep Country mattresses, Porter Airlines, Sleeman, and Upper Canada beer. All of these companies grew with the added partnership of private equity. Then there are the hidden businesses in the economy, such as Vantrix in multimedia, BridgePort developing technology for mobile phones, Spintex manufacturing yarn, Bermingham making construction equipment or companies creating medical devices, supplying nursing homes, creating parts for the auto industry or even shredding paper—and many more.

What all of these companies will tell you is that private equity helped them. By working together, the market-savvy entrepreneur and the experienced investor can create something bigger that neither could do on their own—a growth business that explodes like dazzling fireworks, lighting up the horizons far beyond the familiar backyard.

Money for All Sizes

The first good news is that private equity is available to a broad swath of businesses, not just IPO-sized companies. Private investors will look at startups needing $500,000, mature family entities wanting $10,000M input of capital right up to $100,000M for large companies wanting capital for new projects. That's novel. What you need to know is that each level is matched by a different type of investor that you will come to recognize by the time you finish this book.

There's a growing realization that something different is happening. Entrepreneurs are the new heroes. According to Industry Canada, there are 2.3 million small and medium enterprises (SMEs) hiring 65% of working Canadians. It is time for provincial governments to bend over backwards to do more for investment in entrepreneurship, but people are certainly not sitting around waiting. Ambitious youngsters attend seminars to learn to do their own thing, without needing an uncle in the business to give them a leg up. New entrepreneurs are getting more sophisticated about operations and are learning that the old ways of getting money are no longer the only ways.

As if business owners are not busy enough, they are urged to become serious about their expertise and sign up for university courses like "entrepreneurship and making money." Business schools run jam-packed sessions on entrepreneurship with competitions for business plans—the winners receiving $40,000 in start-up capital.

These are all little smoke signals that build up to the big message: there is serious money for the owners of real businesses whether they are new startups or 100-year-old manufacturing companies.

The point: for business owners and CEOs of small- to mid-sized companies, there is a brand new buffet table with a delicious variety of ways to attract money to your business (and your retirement accounts) to pay for the lifestyle you and your spouse want to enjoy.

Private Equity Is One Arrow in Your Bow

Money comes in a huge variety of forms from low or highly leveraged bank debt to private capital to the public market. We will be dealing with private equity but recognize it is only one of a whole range of options available to you; your situation might be suited to the public market or the bank. The range can get confusing. Calm down and breathe deeply, and look at the table in Figure 1.2. It gives an important snapshot of the sources of capital.

Things are actually getting simpler. Business financing is getting more democratic. It is how money lending should be. Indeed, many

Figure 1.2: Your Finance Options

Angel Investor/Venture Capital	Private Equity
☐ Higher Risk Tolerance	☐ Patient and Long-Term Investment
☐ Higher Target Returns	☐ Allied Interest with the Growth of Your Business
☐ Active Investor	☐ Strategic Partner with Experience in Your Industry
☐ More Ownership Given Up	☐ Flexible Deal Structure (Equity or Debt)
Bank Debt	**Public Market / IPO**
☐ Lower Risk Tolerance	☐ For Later Stage Companies
☐ Lower Interest Cost	☐ Public Market Regulations Apply
☐ Collateral and Covenant Applied	☐ Higher Financing Cost
☐ Higher Leverage, Less Flexibility	☐ Higher Reputation
☐ Loan Called if in Default	

Source: Loewen & Partners

business owners can get more optimistic about their future, as *never* in the history of commerce has so much financial opportunity been made available to previously neglected stages of business.

At first blush, most entrepreneurs assume that private equity is for only the big buyouts by the large firms such as KKR's historic take over of RJR Nabisco, or from the extensive newspaper coverage of the offer for BCE shares—a 1.8 billion dollar potential deal—by Teacher's Pension Fund, Torstar, and Woodbridge. Headlines are full of private equity deals, such as Ford, Dunkin' Donuts, Domino's, Hertz, Toys-R-Us and other Fortune 500-sized businesses, which may be *a bit* above your league. It is true that the private equity source of capital has experienced unprecedented growth since 2001, but it is not only headline grabbing deals that account for it.

"These billion dollar deals are about 1% of the all private equity deals in terms of number of deals done, not by the dollar amount," says Ed Rieckleman, a former partner at Oncap, one of Canada's leading private equity firms—Jerry Schwartz's Onex. In reality, according to research by McKinsey & Company's Private Equity Canada 2006 survey, the best prospects for private equity in Canada are with thousands of small, privately-owned companies that are currently experiencing competitive and succession transitions.

Though the majority of deals are in the small- to mid-sized market, they do not make the front pages. After all, where's the glamour in a $10M revenue trucking company where the CEO makes a fair wage and the highest extravagance is buying warehouses to develop supply chain expertise?[2] But when you research what falls into the bucket of private capital, it becomes as obvious as the nose on your face that large deals make up a very small part of most of the deals available for companies like yours: that's good news for you as an entrepreneur.

Traditional Finance May Follow the Record Industry

Conventional financing—the bank at the corner of the street with their lending ratios and tables, the public stock markets with their lists of regulations and pressure for quarterly results—can be a stress on a growing business. The finance industry's days of full harvest moons the colour of honey and sweet winds carrying the smell of summer hay are drawing to a close. In the air is the first feel of winter.

Meanwhile, sources of money for smaller, riskier companies are growing rapidly as new players such as entrepreneurs who sold out at the top of the tech boom bring their money to the market place. These investors, as well as the larger institutional funds created with pools of outside investors' capital, are creating more flexible ways of rewarding those who take the risk of building companies—people like you. They are also able to take on riskier industries such as software, which the traditional banks quite rightly know would put the bank customers'

[2] McKinsey & Co, 2007 study of private equity.

money too much at risk. Indeed, banks are open to financing deals where they take a lower percentage of the risk, and syndicate a portion to private equity investors.

To give you an idea of the changes occurring, try to imagine a billion years ago, when the world's land mass was all one lump, called *Pangaea*, surrounded by the salty waves of the Panthalassen Sea. Then something happened, a trigger event, perhaps a volcano erupting, and the land began to split into awkwardly shaped lumps, forming the individual land masses of the continents we know today. How unthinkable that what seems so permanent can change into something entirely different, previously unimaginable.

Something similar has happened to the finance industry model. Its trigger event was the arrival of personal computers and the Internet. Just as technology knocked typewriters out of the ballpark as a way to get ideas into print, so it has knocked the old-style business of finance. Exactly like Pangaea's slow breakup and its transformation into a whole new world, investment money is breaking away from the mass of public capital pools and collecting into odd-sized chunks of private cash, otherwise known as private equity. These funds made up of teams of people with expertise in an industry can set up a fund and invest in businesses that would use their skill set. They can manage to do this successfully as the technology is now available to watch daily performance with access to spreadsheets and the ability to do a detailed drill-down into financial spreadsheets. This financial overview was just not available even twenty years ago. The Internet has opened up the ability to research industries, managers, and customers very, very quickly and in fact-crunching detail. As a result, the money available to invest in companies such as yours is going to be tracked, issues attacked quickly, and performance managed better with more financial rewards for everyone all round.

Frankly, it is "Quartitis" that is hurting the public markets the most. Shareholders' demands for higher results every quarter takes away the fun of growing a company as any new project will reduce the results. The uninvolved investor who demands that the company gives out money and treats the company as an ATM machine is tearing apart public money. CEOs are motivated to escape the public shareholders' attitude.

Unlike public money, which allows companies to list and then may end up ignored by investors, private equity gets involved with the business in a way the public market doesn't by taking the long-term risk to invest in non-tangibles of R&D and innovation.

You may have noticed that the music industry is crumbling, despite the frantic efforts of the big boys desperately propping up the crumbling walls. It's like the sagging Tower of Pisa, except the music business is collapsing much faster. They try anything they can think of to legislate the old business model into permanence, even to such ridiculous extremes as suing teenagers (their primary clients!) for downloading tunes illegally. Come on, record guys, use your brains. It's over.

While the traditional recording industry is one of the highest-profile casualties of the new information era, the public capital markets, the Dow Jones and all that, are also finding technology altering their game too. Technology allows music lovers to access their favourite tunes in a hundred different ways, such as downloading music from the rock groups themselves, purchasing albums directly from small labels, or buying just one hit song from Apple's iTunes. No longer do you have to buy an album full of lousy B-siders to get your one hit. In the same way, no longer is the IPO the be-all and end-all for ambitious business owners. Today, entrepreneurs can access capital for their companies from a hundred different funds.

Business owners' antiquated ways of thinking is catching up to the new geography of money as they realize companies no longer have to get listed on the stock market to gain access to money.

Challenges Facing CEOs and Owners

Before we go into detail about private capital—private equity—it is worthwhile looking a little closer at the reasons why the stock market is no longer the primary place to access money.

First of all, public companies are being legislated to the eyeballs as regulators try to smooth the turmoil from the bad apples (Enron) who spoil the whole of the stock market. Companies pick up the tab as they grapple with the costs of complying with ever-tightening rules and regulations thought up by bureaucrats and regulations such as Sarbanes-Oxley do have an impact on the Wall Street stock market. Market forces are begging for a better way of doing things because public companies are drowning in the sea of paperwork and sucking out time, money, and energy filing reports that prove they are not embezzling funds through the compensation committee or money laundering for terrorists. Board members arrive with their own lawyers and want little risk in steering the business for fear that the earnings will take a fall. Managers' time is taken away from the competitive battle. The New York Stock Exchange has lost 80% of the world market in equity offerings in four years. Stephen Schwarzman of The Blackstone Group believes that will wake up someone to make the public market more attractive. Canada (TSX) and the UK (AIM) have so far not subjected their venture capital exchanges to such a level of bureaucracy—yet.

Another knock against the current industry model is the short-term outlook of the public stock markets. CEOs are hounded to raise revenues every quarter, which is rarely good for any business's long-term value. And no one can make excuses and say, "How could we have known that this quarterly braying for rising revenues would cause the markets to not fully invest in new projects or R&D?"

The alarm bells were sounding more than a decade ago when MBA finance professors' favourite exam question was, "For 30% of your marks, show how a CEO can boost the stock in their publicly traded company." It was a clever exercise and it aptly demonstrated how a quarterly earnings focus wears a company thin. After all, there are only so many times you can water the wine. The problem is that this common question—designed to teach students how to recognize a company being asset-stripped—has now become the actual demand of shareholders playing the stock market. They have influence as shareholders are owners of the public businesses.

Who can blame the CEO either? Show beleaguered CEOs a public shareholder who is willing to wait for a long-term R&D strategy to take effect while the balance sheet flatlines, and they will gasp in disbelief.

Shareholders have proven to have the attention span of a kindergarten class with the ice-cream van driving past; they run to the next attractive deal as fast as their little legs can carry them. At Berkshire Hathaway Inc., Warren Buffett's strategy was the opposite of the rest of Wall Street—he actually invests and holds—for years. What a radical strategy. Who would have thought?

Inevitably, the costs of this alarming popularity of such short-term investment strategies, with their rigid quarterly focus, caught up with the public markets—which once enjoyed a monopoly on efficient capital.

New Ways to Add Value

Wall Street and Bay Street's purpose is raising money to throw at innovation. It does achieve this and has done a wonderful job for decades. But a rock has been thrown into the pond—the rise of private equity. Banks are no longer the guild controlling the lending business. The ripple effect is that the market has found a new way to be more efficient. Goodbye to those uninvolved shareholders whose prime question is "Is this company being run to feed me dividends today?" Now you have private equity teams, with their skills and global Rolodex, whose prime question is "How can we work with a long-term horizon? How can we collaborate with the management team and current owners to grow the business?"

The KPMG report, titled *Building Private Equity Value*, says, "In the past, Private Equity firms tended to be highly deal focused: their success depended mainly on identification and completion of transactions. Today, however, the emphasis has shifted to building value and managing performance within existing assets. The private equity firm's core objective is to add value to a deal above and beyond historical returns."[3] Who can blame companies for dumping the old for this new model?

How, you ask, does this private equity money work? What is so new? Does it cost more? How can you get some?

---

[3] KPMG in Canada, *Building Private Equity Value*, 2007, www.kpmg.ca/en/issues/durabilityPrivateEquity.html.

The Big Difference Private Equity Brings

The common attribute of leading private equity players around the world is exactly as KPMG put it; they are using their skills inside the company. The best people in private equity have been those who cashed out of their own company and have been out there toiling themselves. They can relate to you. They can walk through the soil of an unknown field and instantly know the blood and sweat involved in getting that level of sweet, moist richness. They have planted their own business seeds in the topsoil of loans and bank financing. They have lived through the seasons it takes to germinate and grow a good crop, to get past the heartbreak of hailstorms, and reap the rich harvest. They know seeds can not be expected to produce green fields the very next quarter—they do not suffer from "quarteritis." They appreciate the life flow of business. They know what it takes to bring seeds and plants to maturity. They respect what has gone into making your business.

USE PRIVATE EQUITY TO . . .

- Buy or recapitalize companies
- Inject capital for growth (minority investment)
- Give liquidity to owner
- Possibly buy out control of owner
- Make transition from your business supporting your lifestyle to the discipline of a professionally managed business
- Change or step up strategy
- Add to communication competence
- Re-energize the business and refresh the team
- Manage risks.

John Seminerio, an engineering graduate from the University of Waterloo, started up the high-tech business Abatis in Vancouver and partnered with the private equity firm Celtic House to get seed money. Abatis sold for over $2 billion and Seminerio went on to repeat his success. Now Seminerio has a hand in the venture capital funds Yaletown and Magellan Angel Partners, where he puts his remarkable leadership talent into the growth of the high-tech sector of the economy.[4] Imagine having the privilege of receiving personal attention from such a successful serial entrepreneur. So you see how private equity can do far more than lend you money. Private equity can help you grow revenues more than you could on your own or with a bank loan. The impact to your business is that private equity wants to see your business do well because they get their money back and a whole lot more. They also reap the uplift of bonus performance. They are in it for the same end-game profits as seriously as the owner.

This shift in financing attitude is not only radical, it's downright revolutionary. It's dangerous and dazzling. It's the biggest *wowza* benefit of private equity. This is the true win-win partnership.

Lender *and* Owner

You may ask why you would want private equity investors if the bank will lend money for less and your business is ticking along well enough. Why invite trouble? *I would have to give up equity in my business in the form of shares, right? Is it really worth giving up precious equity for this unknown partner?*

The simple answer is *yes*.

Like banks or public markets, most private equity money is held by professional funds, former entrepreneurs, or wealthy individuals. The difference is that these investors are looking to become directly involved in your business. Some owners find this extremely alarming. They imagine an invading army rushing into their business, boots and clattering armour echoing around their offices and plants, while employees hide behind their desks trembling and praying that these newcomers will be nice and not shoot anyone.

In reality, a CEO will enjoy running a company with capital to complete the big vision and with a smart private equity team bringing skills to the business, such as helping hire that CFO or setting up a trip to China with trusted contacts. Some private equity gets better returns by leveraging the balance sheet and other financial shenanigans. In other

---

[4] Gosia Brestovacki, Alumni Communication Officer, University of Waterloo Engineering http://newsrelease.uwaterloo.ca/news.php?id=4600 2005, December Achievements.

cases, Robert Pozen of MFS Investment Management cites McKinsey's research, which reported that the "prime driver of value creation in a majority of the private equity deals studied was company out performance rather than financial leverage."[5]

This reluctance to share ownership is the understandable instinct of a business owner. Yet the ownership does not have to be forever. You have the option of buying back your company, earning shares as the time period ticks away. Before you stop reading in frustration, do give private equity fair consideration. Get to know the players, their needs, and, most of all, their motivation. They do it because they are as passionate and crazy about business as you are.

The Benefits of Private Equity

When the announcer yelled out, "The winner of the Media category, Ernst & Young Entrepreneur of the Year—*Somerset Entertainment!*" Andy Burgess grinned and bounded up to the stage to collect the award. It all looked so easy to be standing there in a tuxedo waving the trophy, but this moment of appreciation came from painful years of slogging late into the night.

Andy Burgess is one of the owners of Somerset Entertainment, which produces and distributes specialty music to gift stores and other non-traditional retailers using interactive displays where you can push a button and listen to the CDs. They have 28,000 displays in over 18,500 locations that now include mass merchants and specialty stores.

With business and Juno awards filling their shelves, Somerset Entertainment did various acquisitions and moved from $5M in revenues to $11M, until eventually they were achieving $21M in revenues. They bought a distributor and, in 1998, levered up with four flavours of debt: term debt, debt at 17% interest, revolving credit, and a vendor takeback loan. Then the cracks began to show.

The Buffalo distribution fulfillment centre had been shipping comfortably to over one hundred different retail points when Andy asked,

---

[5] For Pozen's article, see www.hbsp.harvard.edu/hbsp/hbr/articles/article.jsp?articleID=R0711D&ml_action=get-article&print=true, page 3 of 8.

"Can you do higher volume?" Naturally, they answered, "Yes!" when in fact that was far from the truth. Somerset had been a company with $8M revenues and $2M in EBITDA (earnings before interest, tax, depreciation, and amortization—see glossary) but had grown into the supply chain approach with a distributor turning out to be slow and with the uncanny ability to mess up orders. They would say they had shipped goods—the display case with CDs—and Somerset would then invoice the retailer who, it turned out, had not received anything except a bill. It was October—prime pre-holiday selling time with the Christmas season around the corner. Not good!

American retailers are the toughest sons of guns and were furious at being bamboozled. They told Andy they did not get the goods, but then told him not to bother coming around any more—they were through. Yikes! In one fell swoop, Somerset had gone from being swift deliverers of orders to slow, unreliable duds.

"We hit $36M in sales with $8.5M EBITDA but our debt was at $15M and for the first time, we stressed about breaking covenants. We got a valuation of $15M and, with reluctance, we decided to go with a private equity investment of $21M."

In hindsight, Andy says getting private equity was good for the owners' motivation. It took the edge off the worry about money and retirement. "With private equity buying part ownership, we were allowed to take a large chunk out for ourselves straight away but still retain control. I had been working very hard and it was good to get $6M out for the founder and owners."

The money meant Somerset could pay off their debt straight away and still have $4M to make acquisitions. Andy says, "With that extra cash, we set up an office in Chicago that has turned out to be the vital springboard into the American market, taking Somerset to the next level. We've had a bad year in there, but we did not have to worry about the business blowing up. The peace of mind meant we could focus on battening down the hatches to the storm and finding a new way forward."

The private equity partners proved to be great sounding boards when Somerset was making acquisitions. The investors were more aggressive in wanting growth but respected Somerset's decision to step away from some identified targets.

"Also, when we nearly lost a key person," Andy adds, "The investors did bring him around and get him to stay."

Andy says, "When you are an entrepreneur working your butt off, it is great to get that cash pay out as well as have cash to grow the business. With private equity you get the best of both worlds—the cash liquidity without the rigorous scrutiny of the public market."

"Not every company can go public," says Andy. "Private equity will transition you." See if you can go public. Take Andy's test and put the necessary tick marks next to your chart.

- ☐ You are making enough money to pay for public listing and accounting.
- ☐ You are profitable.
- ☐ You have a strong growth curve for your revenues.
- ☐ You have a decent management team.
- ☐ You are a good size.

Andy says, "At the time of the private equity deal, we were too small to go public. With private equity investors, we got to retain control *and* we got liquidity. Private equity took us back from the brink with risky debt and looming covenants. They were the stepping stone to getting big enough until in 2005, Somerset did our initial public offering (IPO). Selling those secondary shares was sweet, too."

As Andy Burgess stood on the stage and let the applause of the audience sweep over him, it struck him how far Somerset Entertainment had come and what a ride it had been so far.

Your Competitors Will Get Private Money

Make no mistake. Watch out for your competitor. You need to keep up with the Joneses. They will also be studying private equity. They might already be meeting with potential equity partners. What would be the worst thing they could do to your business if they suddenly got a cash injection of $1M? Or, if you have revenues in the $6M range, what could the Joneses do with $5M?

A lot of damage, did you say?

What if the Joneses' new, best friend was perhaps John Seminerio (mentioned earlier), an industry expert in your field and with a bigger vision of the global market? Imagine if the Jones family now had the experienced help to manage the long supply chain from China and move most manufacturing to Mr. Private Equity's long-established contacts in Shanghai? What if, like the profitable Cineplex Galaxy, they had Jerry Schwartz, CEO of Onex, one of the leading lights in private equity, paying attention to their board meetings and opening his Rolodex?

How do you like private equity so far?

By the way, if your business can't possibly move production to China because you are in service or transportation or because your products are too heavy or bulky to be flown economically across the Pacific, equity players will really, really like you because it would be hard to have your business get clobbered by cheaper imports.

It's the Baby Boomers Again

There is a caveat to all of this. The python digesting that huge lump known as the Baby Boomers is finally getting close to the end of its meal. It is retirement time for the Boomers. And that means that they are already offloading their businesses, and it will accelerate over the next five years as they reach their golden years on the porch.

As with every market before it, the Baby Boomer life cycle will distort the private financing market. Since much money stems from business trends, these happy times for private equity will come to an end. It's as predictable as a Hollywood summer blockbuster. Just as we had tulip mania in Holland during the 17th century, or the dot.com bubble of 2000, now we have the private equity boom. In the middle of a bubble, it is hard to remember that all things eventually go "pop."

"Scaling up" means your company becomes more attractive to private equity. If you're serious about attracting equity, you need to start today. There has never been a better opportunity for business owners and CEOs to access investment money. The emerging options of finance will change within five years. Ride the tsunami wave of private investment and make sure you are not one of those business owners left far behind, gasping for help on the rocks.

Your Business is More Attractive Than You Think

Are you a business owner who wants to grow your empire but lacks the manpower, contacts, or ideas? Perhaps you are approaching retirement and making the classic mistake of thinking no one would want your business. Perhaps you plan to pass it along to the kids without realizing that there are investors eager to take it over and give the business a fresh run.

It is tougher to start with an idea and create a business around it. Geoffrey A. Moore's excellent book, *Crossing the Chasm*, brilliantly captures the difficulty of scrambling up that cliff edge and having to jump across the chasm to the other side. Harness your sheer tenacity to cross the chasm. Gird up to attract investors!

The key to attracting private equity is to match your situation to the right investor and win their approval. This book will help you do that.

Before we get to finance details of your business, we need to first understand exactly how private equity works and the reasons investors put money into some companies, but not others. You will find out why your company should choose the private equity option and how it actually works in a real life business case. You will also learn how to avoid those pirate equity types who lurk in the darker areas of the finance world, waiting to prey on founders and entrepreneurs who do not understand how private equity could hurt them.

Next, this book will introduce you to some of the characters in the business of money and teach you their special language to help you gain their support. It will also help you to spot the best investor partner. You will learn about the world of private equity through this exclusive club and meet the people—the money magicians—who can take your business and transform it from a lifestyle to a legacy.

Finally, you will discover the mechanics of the written investment proposal and learn how to prepare for and present at the investor meeting. Getting "investor ready" will teach you what to have in place to attract the investors you want. Most of all, through *Money Magnet*, you will learn how your company can crack open the private equity vault and get you the money your company deserves.

TAKE AWAYS

The traditional financing structure is changing. Banks or the public market used to be the places to get capital, but now there are alternative pools of capital held by private funds and individuals that were not available twenty years ago. This is privately-held money and seed, start-up, angel, venture capital, and institutional funds all fall under the one label—private equity.

CHAPTER 2

THE BIG DIFFERENCE: OTHER PEOPLE'S MONEY

If you want to run fast, run alone.
If you want to run far, run with a team.

African Proverb

Business is all about momentum. It was film director Woody Allen who said that a relationship is like a shark: it either moves forward or it dies. While Mr. Allen is a dubious expert on relationships, he knows how to make a point and this observation applies particularly well in business. Moving from a business model that merely supports an owner's lifestyle to a business that survives beyond the owner is difficult, but it can mean the difference between the life and death of a company. Private equity partners can be a valuable source not only of money, but of the talent that could give your business the extra propulsion needed to grow.

Other People's Money Gets You Moving

Are you clear on what you want to do? Every business, surprisingly even a failing one, has opportunities that could be seized with an infusion of other people's money (OPM). Attracting investment is rather daunting—much like your first time learning to play golf but with the top-ranked players of the club watching you. Perhaps you are feeling stuck, too. Perhaps your company is trapped in an eddy. It is time to stop hiding from the open waters and get in the flow rushing down to the ringing sea. It's time to get investors.

If you own a business you may have heard of this private equity financing idea and know it is a growing source of money for entrepreneurs in North America. Perhaps you dismiss using OPM based on the odd gruesome story loved by the media where owners start off with high hopes and are later found destitute.

"There are the popular myths," says Markus Luft, the bristling-with-energy entrepreneur-in-residence for Roynat Capital. You, the entrepreneur, have invested your life in your company and now you believe if you invite in partners they will take over power, get you to do things you wouldn't do blind drunk, and trick you into signing over your life, leaving you penniless on the street. Luft says, "There are stories of unimaginable happenings once you cash that venture capital cheque, stories of private equity investors who switch from the passionate love affair to the bossy marriage, stripping out all the good bits, greedy for your cash."

Luft looks serious, "Yes, finance has its rattlesnakes, as do all parts of life. There *are* opportunists lurking out there, profiteers who dismantle businesses and sell them off for a quick profit." These investors push in a new management team with all the morals of Vlad the Impaler. They don't care if Stan the bookkeeper has served you loyally through all the bad times. There is the dark side with the pirates of equity who replace their hearts with calculators directly connected to quarterly results. "But these private equity funds' track records will not survive today's competitive markets. Management by greed is doomed to failure because they are not powered by passion," says Luft. "Let's be clear; you do hold the power. You run the business."

Time to Take Your Business Further

There comes a time when every business has developed as far as an owner can take it. First, it is important to recognize that all companies have a life cycle. In the evolution of a business, there are recognizable stages of growth: from that one-person band, through to the group with four guitars and a set of drums, right up to the full-blown concert complete with back-up orchestra selling out Carnegie Hall. Some companies never make it past the one guy with a guitar.

Secondly, if you are serious about moving beyond the bank to acquire growth financing, you will need to change your mindset. You need to go beyond you. At the height of their popularity, The Beatles recognized that most of their music was not being heard over their fans' shrieks of delight, so they made the astonishing decision to stop touring and record mainly in a studio. Counter-intuitive and crazy! Few other performers would turn their back on such easy money. The Fab Four also made another important decision. They surrounded themselves with professional management who had similar artistic aims and complementary skills—so they would support, and indeed push, their growth. As a result of focusing on their legacy—their art—The Beatles grew far beyond a rock-and-roll touring act and their music will survive us all. If they had kept all the control over decision making to their original band, without outsider help, they would not have achieved as much notoriety or wealth.

Make no mistake: fund managers and venture capitalists seek out companies that appear to promise a good investment. They do want to fund a business where you are deeply committed and passionate. They want leaders who want to grow the business into a legacy that goes way beyond them.

Are you at that stage where you wish to let your business grow beyond you? Perhaps you are ambitious enough to want your business to grow beyond your lifetime. You know that time creeps up awfully fast. Private equity can transform your business from an asset that merely supports a lifestyle to a professional business that can afford the rigour required to make it up to the public stock market. With private equity experts, such as Markus Luft on your board, you gain his brains and experience as the business grows because he has been there himself. With private equity assisting your company, the odds of making it are increased.

Figure 2.1: Three Stages of Business

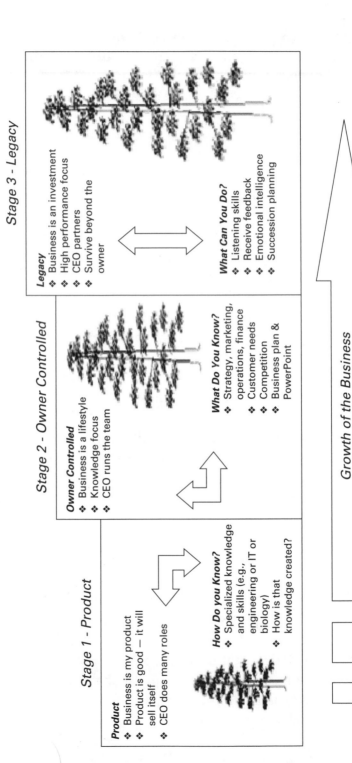

Stage 3 - Legacy

Legacy
❖ Business is an investment
❖ High performance focus
❖ CEO partners
❖ Survive beyond the owner

What Can You Do?
❖ Listening skills
❖ Receive feedback
❖ Emotional intelligence
❖ Succession planning

Stage 2 - Owner Controlled

Owner Controlled
❖ Business is a lifestyle
❖ Knowledge focus
❖ CEO runs the team

What Do You Know?
❖ Strategy, marketing, operations, finance
❖ Customer needs
❖ Competition
❖ Business plan & PowerPoint

Stage 1 - Product

Product
❖ Business is my product
❖ Product is good — it will sell itself
❖ CEO does many roles

How Do you Know?
❖ Specialized knowledge and skills (e.g., engineering or IT or biology)
❖ How is that knowledge created?

Growth of the Business

Source: Jacoline Loewen

What Will Make or Break You

It's an astounding fact that your attitude toward outside investors may be the most critical determinant to getting financing. Alan McMillan, serial entrepreneur, says, "80% of deals are turned down because of the attitude of the person making the pitch. Entrepreneurs are head strong, they don't listen, and the private equity guys don't want to work with someone who will not be a team player."

Do you believe an investor will be domineering? A Donald Trump–type telling you what to do? Perhaps you worry, *I'm not making enough money for investors*. Maybe you don't understand financial markets and have never explored the prospects beyond the bank. These are all common worries and it is your ego speaking. To be ready for investors, however, you first need to understand what it takes to put aside your ego and to share control in order to transition up the growth curve to be a Stage 3 Legacy Business. The chart in Figure 2.1 provides a visual representation of the growth required by you, the leader, to develop from a sapling to a fully grown evergreen tree, standing tall.

Stage 1: Product

In Stage 1, Product, the business is dominated by the specialized knowledge of the owner, whether he or she is an engineer, scientist, or baker. The engineer, scientist, or pie-making specialist is trained to think and speak the language of the product they love—the technology, the science, or loaves of bread. They do what they know—invent new technologies, develop new medicines, or bake award-winning French bread. Many

---

ARE YOU READY FOR INVESTORS? A QUICK SELF-TEST

- Does the business need broader skills?
- Can you share decision making?
- Can you take advice and act on it?
- Do you have a succession plan?
- Do you have a written description of how partnership would look to you?
- Have you got legal information, financials organized?

smart people stay at this level because they are fascinated—smitten, actually—with their product and, frankly, are quite good at being specialists. They believe the product is so strong it will sell itself.

These people do not get caught up in managing their business—or, all too often, even themselves. If they are fortunate, they find managers to do all of the company-building, such as administration, accounting, marketing, and watching the bottom-line figures. To assess how ready you are to move up to the next stage of business, answer these questions:

1. What's your idea of success? Are you in business to get wealthy? Many people really want a nine-to-five type of job so they can play in the jazz band on Mondays, go to their kid's soccer game, volunteer, or whatever. There's no room at the top if you are in business for lifestyle reasons.

2. Are you doing this for your ego? Most entrepreneurs start out wanting to make money *and* run the show. Research proves that if you do not decide which is more important, you will end up being neither wealthy nor controlling a strong business. Be able, when the time comes, to invite in partners and share the control to grow to the next stage.

3. Could you do better working for someone else? Engineers can create the best technology that never gets bought by a customer because it is simply too risky to award the project to a small, untested company. They would achieve more by going under the umbrella of a larger business that can protect their inventions with patents and take them to market faster through the sheer power of their brand.

4. How are you with cash flow? In your business plan (here's hoping you've got one), do you make assumptions about money coming in and flowing out. Like a renovation project for your home, think about the advice "Double the contractor's estimate of the time and the cost." That applies to business plans too.

5. Does money matter? Yes, it does. You must charge for your work, as you need to pay the bills. Otherwise, you are not an entrepreneur; you are a hobbyist. The toughest skill is to convince someone to put her hand in her pocket and hand money to you. Top entrepreneurs get clients to pay again and again for more and more.

ARE YOU READY TO MOVE TO STAGE 2?

1. Which do you want—to control your business or to get wealthy? This is the decision you need to make early on as it will influence your decisions.
2. Have you delegated your work to others or are you still writing your own marketing material, etc?
3. Do you focus on cash flow?
4. Are you charging enough for your products or services?

Stage 2: Owner-Controlled

Moving up, a Stage 2 Owner-Controlled business involves a more formal structure. Knowledge is built up around the product or service, and converted into formal strategy, policies, plans, and budgets in order for more people to create the products. Stage 2 encompasses marketing plans, accounting systems, operating processes, and so on. You can demonstrate that your management team skills go beyond the "product coolness" focus of Stage 1. The "doing more" forces your business to move beyond the one man with a hamburger joint up to a chain of branded McDonald's, or from that one bakery up to Ace Bakery supplying French loaves to grocery chains, or from a club of programmers sharing photographs with each other for kicks up to the online photograph community called Flickr (a Canadian start-up eventually bought out by Yahoo! Inc. in 2005). But even a Stage 2 Owner-Controlled business, with its systems and controls, may not yet be ready for formal investors.

Here is the crux of how to attract financing: the difference in performance between Stage 2 and Stage 3 companies is the attitude of the leader. *It all starts with you.*

Stage 3 Legacy leaders are ambitious enough to put aside their own egos in order to create a company that can succeed without them always sitting in the captain's chair. They recognize that for the company

Many businesses that make the transition from Owner Controlled to Legacy, from making a living to building a long-term, sustainable business, take on investment partners.

to grow, they must move beyond being the only star and embrace the change introduced by private equity partners.

Stage 3: Legacy

The Stage 3 Legacy Company refers to the state in which a business is best able to receive funding from private equity, including venture capital. Leaders of Stage 3 Legacy companies understand the evolution of their business. They know that in order to make the transition to Legacy status changes will be required—equity partnership being one. The owner-entrepreneur who makes the conscious decision to move from an Owner-Controlled to a Legacy business will discover private equity partners can move them to the next level of wealth.

New Rules for Your Leadership Style

Love it or hate it, contestants on *American Idol* have to endure pitiless and very public critiques of their performance by a panel of judges. The judge's role is not to coach the performers, but to decide which singers can possibly sell a massive number of records—in other words, make money. After all, judge Simon Cowell has put his *own* cash into winning performers.

Yet, invariably most singers (and much of the audience) seem confused about Simon's role, looking for slobbering approval as if he were their patient, supportive coach. Wrong. Think about the many cringe-worthy singers who angrily responded to Simon's criticism by saying, "What do you know, anyway?" (Presumably, a great deal about what it takes to get music fans to shell out twenty bucks for an album.) These sulky singers would have benefited far more by demonstrating the emotional maturity to listen and actually prompt Simon for more comments, as he is well worth hearing out—albeit ruthlessly blunt.

Take a good, long look in the mirror. Do you take feedback as a massive assault? Do you immediately launch a missile at your attackers, thinking, "This will show them?"

A private equity relationship begins with the intensity and candidness of Simon. Investors will hold you up to the cold, unforgiving light of day to judge if your business could make money in the future. As they go through the steps of deciding whether to give you their cash, they are not going to coach you on your next steps or how to improve.

When their criticisms flow, will you have what it takes to listen? Will you move on to the next round or are you one of those Idol wannabees furiously stomping off the stage, too insecure to hear the realistic comments you need, oh so badly, to hear?

"Ninety-five per cent of people are just not built the same as entrepreneurs," says Alan McMillan, serial entrepreneur. "They would get too discouraged from all the rejection to continue. But those who succeed are able to treat criticism well—almost with the dual ability of treating it as water off a duck's back while also absorbing the important points. Those emotionally developed entrepreneurs get financing. Emotional control can be learned."

Can You Attract First-Round Money?

> ### SHOULD I LOOK FOR OUTSIDE CAPITAL?
> . . . If you answer yes to one or more of these questions:
> - Do you need money to grow or for an acquisition?
> - Should you be reducing your personal risk and taking some money out of the company?
> - Could your knowledge or strategy benefit from outside expertise?
> - Do you have new ideas that will require capital to fund?

Not surprisingly, the start-up company spends a healthy proportion of its time at Stage 1, Product. But to attract the first round of money (venture capitalists or private equity fund managers), the owner needs to move at least to Stage 2. In order to move from the first stage of Product upwards, you need to face a critical dilemma. Answer honestly, as early as possible, how you define your success. Is it being king of the joint or making money? Research by Noam Wasserman shows that except for the few stars like Richard Branson and Anita Roddick, it is rare for founders to take their business to an enduring, wealth level of business. Wasserman says, "A founder who gives up more equity to attract investors builds a more valuable company than one who parts with less."[1] If you decide you

---

[1] Noam Wasserman, The Founder's Dilemma, hbr.org, February, 2008, page 105.

want to make money, you will realize that there comes a time when you cannot do it all and you need to give over equity to partners.

This first round of financing tends to focus on the business plan, the two-minute description of the business purpose (elevator pitch), and the PowerPoint presentation. The entrepreneur who is certain to get the approval, never mind the stage of development, is the one who can combine business acumen with emotional maturity that appeals to investors—and that's Level 3, Legacy. These CEOs manage all the steps in Stage 1 and Stage 2 but know that the crucial decision to invest will only be made if they can accept rejection of their ideas and business, learn from feedback, and know that getting investors is a privilege.

As you enter the negotiation process, you will be tested to see if you are able to learn (are you curious about different ways of doing business, rather than grimacing uncomfortably at suggestions, as if your mother had just asked if you've brushed your teeth and tidied your room?). From the first moment of contact, the investor is examining your response to curve balls and interrogative comments. Do you get defensive? Are you touchy about questions regarding past performance, making excuses for what happened rather than exploring the problem in depth? Do you embrace dissenting opinions? Are you a good listener? The answers to these touchy-feely questions will help the investors decide whether they would enjoy working with you over the next five years.

Reality TV, despite the criticism, does attract loyal audiences because viewers are intrigued by the raw human interaction. If *American Idol* is not your taste, then there's CBC's *Dragons' Den* where five seasoned, self-made gazillionaires listen to early stage company owners pitch for investment money. The fieriest Dragon, Kevin O'Leary, believes the attitude of the leader when getting grilled by investors is the most influential factor in attracting investment. He says, "I don't know why fortune smiles on some and sets the rest free, but maybe the answer lies in the strength an individual gets in dealing with rejection."[2]

---

[2] Kevin O'Leary, "Lessons from the Dragons' Den," *InTouch*, Richard Ivey School of Business, Winter 2007, page 60.

The New Competitive Advantage: Skills

Stage 3 Legacy companies recognize that with the availability of private equity to smaller companies, a CEO's number one skill must shift from sourcing capital to pulling together the world's best skills. Over the past twenty years, capital has been reduced to a commodity. Smart owners and CEOs recognize that competitive advantage in the future will arise from the business's ability to partner with talented people. Here's the beauty of private equity—they share the capital risk as well as bring an extraordinary range of creative contributors to learn together and risk new ideas (some whacky, some strange) to grow the business.

> Stage 3 company owners recognize this shift from capital to skills and that private equity underpins with capital and reinforces team skills.

How do you decide if you want to consider private equity? That question isn't enough by itself. It needs to be paired with a second question: How do you judge success? Do you say, "I want to partner with private equity and get a bunch of money," while rubbing your hands together and grinning like Jim Carrey? Or are you the Stage 3 CEO who says, "I want to build an enduring legacy—a business that works without me."

Face Up to Your Financial Reality

Whether you are part of a family running a business, a lone entrepreneur, or a manager in a neglected corporate division, you can benefit from additional capital and professional stewardship. If you want the business to grow or you wish to reduce your risk exposure, or both, it may be wise to diversify your assets. Private equity will allow you to take some money off the table so that your business does not represent all your net worth. Some owners do it early in the business, some close to retirement. "CEOs who sign up with private equity funds often have 99% of their net worth in their company—the equivalent of putting all your money into one stock," says Greg Milavasky of Canterbury Park Management. "The CEO who signs up with a fund now gets the benefit of taking some money out to diversify elsewhere but also benefits from the discipline that private equity brings to develop their business."

Running your own business is deeply personal, and you are not alone in being reluctant to bring in partners, because then you will have to face your financial realities. It's a scorecard that reveals your level of success and the majority of owners, whether they are pulling down a six-figure income or not, think that their scorecard should be larger, better, and more impressive.

When you need expert advice on a particular health issue, you visit the doctor. Before the examination, you may feel embarrassed to bring up your "problem." But once the doctor elicits a description of your symptoms, you usually feel relieved and much more at ease at having learned what is really going on. You may even wonder why you ever thought you couldn't face the "problem." It's much the same process with private equity.

Are you afraid of being told no, your business is not worth that much, that you are washed-up, that you can never retire, that you've wasted your life?

Big—and costly—mistakes happen if you are the sales-focused entrepreneur who ignores the company's future financial growth. Just because you cannot see the potential of your business, don't make the common mistake of thinking your business does not have enough to interest investors. If you have paying customers, trust me, there will be interest.

Make the Two Most Important Decisions

"OK," so the Stage 3 Legacy owner says, "I want to see this business expand aggressively. This is not an Owner-Controlled business. I want to see how far this business can go—maybe even to being a Fortune 500 company." This is a fundamental and deeply personal decision, to go for the Stage 3 Legacy and seek private equity partners, as each owner has a widely differing set of decision criteria and risk parameters.

It is impossible to reach Level 3, and take on private equity, without answering two questions honestly:

Decision 1: Do I need to be in personal control of the business?
Do I have personal comfort with a partnership with strong, talented people? Will I be able to let go of control? Do I have the

skills to be a team player? Does success mean leading my own team or can I step aside to share control or even move out of the CEO role?

Decision 2: What level of risk can I bear?
How much of this company do I want to personally carry? Could I do more for the business with other people's money (OPM)? How much money does the business realistically need—$500,000, $1M, $2M, $5M, $10M, $21M, or more? How much do I want my partners to help me? Would I like to reduce my risk by selling off an equity stake by 25% or maybe 75%?

Decision 1: If Personal Control Comes First

Ten years ago, a food company in the U.S.A. had aspirations to grow and build a new plant. It was getting close to signing up private equity partners, with 51% control over to private equity partners, when the CEO called Ed Rieckelman, who now heads up True North Investors, for a meeting. He said, "You know guys, I've run this business by myself for twenty years and I don't think I'm able to answer to anyone else. I don't think I would make a good partner. At first I was excited about it, but then I realized I'm too set in my ways. I think I'm going to stick with bank debt, which requires nothing of me."

This feisty entrepreneur knew that he was a Stage 2 business and content to remain as captain of his own ship. A Stage 3 owner would be ambitious enough to put aside his ego and move over to make room for other experts giving strategic opinions. This food company expert knew he had taken the business as far as he could on his own. For his business to move to the next stage of investment, he knew it would require partners, but he preferred to stay with what he knew and could control. He worried that if he opened the gate to private equity, the horse would bolt—with equity as the surprise jockey wielding the whip and charging off toward the horizon.

"We respect that owner's honesty," says Rieckelman. "Absolutely. When dealing with private equity, it is important to understand what being a partner means." Rieckelman advises owners that if personal control is very important, private equity is not for you.

The Dilemma of Leadership

The irony of owner-run companies is that their current success has often grown as a result of their autocratic leadership style. The challenge of moving to Stage 3 is adapting to a team of peers—partners—and learning together. It is not an easy evolution and there will be hurt egos—probably yours. Business founders will need to rein in and even put aside that very same dominating ego and personality that pushed, prodded, and pulled the business to its current level. Only then are they ready to invite in partners. Ironic, yes, and very hard to do.

Stage 3 company owners understand the paradox of future success: transforming from autocracy to partnership will grow the business. Yet, it can be excruciatingly difficult for owners of a business to allow in partners.

Stage 3 means working hard on integrative skills from which the foundation of a Legacy business can be built. Integrative skills such as teamwork, listening, and the ability to learn by taking feedback—without feeling threatened—are the essential skills necessary to incorporate a talented team into a common vision that builds a lasting legacy. The food company owner was fond of his Owner-Controlled lifestyle and would not be able to handle other people telling him what to do—or that was what he believed, anyway. He did not want to evolve the business beyond its current size. He was happy where he was. But he could be leaving a great deal of money on the table, as well as missing out on the opportunity to grow the business into something greater, and maybe growing as a person as well.

Decision 2: Your Level of Investment and Risk

The second question entrepreneurs or CEOs need to ask is how much risk are they willing to carry on their own. Being the sole decision-maker, with the bulk of ownership, raises the risk profile of the food company expert's business. What would happen if he got hit by the proverbial bus? With strategic private equity partners, his business would not need to die too. His family and employees might appreciate that spread of the risk!

Also, there is the stretch of growing a business. A manufacturing company's CEO was happily engrossed by his business and making a great deal of money. Inspired by a speech by Apple founder, Steve Jobs, however, his dream became to grow the company more. This CEO knew that he had the drive but worried about putting so much of his personal money at stake. He could not afford to take the risk, nor could he go to the public markets at that stage. To help his company evolve, the CEO sold 75% of the company's shares to private equity partners. They helped build up the staff, create systems, and identify acquisitions. Ironically, his 25% share ownership ended up giving him *more* financial return than if he had kept 100% to himself. How incredibly satisfying when the difficult course turns out also to be the best! Of course, if you're following Steve Jobs' advice you must know the risks to growing. One additional point—Jobs may have lost his spot at Apple for a decade but he says the company made it through that period due to the private equity financial partners in place.

Risk is relative. A medical device company wanted to launch a new product. As the owner knew it would cost $5M to bring to market, he weighed the risks. "Right now, I'm profitable. If all goes well, the product will grow my $10M company to $30M, with a cash flow of $1M. If it does not go well, I'm in the hole for $5M and it will take me five years to break even and get back to where I am now."

Pass!

But private equity partners will be lured to the possibility of growth. They catch a glimpse of the big fish in the dark water and appreciate the gleam of its scales; they will pick up the harpoon and take on the struggle, bleeding from holding the line, facing unbelievable adversity to bring home the fish others can only admire from the shoreline. That medical device company's CEO settled on admitting to the conservative nature of his personal and financial goals. "I built this business in my garage and now it has to fly without just me. Let's get in partners and share the risk." He got enough cash off the table to cover his retirement and compensate for all the hungry years, but he was still able to stay around to enjoy the new growth with the partners who brought valuable new skills—vision, contacts, and patient capital through the storm.

Decrease Ownership but Gain Growth

As a business owner, you set your risk by the amount of shares you sell to a private equity firm. It is vital to realize that you control the level of effort the fund will bring to your revenue growth.

Figure 2.2: Valuation and Future Value

	Controlled	**Shared**	**Majority**	**Sell**
Ownership	30%	50%	75%	100%
Partnership role	Likely more silent	Board skills and strategy	"Heavy lifting" and active participation	Take over and you walk away

You can sell:

- 100% or 90% and walk away from the company. By selling 90%, you can keep shares and get some upside to the new ownership.
- 75% and keep some control but benefit from the skills and Herculean effort put in by your new partners.
- 30% and take on a minority shareholder—you cannot expect these partners to be seriously hands-on for that amount.

Private equity partners will not be motivated to do a great deal of heavy lifting for just 30% of the rewards. Stage 3 owners appreciate that the more ownership is shared by the investor, the more effort they'll make to help build revenues (see Figure 2.2). This is your decision to make, not the private equity fund's. You have the control.

The level of ownership by financial partners will determine how much motivation and skills you can expect from them.

TAKE AWAYS

Gathering together skills and talent of the private equity investor is the competitive advantage. Your attitude is the top factor to attracting investors to your business. Your openness to moving over and sharing control is key for investors.

Decide if you want to control your business or get rich—research shows few founders achieve both.

CHAPTER 3

TAKING ON A PRIVATE EQUITY PARTNER: HOW IT WORKS

Decide on three things at the start: the rules of the game, the stakes, and the quitting time.

Chinese Proverb

A Case Study: Sassy Seeds

The first year a company (we will call it Sassy Seeds) had a drop in profits, Tom, the owner, blamed it on the rising Canadian dollar. An alarming plunge in the second year signalled that Tom could no longer ignore the fact that trouble was brewing. Up until this point, Tom was fierce in his leadership of Sassy Seeds. He was following in the footsteps of his grandfather who had started the business to "Keep up with the future—because business is always unpredictable."

Hadn't Tom done that? From automating the seed packaging to boldly going where no seed-grower had gone before with information technology, Tom was the leader in his industry every time. When the heady opportunities of the Internet came along, Tom uploaded Sassy Seeds' catalogue and kicked open the door to foreign markets. The first time a British online gardening club selected Sassy Seeds' *Daisy Glory* for its "best seed" prize, you'd have thought Tom's team had won the Stanley Cup. Yet, despite all this good will and a great team running production systems and marketing plans, profits were sliding at a giddy pace. One evening at his CEO Group Advisory meeting, Tom learned about "paradigm shifts" and admitted with pain that his customers no longer had the time or space to garden. China was also biting at his profits, but he was at a complete loss as to what to do, all of which stepped up his urgency to sell the business before revenues surged off the cliff faster than crazed lemmings. "This is so over," he thought with dismay, and picked up the phone to call a private equity fund that had presented at a conference he had attended.

No one was more surprised than Tom when the investor, Mr. Private Equity, arrived at his packaging plant eager to become a partner and told Tom there was no need to sell the whole thing. Little did Tom realize back then that even as he sold 75% of his stake in the company, his remaining 25% ownership would be worth more than the company's entire value before the sale. While Tom was relieved to take a large chunk of money off the table to cover his retirement, he was concerned about giving up equity and staying on as CEO—how would it work with Mr. Private Equity as his new partner? Would it turn out to be a partnership like *The X-Files'* Scully and Mulder—taking on the dark competitive forces together—or more of a master-servant relationship, with the investor as Lone Ranger and Tom as Tonto, or would he be fired? What would Mr. Private Equity do? It would be untrue to say it was easy: the first year was a real test for Tom.

First, there were production issues—housekeeping changes that Tom kicked himself for not addressing earlier. But what got Tom, more than the plant visits with Mr. Private Equity's incessant note-taking and thirst for details, was his use of jargon. "We need to focus on the few key measures—our operational dashboard—that can be understood by all." It took a while, but Tom reluctantly began keeping track of numbers and grudgingly admitted that this information helped nudge his team when Sassy Seeds headed off track.

As Tom found his team needing him less and defining for themselves the activities that drove revenues and costs, he saw that what gets measured, gets done. Getting the metrics right meant bored sales representatives had their uncoordinated methods replaced. Customer service representatives and individual account managers now set priorities by determining the numbers of calls to achieve and who were valuable customers. An incentive—sales targeted compensation—rewarded the stars who previously felt ignored and gave them an extra hearty push. Revenues began to creep upwards.

Fast-forward ten months and Tom had to admit that the monthly board meetings with Mr. Private Equity and two fund managers rubbed him the wrong way with their insistent pressure to bring a discipline to the business it had never seen before. It did irk him when his management team mentioned how much they *liked* the changes. Now, the focus was absolutely on growing the revenues. Tom knew he had missed the forest for the trees, and he was miffed that it took these new partners to see that the rise in production costs pointed at bringing China into their packaging process. It was the new systems introduced by Mr. Private Equity (which he had resisted) that had highlighted the cost troubles too.

Some investors want to help you grow the business at a higher clip than 20% a year, while some want 25%, and higher. Before you gasp in horror, keep in mind that private equity investors can help you achieve this growth rate. Not all investors have experience in your industry, but if they like your business, they will apply templates and solutions that have worked for them previously and bring success to your company too. They can bring in an experienced CFO and take you to new markets. Along the way they'll cajole you to overcome your fear of success (or failure, or whatever it is), pierce through the barriers that have held you back, and ensure you get the right work done.

With Mr. Private Equity's encouragement and his newly appointed CFO's ability to build forward-looking financial models, the team analyzed the business for the first time, seeing what brought in the cash, and where it got spent. Together, they cooked up a strategy at a sophisticated level that Tom had never thought possible before. Prior to Mr. Private Equity's new style of governance, Tom wrote out the year's goals in his office and chatted to his senior team about them over a game of golf. He did not believe everyone needed to know the direction in which the business was headed (he was afraid it would scare them). Now there was Dave, the operations manager, happily coming up with suggestions for ways to expand business.

The new COO, brought in by Mr. Private Equity's blue chip executive search agency, applied his top-notch experience running businesses in other countries. Mr. Private Equity said to Tom, "Private equity is especially good at accessing a substantial network of professionals and business individuals, who can be made available to provide help to Sassy Seeds."

The injection of new talent boosted spirits and changed Sassy Seeds' strategy ninety degrees. Instead of growing seeds, they now sourced specimens from Mr. Private Equity's global network, in their case, suppliers in both China and South America, packaging them under the Sassy brand—which gave the team more time to boost sales and expand the range of package designs. Each manager had clear goals to bring Sassy Seeds closer to the five-year vision of growth that Tom knew should have been spelled out years ago but somehow never got done. Now, do understand that Mr. Private Equity is not a divine being. The process itself was what pushed Tom and his team to focus on the activities that would have the most impact.

Then it happened. At a board of directors meeting, Mr. Private Equity started by saying, "Sassy Seeds has a serious problem with its traditional line of business." Tom took a sudden interest, but Mr. Private Equity was not finished. "We have an idea for the whole team. Are you game?"

Tom knew it was time to say what had worried him for so long. "Aren't we whistling past the graveyard? Isn't Sassy Seeds in a declining industry?"

Mr. Private Equity looked at Tom. "I'm glad you are so honest. But Sassy Seeds is a great brand name that can be used with different products."

"But what about cash flow? How can we afford to fund new projects?"

Mr. Private Equity leaned back and laughed, "Tom, you forget that we are not a bank. We don't provide capital based on past revenue, but on future potential possibilities. Your traditional business needed to change its product offering, but the brand name is strong enough to support a transition to new products. This is just a sudden bump in the road and I've been through worse, my friend. We have a five-year game plan that gives us the space to shut off the old way and go in a completely new direction."

For the first time, Tom understood the description "patient capital." The relief that flooded through him made him feel like hitting a home run. He had been irritated with the time and energy it took to develop a detailed five-year plan with future earnings defined right down to how much to spend on marketing brochures. Of course, he had been aware the private equity fund valued his business and paid him equity based not on the past earnings but on what they could see Sassy Seeds earning in the future. The financial future goal was established, but markets were changing faster than anticipated. There were still four years to make the plan, and it was becoming apparent to Tom that his ideas were not the only way. Now he peered at the five-year goals with serious intent and listened as Mr. Private Equity read aloud the top line—acquisition of a supplier in the industry.

Tom said, "Never thought I would be buying a business, but OK."

Lunch was set up for Tom to meet Sarah, CEO of Lots of Pots, a garden container business that the private equity fund team had targeted as a good acquisition. At first, Tom was skeptical (to put it mildly). But despite his fears, the two got along like two peas in a pod. Over lunch, Mr. Private Equity shared what he had in mind: Sassy Seeds would supply seeds for Lots of Pots to place in their containers. Since Sassy Seeds' brand was stronger, the arrangements would have tags splashed with "Sassy Seed—Garden in a Container." Lots of Pots brought to the party strong marketing relationships with new clients—all the major retailers. Plus, they knew well how to get small pallets of products delivered to many locations across the country.

Mr. Private Equity's lawyer—another professional whom Tom would never have afforded—saw the deal through to signing. That summer, both Tom and Sarah were astonished as their instant flowerpots for patios, front doors, and apartment balconies sold. Tom's buddies at the golf club ribbed him about all the positive newspaper articles featuring photos of a beaming Tom holding a Sassy Seeds balcony pot of flowers and the glowing descriptions of his company's radical make-over—all arranged by Mr. Private Equity.

Ironically, Sassy was now selling seeds at about ten times the old price because they had been artfully combined in a range of pots. With Mr. Private Equity's centralized buying and engineering expertise brought in, margins were greatly improved. As a bonus, Sarah had earned her stripes, so Tom agreed to Mr. Private Equity's suggestion that she should take over as CEO as part of the new Succession Plan to buy out Tom's remaining 25% ownership when he retired in three years. Tom was over the moon.

Sipping chardonnay on the patio with his wife, Tom said, "It got my goat that someone else could grow my business and manage the people. But from now on, Mr. Private Equity has my vote." Tom knew the mentorship of the private equity team was far from the mechanistic, "ignore all humans" economic model of the character from Wall Street—the Gordon Gekko stereotype beloved by Hollywood. With Mr. Private Equity, Tom was confident that Sassy Seeds would survive his departure—and continue to thrive.

Sassy Seeds is a combination of several companies' true stories and illustrates the method used by KKR and Bain, which has raised the bar in how to invest capital. It is the best-case scenario that other private investors are trying to follow with varied results. Figure 3.1 summarizes how private equity *could* add value to your business, similar to that explained in the Sassy Seeds example and other cases to follow. Do keep in mind that you will not get all the value-added features listed in the chart. You may not get even a few. Understand that this is the top standard. As you pick your partners, keep "The Private Equity Value-Add" list handy and question your investor about what they would do for you.

Figure 3.1: The Private Equity Value-Add

THE SKILLS

- ◆ **Network**
- ◇ Network of contacts (suppliers, customers, etc.)
- ◇ Expanding markets beyond familiar geographical borders
- ◇ Network of talent to boost management

- ◆ **Operations**
- ◇ Mentorship
- ◇ Knowledge about operational processes and managing supply chains
- ◇ Creating new ways of producing goods

- ◆ **Cost Savings and Support**
- ◇ Access to top professional services— patent lawyer, accountant, etc.
- ◇ Buying centre for shared costs across all portfolio companies

- ◆ **Strategy**
- ◇ Acquisition support
- ◇ Inject high-level CFO skills
- ◇ Growth to the partnership
- ◇ Discipline of board meetings and strategy
- ◇ Clear goals and milestones for five-year vision

THE MONEY

- ◇ Obviously, your company gets a large chunk of capital
- ◇ Patient capital
- ◇ Five-year vision for projects— revenue streams analysis
- ◇ Cut costs and expand where returns are higher
- ◇ Useful capital creation skills
- ◇ Assistance with possible acquisitions
- ◇ Timing to exit
- ◇ Increased valuations of business

Use the list as a conversation starter to map out how you would work together and get expectations aligned.

Are You Ready for Private Equity?

If you are starting up or running a long-standing family business, the first thing to do is set up a tough, challenging advisory board. Talk to them about what investors want. Each investor is part of a fund with its own expertise, dynamics, philosophies, and workload that makes getting ready to find an investor a challenge. Curve balls will be thrown.

You are ready if you can talk about why you and your team are the right people, how exactly your company is doing well with a clear path forward, how your technology has a strong niche but there are barriers to entry. Can you get across the complexity of the industry but also the upside and opportunities? You need to know the value of your business and price the deal well. Above all, circling back to the beginning point, *it is all about you and your team.* Investors put money into people, not technology or products, because it is the people who create wealth. Later in the book, we will build your pitch to investors (which is where most finance textbooks begin), but as Adam Smith explained in his book *The Wealth of Nations*, it is the *emotions* of human beings that drive commerce and outcomes. Your emotions will determine your investment success, which is why it is probably more valuable spending your time understanding the investor's attitudes than writing a business plan. Before you even start your presentation, the investor will have decided if they like you enough to consider giving you money. Much of getting people to like you is having empathy for their needs.

Partnership of Money and Skills

Business owners need to know themselves personally—their strengths, their weaknesses, their objectives—but many do not step out of the box and analyze their financial risk. Are they locking up their wealth in a non-liquid form (i.e., the business) to maintain their lifestyle? Are they avoiding the transition of their business into a professional operation? Are they missing the opportunity to grow the brand internationally? Most importantly, would their families benefit from spreading the risk among partners?

Challenging You

As you contemplate whether to grow your business, you may feel uncomfortable, perhaps offended by the thought of the intrusion of investors. Is it possible that you are sensing that you are out of your league and fear the challenge? If so, the research shows you are not alone. Private equity investors may be younger than you or their career track may have given them a great deal more exposure to the big business world than you. They also have made more money. Perhaps they have run their own business and sold it, and now want to invest their money; some are professional money managers with strategic know-how. This can all be intimidating stuff for entrepreneurs content in their domain.

Here's what you need to understand. These equity investors often have the wisdom to ask you all those sacred-cow questions that your staff may not have the courage to ask. This forthrightness will certainly annoy some owners. However, if you dig down deep you will realize that anger is the cover for a deeper emotion—fear of being revealed to be out of your depth. Testing your business skills against those of an investor may seem frightening because it means you will be judged— possibly criticized. It means things will likely change and the business may no longer be under your control.

The Company You Keep

A young student once asked investment guru Warren Buffett, "How do you build a great business?" Buffett answered, "Surround yourself with great people."

You can profit from Buffett's insight by seeking out exposure to the guys in private equity. You will be surrounded by a new, infectious level of ambition. Warren Buffett would tell you that there is nothing wrong with feeling intimidated. Being prodded to look at your business in ways you have resisted before is a good thing. These experienced investors have exactly the skills needed to help you take your company to another level. They will be the catalysts that can turn you from business success to superhero, pushing you to use what Spiderman calls your "Spidey senses" in ways you never knew were possible. Private equity partnerships build more value by sharing resources: expertise, networks of contacts, processes and supply chains, setting milestones, expanding markets beyond familiar geographical borders, and creating new ways of producing goods. Owners, quite understandably, often have trouble seeing beyond their own horizon or goals, believing their own expertise and networks to be the highest level that can reasonably be achieved. They may not recognize that private equity, at heart, respects the spirit of the entrepreneur—they want to work with you, not dominate.

Stage 3 Legacy business owners understand how partnership with a private equity partner looks. They get that this new combination of resources, experience, and skills will produce an exceptional competitive advantage, eclipsing plain bank debt, possibly on a global scale. They get that if they "hang out" with energetic, passionate private equity investors, they will become energized.

How about you? Do you hang out with people who don't threaten or motivate you and then wonder why you can't break out of your current level? Can you imagine working with people who scare you?

The Right Partner Adds Vision

Private equity is about the outsider who can see the situation with greater clarity. Ever notice that the best movies portraying a country's culture are often made by directors who are outsiders? The award winning *American Beauty* was produced by Sam Mendes, a Brit. *Room with a View,* the popular British historic drama, was by Ismail Merchant, an Indian. It's much the same with the investor partner who recognizes the market power of a company's brand name and creates a new alliance.

A big reason for ignorance about private equity investors is that they are lumped in with the traditional banks. Bankers are fond of talking about relationships with their clients but, in fact, it's more like a parent, with *you* as their teenager who's avoiding giving any information whatsoever.

In sharp contrast to traditional bank financing, private equity is neither a master-servant relationship nor an employer-employee dynamic. It is a partnership focused on increasing the value of the business. Together, both take the risk to commit entrepreneurial energy over the next five years. Both could win big or lose it all, unlike banks, which can claw back assets (buildings, equipment) and within months receive a reassuring trickle of monthly payments.

What Investors Want

Private equity partners want to know that you have done your homework to understand why their type of financing is going to help you grow; in other words, why they are different. They want you to respect them and be able to articulate why they have a different status from other people who bring you money.

Private equity investors want your business in four, five, or ten years from now to be worth a great deal more. The only reason your company will be worth a whole lot more is because investors bring in additional talent and energy. Pete Peterson, Chairman of The Blackstone Group, says, "If you look at the typical private equity investment we make . . . the vast majority of the time we invest much more in the future, in development, in research; because what we're interested in is doing those things that are going to make the companies five years from now go faster so they'll be worth more than what we paid for them."[1]

This shake-up will be a challenge for you, but if you understand the following key issues for private equity investors, you will find the road smoother.

A Motivated Board

The investor will want a board with strong reporting capabilities that are likely absent in your business currently. This brings increased process to your workplace. As an entrepreneur, you chose how much information you give. The board is not your team captain, but your coach. Board members are not in a competition to be smarter than you, and once you come to terms with that and their requirement to prepare regular reports, you will realize you are still the glue that makes the board a team.

"Some companies worry about having a fund manager take a seat on their board and interfere in the business," says Bob Roy, the gentle-bear leader of Roynat Capital. "What CEOs may not realize is that most funds do not wish to get in the kitchen and will focus their help at a strategic level." Bob adds, "Owners quickly come to appreciate how the mere presence of the private equity partners on their board brings enhanced prestige and credibility to a business."[2]

---

[1] Recorded on: 7/26/07 at www.bigthink.com/business-economics/343.

[2] Diamonds in the Rough conference, Exit Strategies for Business Owners, Toronto, February, 2005.

> Stage 3 Legacy companies agree that a private equity partner on their board brings professional rigour and discipline to create a vision and ensure the strategy gets done. Legacy companies recognize that they may not set the same standards or bring the same discipline as will be required when partnering with private equity.

Part of strategy is to grow and get access to capital. If an analyst looked at your finances, she wants to see debt. If the balance sheet is not geared (loaded up) with debt, the business risks being static. That is the trick of cash—use it or lose it. If you want to acquire other companies, you must like debt. If you tell an investor, "I'm ungeared—little debt," it shows a lazy approach to business.

As the company develops, there will eventually come a time to adopt the discipline of debt repayments, which has the magical effect of making management of the large private equity partnerships focus on cash flow. The team will be focused as never before on quarterly payments, which gets a company doing the things it needs to do to bring in paying customers.

Recognition of Their Skills

Many private equity investors were entrepreneurs themselves, running Stage 2 businesses, who managed to take them to Stage 3 Legacy and sell out. Their investment in your company and the partnership with you brings those valuable lessons in growing a company to your business.

> The expectations of private equity are that you will see the relationship as a partnership. They recognize that you are used to making the decisions and that you have grown the business to the current level and know what you are doing. Equally, they expect you to respect that they have extensive experience too, albeit in a different area—finance—and that you will respect their decisions too.

Savvy investors have a lot of experience looking at a variety of businesses, being in contact with individuals in those businesses, and studying their operational strategies and management techniques.

Having their perspective in your company will help develop a wider-angle view about your business that may not have been obvious to you. It is why they can add strategy, recruit talent, and find strategic partnerships.

"Private equity touches everything in a business once you get past signing the deal," says the enthusiastic Greg Milavasky of Canterbury Park Management.[3] "Marketing, operations, sales, managing the work force are all part of the ongoing relationship." It is why top private equity investors such as Jerry Schwartz, who runs Onex, are called the Renaissance people of business—because the best funds bring a great deal of expertise and industry knowledge to the business. Good funds must have much more than pure finance skills.

Recognition That Their Risk Is as Big as Yours

Private equity investors want you to recognize that they are taking a high measure of risk with you. According to Milavsky, "This is not some huge bank's money where I can write off a bad investment and go home for the weekend unscathed. It's my own money down the drain." *Ouch!*

The private equity universe comprises large firms that dominate in the media, but it is the thousands of small firms that account for the majority of private equity. Each of these brave companies take on risk and the smart business owner realizes that this means they are asking investors to place their bets on his horse, his business, his word. Private equity investors often borrow money to put into companies they believe have the potential to grow with the added capital, a more savvy strategy, and a boost in skills. This makes investing stressful and brings the decision-making razor blade close to the investor's jugular. If they see a CEO who has not taken the time to prepare well, who has not risked much of his own money in his business, and who has the cheek not to do research on who he is meeting with, why should they hand over cash? Would you?

---

[3] Interview, Greg Milavasky, Canterbury Park Management, Toronto, December 4, 2007.

The risk is substantial for the private equity partnership, and investing in companies is not seen as the opportunity to simply sit back and pull money from an ATM machine. After all their invested time and capital, there is the cold possibility that the private equity group may not make any return, despite taking the same entrepreneurial risk as the company.

They Could Lose It All with You

"Private equity is the nose of the hound dog," says Jeremy Rifkin, futurist and author of *The End of Work*. Rifkin believes there is a third industrial revolution building with the support of this new economic framework. "Private equity is on the vanguard of the revolution. They are there because they can take the risk."[4]

Exactly! The bottom line is that private equity is amazing with the risks it takes and how it gets behind a business owner. After all, private equity puts in a huge dollop of capital and unlike the bank, does not get it back in the form of monthly interest payments within a month or so. They will put their time and energy into building the growth of the business, another activity you will not see your local bank manager doing. This is a serious amount of money and effort invested upfront before getting back their investment or a cent of interest repayment.

You see, private equity sounds awfully glamorous and wealth generating, but in reality, for every successful private equity investment cruising the highway in triumph, there are many driven off the side of the road, burning horribly in the ditch. No wonder they need to see the facts, ma'am, just the facts—the financial story.

Figure 3.2 contains a list of questions investors will want you to disclose quickly when they first hear from you. They will probably want these answered over the phone, before they meet with you. Be ready to lay out this information when asked, "Tell us about yourself." They don't mean where you were born or went to high school. In fact, the investor is asking you to present your business because it illustrates how you sell to your customers. Be factual, honest, and powerful in your knowledge.

---

[4] Jeff Sanford, "Private Equity," Canadian Business Online, March 23, 2007.

Figure 3.2: First Checklist Used by Investors

Your Industry. Is it medical, construction, etc.? Funds are narrow in their industry focus.	**Current Ownership.** Who's got shares? Who do you know and how messy is the ownership? Have you shared equity before?
Market Conditions. The funds can see your problems as their opportunity, e.g., to open new factories outside of Canada.	**Financing Preference.** What is your level of sophistication? What types of debt or equity have you already got? How far from falling off the cliff are you?
List of Products or Services. How deep and wide is your business or are you still with the one software application? Positions you as a start-up or company requiring growth capital.	**Capital Requirements.** How much money needed $_____? Make it higher than you think. As they look at your company, you may start out asking for $10M and end up with $20M.
Number of Employees. Can assess your management depth by number of people you manage and pay.	**Usage of Proceeds.** What will you do with that money? Do you see opportunities such as new markets?
Target Customers. Funds know customer groups in their current fund. Could these apply to you?	**Current Sales Volume $_____.** Give a ballpark and share, as professionals are not shy about their level of revenues.
Your Competition. Who do you know in your industry? How good is your radar?	**Current EBITDA $_____.** This is the true profitability and is the most common measurement.
Competitive Advantages. What do you do well? Can you be copied?	**Current Profit Margin $_____.** Show that you think about this — many don't!
Growth Potential. Do you have big dreams but not the cash to try them?	**Financial Projections $_____.** Show you think ahead and want to grow.
Management Team. What is the depth of team experience? Will the fund have to hire?	**Any Lawsuits Pending.** You can get money even with a lawsuit underway.
Google Search is Clean. No breaking kneecaps of old partners.	**Past Problems.** Shows your ability to face issues honestly.

Source: Loewen & Partners

Financing Mistakes Made by Rookies

Attracting investors is a financial game, but make no mistake, it is also a marketing game. As quickly as investors see you, they will show you the door if you exhibit the typical rookie errors that reveal that you would not make a desirable business partner. In order to market your business well to the private equity investor, you need to avoid the major pitfalls described below.

Assuming You Are Losing Control

"Even with a minority position, you still have control," says Eric Berke, Torquest Partners. "As the CEO, you are the one making the operating decisions and having the ultimate say over strategy."[5] Berke says that when the Torquest private equity investors pushed for Granby Steel Tanks, a company making storage tanks for fuel, to increase their price, the final decision rested with the CEO; he was encouraged to make the choice. Once implemented, customers paid the new rates as they recognized there had not been an increase in decades.

Mistaking Private Equity for the Bank

Each private equity investor takes on the real risk of working side by side with your company for the next five to seven years. They are not collecting a comfortable banker's salary while they wait for you to return their investment. Thomson Financial cites the average holding period of a company investment to be six years. How's that for harsh? It's certainly not for the fainthearted. Why not park that money in real estate instead? Frankly, it's because the best private equity investor lives and breathes business. They are not there for the greed but for the sheer ride.

Not Recognizing It's a Negotiation

Some CEOs make all the usual mistakes of entrepreneurs in love with their business, which is a good thing, but do not realize that when you

---

[5] Eric Berke, Torquest Partners, Canadian Innovators Forum, CEO Retreat, Toronto, March 2006.

are called in for a face-to-face meeting you are now in a negotiation situation, not a sales pitch. If the investor has granted you a meeting, they are interested in buying a share of your business. Do not go into detail about your product. No! You are selling shares in your company and the investors are interested in your company's financial potential, not the details of your products. You are not there to get feedback on your marketing plan; you are there to gain partners.

Not Being a Competent CEO

If you drone on about the product, you show yourself as less than ideal CEO material. The investors want to see a leader who can execute. CEOs need to show they think big and that the business could grow well, even if competitors with deeper pockets tried to copy the products, instilling confidence that others would be unable to wrestle away client contracts. Remember this before you even begin to chat with investors: They *already* assume your product is the better mouse-trap. Now they want to know how you are going to get people to buy it and how much money you could make. History books are littered with tales of smarter products that did not capture the attention of customers and entrepreneurs who did not manage their cash flow and failed.

Even if you are at start-up stage, move from being a marketing guy or a product developer to a CEO. Product guys do not get out enough to the financial community. When they do, too often they stay stuck to their skill topic rather than speaking like a CEO and talking financial projections, cash flow, or balance sheets. Product-focused leaders think numbers are for accountants, but mature leaders can run through the business future cash needs in their sleep. You would be surprised at how many leaders of companies have no idea what drives growth in their businesses or what is eating up the cash. What is your Cost of Goods Sold (COGS)? What are your earnings before interest, taxes, depreciation, and amortization (EBITDA)? What key ratios do you track? (If you do not, start now.) Investors want you to know how many more salespeople you will need if you increase revenues by X% and what their salaries will deduct from the bottom line.

Not Gathering a Team

Investors are betting on the people who are actually involved. You don't need to have big names working in the business nor does your team need to be 100% working in your business. You do need to have names and profiles of solid people willing to be written into your plan and ready at the drop of a hat to support your plan in person when asked.

Not Talking about Return on Investment

"It's not about the money but it's about the money" is a common phrase that seems to make no sense whatsoever. It means that finance people invest in the people—you—but if you do not know your Return on Investment (ROI) then you are not a good investment. Simple as that. Your lack of financial knowledge shows your management skills are lacking. You are probably a techie person who has not taken the trouble to learn that tracking a few financial ratios is not that difficult. Simultaneously, as the investor sees if the size of investment fits his own Internal Rate of Return (IRR) goals, he will take that into account far more than the pure financial valuation. He will consider the possibilities for the next five years. How much could the business grow? And this is determined more by the industry size than your past performance.

The investor's IRR is the rate of growth a project (in this case, investment in your business) is expected to generate. The higher this number is, the more interested an investor will be to invest in your company. This number will also give the investor an indication of how many years it will take to get his principal back. Weighing up all of this, the investor now looks at the market. He asks himself, what is the value of my money now? I want an IRR of 25% to 30%. Why should I take the risk with this company when I can get an income fund for 10%? If the lower risk is 10% to 12% return, then I want 30% on my money because I am not getting any security on equipment to sell if things go south.

The absolute keystone is the additional money to be made beyond the initial investment. What future revenues and rate of return can the investors expect? In a nutshell, the people holding the cash want to know "How much money will I make?" and "What is my risk?" They will want to know the yield. It is much like a mortgage, which returns 5% a year.

Assuming Valuation of the Business Is Just the Money

As one investor said, "More so than a bank, private equity will recognize a strong CEO and team. If I believe in the leader, but the business is struggling or even failing, I will invest and give that business a new life with my time, effort, and vision." The value of the business is based on the *potential* future earnings, not on the present situation.

Not Being Clear about What You Want from Private Equity

"A huge destroyer of value in a business is if you are not clear about the role private equity will play," says Peter Carrescia of VenGrowth Capital Management Inc. "I have the most important piece of advice for owners looking for capital—you really want it? Be clear and understand that if you are not clear, then it is inevitable that infighting breaks out between investors and the company team."[6]

Imagine if you can (and you probably don't want to) the day you get a cheque for your business. That's right, a cheque signed by someone interested in your business. Perhaps you imagine it's a 10% or 75% partnership. Whatever. Pick a figure. It's money for your business. How much do you want to see?

On your desk, next to the money, your business plan lies gleaming. Inside is the outline of the remarkable growth of a well-planned and executed strategy. In fact, it tells the tale of a business started from

---

[6] Peter Carrescia of VenGrowth Capital Management Inc., ACG Conference, Toronto, November 2006.

Figure 3.3: Your Exit Strategy
Write down the amount you would like for your company.

I would like to get $ _____ for shares in my business.
I could give _____% ownership to a private equity investor.
I want to achieve this by_____(write down a year).

the kernel of an idea with a few people that has grown (with pain and horrors) to a full oak. Excellent! Now imagine the last day in your business. Write down the year. Don't panic. No one is going to hold a gun to your head and force you to sell. Whatever you do is not the point. With that final day in mind, and the final money value in dollars clearly set, you are ready to get the financing your business deserves. It's that simple.

Close your office door, get out a pen and paper and write down the exact date and strategy of your exit (see Figure 3.3); it may be five years or ten, and state if you would be selling to a competitor or having your daughter take over. The specific details and timing are not important—it is the psychological power of having a date and a rough plan that will wake you up to the fact that one day you need to exit your business. A written plan and potential exit date will assist your management team and advisors in a course of action.

What to Do If You Hit a Brick Wall

Resilience and dogged belief will be required through the dark hours when a Level 3 Legacy company confronts the reality that their business, in its current form, may not be suitable for private equity. They seek to understand how to build the features they need into their business. The finance community is small and you rarely get more than one bite at the apple. What this means is that there are loads of money out there to invest in you at the drop of a hat. The bad news is that money can drain away just as quickly as the tide pulls back into the ocean.

Randy Pausch, a Carnegie Mellon University professor who created the Alice program, which allows anyone to create onscreen animation characters, was given a shocking diagnosis of cancer with a few months to live. When he gave his poignant last lecture,[7] he chose to talk about attitude. "I believe that when you are told no, when you hit a brick wall, that it's put there to help you decide what you really want." If you really want the financing, find out how to get around that brick wall and try new ways. Do not see it as a final no, but as a temporary block in your journey.

> Taking a company from Stage 2 Owner-Controlled to Stage 3 Legacy is a challenge to everything you do today. As you begin to meet private equity investors, pursue their opinions of your business and what would make it a better investment.

When you hit a brick wall with a private equity fund, ask (nicely) why they do not see an investment opportunity. You may be surprised. Perhaps you have put too much cash into a building rather than growing the company. That conservative approach to looking after the value of your business may signal that you are comfortable at a Stage 2 Lifestyle business and do not have the guts to take the risks the private equity guys require.

A day care business, Kids + Company, had seven centres and a long track record of steady revenues, but the CEO, Victoria Sopik, thought they were too mundane a service company for private equity investors. However, despite spending more than their revenues they attracted private equity by developing a five-year plan to roll out a national day care chain and put in place a committed team.

Accept That It's Oil and Water

Level 3 Legacy companies know that the first step in putting together a private equity relationship is understanding how different their view will be in comparison to the investor. When dealing with private equity, the owner must realize that investors are very different, which makes

---

[7] Randy Pausch Last Lecture at www.youtube.com/watch?v=4HqdnjgkExY.

the relationship challenging. This creative tension does bring more to the business than the entrepreneur smoothly sailing on her own.

Gaining the investor's attention requires an understanding of the differences in order for the entrepreneurs to build the relationship.

- Ditch the sales pitch and lead with the financial story.
- Think Return on Investment (ROI).
- Respect the risk taken by private equity—and if you are not investing in your own business, why should they?
- Listen and take feedback as this will be the most useful and honest analysis about the long-term viability of the company.

TAKE AWAYS

Entrepreneurs, business owners, and CEOs of companies will discover they are very different from investors.

Do not mistake cool financial acumen of the fund managers for coldness towards the business opportunity. Rather, ask about their perception of your business as a long-term, exciting investment opportunity.

There are many myths and fears holding back entrepreneurs from exploring private equity.

Smart entrepreneurs know that the full value of other people's money to grow their companies goes beyond cash. Stage 3 Legacy business owners recognize that private equity brings not only expertise but mentorship, exposure to a new universe of contacts, and patient capital that can wait for its reward.

Summary Points: Achieving Mutual Understanding

1. Private equity investors will make an investment decision based on facts about the finances of the business as their job is to generate investment return from the assets they manage. Level 3

companies understand the strength that private equity brings to their partnership is superior financial ability. Level 3 companies know why it is imperative that private equity's focus be on the financial disclosure.

2. Level 3 Legacy companies recognize that private equity investors use their own money, as well as borrowed money, to invest into companies they believe have the potential to grow with the added capital, a more savvy strategy, and a boost in skills.

3. Private equity will resurrect or rejuvenate a struggling or failing business with time, effort, and vision.

4. The risk is substantial for the private equity partnership, and investing in companies is not seen as the opportunity to simply sit back and pull money from an ATM machine. After all their invested time and capital, there is the cold possibility the private equity group may not make any return despite taking the same entrepreneurial risk as the company to create and build assets.

5. Private equity is not an employer-employee relationship. It is an entrepreneurial partnership focused on increasing the value of the business together. Level 3 Legacy companies understand that dynamic and appreciate why investors are seeking companies run by mature team players with a different skill set than they have.

Resilience and dogged belief will be required through the dark hours but Level 3 Legacy companies confront the reality that their business, in its current form, may not be suitable for private equity. They seek to understand what makes a legacy business and to build those features into their business.

In closing Part I, the good news is that by now you are beginning to understand how to get private equity partners to invest in your business. You know the first steps to proving that it is to their benefit to invest in a person like you. Adam Smith advised how to get others to co-operate: "Never talk to them of our own necessities but of their advantages."

In your case, you can now show investors that you understand how the partnership will work and that they will have the advantage of a partner who understands private equity.

As we are about to see, there is a distinct group of investors for every size of business, each with their requirements from you, the entrepreneur.

PART II
BUILDING BLOCKS OF MONEY MAGNET

CHAPTER 4

THE FOOD CHAIN: MATCH YOUR BUSINESS WITH THE RIGHT INVESTORS

My rich dad trained his son and me to be capitalists, and we became entrepreneurs and real estate investors. Instead of working at jobs, we create jobs.

My poor dad encouraged me to be an employee and trust my money to a pension plan.

Simply put, one dad pointed to the top of the investing food chain, the other to the bottom.

My question to you, then, is, "Where are you on the food chain?"[1]

Robert Kiyosaki, author of *Rich Dad, Poor Dad*

By understanding the stages of the process in attracting investors and the best route to take, it will be less harrowing and you will not feel like a little furry animal running on a treadmill. You may even get to a grander destination than you thought possible.

---

[1] Robert Kiyosaki, Adventures in the Investing Food Chain, Web site, at finance.yahoo. com/expert/article/richricher/36074.

For most, it's a hard slog. Try sending out loads of business plans to financial people who do not know you from Nelly. Maybe one or two will want to chat. The more common response from investors, sadly, is returned envelopes, requests denied. consider the fact that each investor receives a mind-numbing pile of "opportunities" in business plans that would make anyone want to bang their head against their desk.

Spot Investors Who Fit Your Business

This is where the trick of knowing the "mathematical fit" of the investor with the size and type of business you have. Wael Mohamed, CEO of the successful startup Third Brigade says when finding investors, ask "What stage of firm do they invest in, what is their average investment, what kind of returns do they look for, where are they in their fund's stage? If there is no mathematical fit it will take an exception for them to invest in you."[2]

Knowing what range of investors would be interested in your stage on the growth curve would put you ahead of many owners. The new business reality is that no matter what your size of business, you can find private equity, but those who figure out their stage of business will quickly target the correct level of private equity.

All of the types of private equity investment—from seed right up to buyout—can fall under the nomenclature of private equity, although some will debate where the line is drawn and whether venture capital is the same as private equity. There are shades of gray, but it is all privately-held money with a similar psychological underpinning shared by investors no matter the size of deal.

Determining your company's Mathematical Fit is set by two simple measures. First, define where you are on the business growth curve (use Figure 4.1). Second, try to estimate the dollar amount of money you

[2] Bob Herbert, *Anatomy of a Textbook Startup*, Stonewood Interviews email, the Stonewood Group, 2007.

Figure 4.1: Types of Private Equity Investment

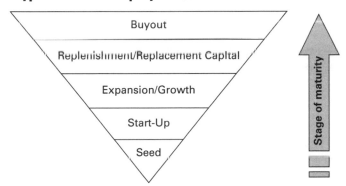

wish to raise. By carefully defining these two criteria, you will be able to match your business to the right investors.

Let's take a look at the food chain (see Figure 4.2) and determine your stage on the growth curve and who should get your investment proposal.

Excellent. Now, you may ask, "Since I am at the growth stage, can we go and meet a venture capitalist (VC) or fund manager? Should I print off my business plan and hand it out to any and all interested bright sparks?"

Whoa—hold on! You need to do a bit more investigating and preparation before you get on the phone. It is illegal to sell shares in your business and, besides, any investor worth his salt would not want to do business with someone who does not even know the law.

Do keep in mind the investors you meet need to source money for their fund from somewhere. You may believe you are the only person begging, but financing companies have had to beg for their money too. It may surprise you, but private equity is one long food chain. Getting private equity funding is about knowing your place in that food chain—you need to know quite a bit more about where you fit!

Figure 4.2: Financial Food Chain

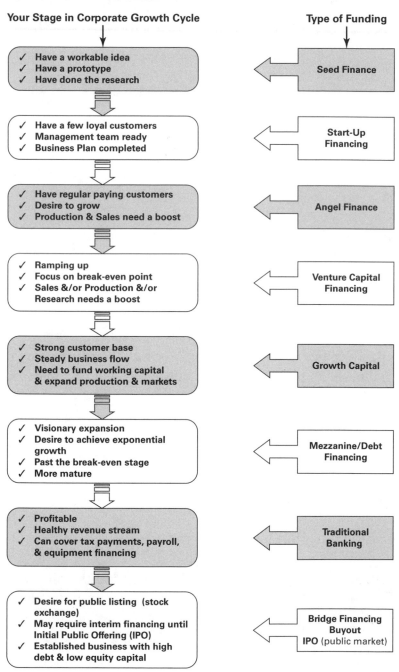

Your Stage in Corporate Growth Cycle   Type of Funding

✓ Have a workable idea
✓ Have a prototype
✓ Have done the research
— Seed Finance

✓ Have a few loyal customers
✓ Management team ready
✓ Business Plan completed
— Start-Up Financing

✓ Have regular paying customers
✓ Desire to grow
✓ Production & Sales need a boost
— Angel Finance

✓ Ramping up
✓ Focus on break-even point
✓ Sales &/or Production &/or Research needs a boost
— Venture Capital Financing

✓ Strong customer base
✓ Steady business flow
✓ Need to fund working capital & expand production & markets
— Growth Capital

✓ Visionary expansion
✓ Desire to achieve exponential growth
✓ Past the break-even stage
✓ More mature
— Mezzanine/Debt Financing

✓ Profitable
✓ Healthy revenue stream
✓ Can cover tax payments, payroll, & equipment financing
— Traditional Banking

✓ Desire for public listing (stock exchange)
✓ May require interim financing until Initial Public Offering (IPO)
✓ Established business with high debt & low equity capital
— Bridge Financing Buyout IPO (public market)

Source: Loewen & Partners

Accessing Private Equity

Being in private equity, you may imagine, is an easy job—handing out cash to grateful business owners. Investors do cope with more challenges than paper cuts as they count cash: a pet peeve is the relentless phone calls made by entrepreneurs (no, they don't fund start-up airlines in Australia or ideas you got last weekend). Investors are driven to boredom by the slew of jargon in business plans and overly wordy presentations made in first meetings that make Hugo Chavez seem quiet. You can make their job easy by getting to know which fund would like your industry and then crafting your message to meet their interests.

Before we go into further detail, let's run through a quick summary of the types of investors.

- *Angel and Seed* put money into new companies with the potential to grow explosively.
- *Venture Capitalists* invest in companies and people who are ten to fifteen years in business and have a background of profitability. They will invest in an idea.
- *Growth Capital* private equity will invest in companies that are well-established and profitable.
- *Mezzanine Capital* is quasi-equity where, usually, a company will not have to give up any equity, or, sometimes, will give up a small percentage of equity.
- *Buy-out* private equity is interested in buying businesses and improving them. In earlier years they would take over a business, break it up, and sell by pieces; the movie *Wall Street* takes you through that process. Today, private equity will grow and improve business in 99% of the deals.

Your stage of business—from startup to mature business—determines how much money you can expect to get and from what type of investor (see Figure 4.3). Each category of investor is distinctive in her risk tolerance and expectations of you.

Figure 4.3: Four Types of Investors

Development	Venture	Growth		Established	
Seed & Angel	Early	1st Stage	2nd Stage	Mezzanine	Equity, Debt, Derivatives
Proves a concept	Product Development	Commercial Products and Sales	Expansion	Expansion Consolidation Pre IPO	Recapitalization Buyout Slower Growth
Not yet profitable	Not Yet Profitable	Not Yet Profitable	Not Yet Profitable	Profitable	Revenue Maturity Competitiveness
Startup	Expansion	Consolidation		Corporate Mature: Liquid Markets	
$50, $100k, $250k to $750k	$1M–$5M	$3M–$50M		$3M–$100M	$3M–$100M

Source: Adapted from GrowthWorks' Web site

If You Are an Early Operating Company . . .

Looking at the types of private equity, an early operating company belongs in development capital where the seed funds and angels understand how to manage with the smaller amounts of capital required and can set the bare essential priorities as you begin to grow. In the early stages of your business, you may be encouraged by others to go to your family and friends with a good idea. Family and friends will give you money because they know and love you—hence the tag, "love money." Their investment is often for more than pecuniary reasons; Mom wants you out of her basement and into an adult lifestyle. This is the easiest stage to attract investors but it can also cause more stress for you than it's worth. Mark Twain knew what he was talking about with his wise advice, "Friendship will last a whole lifetime if not asked to lend money." Putting all of Great-Aunt Bessie's retirement money into your risky business venture is just plain foolish, particularly when there are other options, such as angels. Then you can rest assured you will also always be welcome at Thanksgiving dinner with the whole family, rather than blackballed for life. There are a variety of development capital options.

Tough Angels

Perhaps your product development is nearly complete, a few customers are buying, and there is a sketchy business plan. If you are at the stage of asking, "How do I? Who Do I? Where do I go?" then you may be ready to try approaching an angel. No, this is not some seventies TV show. Angel investors give you money out of their own pockets. They are high net worth individuals who want a piece of your long-term dream— that growth that will make you rich and put you on the cover of *Profit* magazine.

Why go to angels? There are many more benefits (besides piles of cash). Angels will be excited by your business and are also a wealth of knowledge and real-life experience. Most importantly, they have the drive to help your company grow. Angels offer more than money—they are the coach, the cheering squad, and will be tough on any entrepreneur who probably has a bit of an ego. An angel has been around the block and earned his wings!

There are angels all around and you find them by talking to your suppliers and downstream to customers. Mike Lazaridis founded Research in Motion in 1984 and got going with early funding from Innovation Ontario—a government funding program which is now closed. Lazardis also asked upstream to his customers, one of whom was Jim Balsillie, now the co-CEO of RIM, who bought shares early when revenues were $500,000. Balsillie brought his Harvard MBA skills and narrowed BlackBerry's focus to be "the wireless wallet," an absurd dream back in 1992. Balsillie is the angel who stayed.

Seed and Start-Up

Seed is for when your company is pre-revenue, alpha testing in Saskatchewan, beta testing, or commercializing. Early stage is when you have a few clients paying for your idea. You might have little more than a prototype and need to do marketing and more development work. This is the time to seek seed funds or so-called "embryonic funds."

Government-backed funding can also become available through the Business Development Bank of Canada (BDC) if you are willing to do the paperwork and wait a long, long time for approval. It is well worth the work though. If you have any clients outside of Canada, swing by Export Development Canada (EDC), which backs up bank loans and is innovative in its lending practices.

Grants are a common source of funds, often ignored even by your tax accountant. Make sure you access federal IRAP and SREDS tax credit programs, which are tax refunds on payroll costs and can be applicable at all stages, depending on your industry (see Appendix for Web sites). Check out the variety of government tax loopholes to help small businesses. There are a range of government grants, tax credits, and other innovations.

Banks like it if you have assets such as a building or if you have EDC backing up a loan. They may lend money in difficult situations and some banks, such as HSBC, have set up niche services for entrepreneurs as they recognize this niche is also most likely to grow their business (see Appendix).

Your bank manager may have a face that frightens babies, and when he phones, you know your day is getting grey. You are not alone. This stomach-churning relationship with the bank begins as you are generally seriously underfunded and credit cards—AMEX, VISA, and MasterCard—are maxed to the hilt to get the startup rolling. Most banks will want a guarantee of liquidity, and you may begin by accessing your RRSPs, life insurance, and mortgaging your home.

The first question lenders down the road will ask is, "How much do you have personally invested?" It's a smart question because private equity investors want you to be in deep to keep up your motivation. They don't want you running off to a job at Cisco if (and it always does) the going gets tough. But get this clear:

Private Equity Funding Does Not Start at the Bank

The bank is where big, established successful companies or businesses buying capital assets go. If your startup was collateralized by deposits and you have a wealthy partner, banks may be reassured enough to lend.

Generally, there are other options to expensive and difficult bank financing that will not give your spouse a nervous breakdown while you pursue your dream. Sleeman Breweries owner, John Sleeman, was about to ship his first batch of beer when his banker called his loan against the mortgage. It cost him his house and, tragically, his marriage too. It seems that the bank figured beer was not a good business. "Why they didn't tell us earlier, I don't know,"[3] says John. Ironically, today, Sleeman is TSX listed with four breweries and has sales of 1.1 million hectolitres of beer.

You can think big at the start-up stage like Robert Deluce who created Porter Airlines flying out of Toronto Island, minutes from downtown offices. With the private equity backing of Edgestone Capital, Borealis Infrastructure, GE Asset Management, and Dancap, Porter is well capitalized, raising $135M to date. Could you pull this off? Yes, if, like Deluce, you were a pilot and ran a previous airline. At 56, Deluce is a well-seasoned entrepreneur with whom private equity stakeholders have the confidence to partner.

If You Are a High-Growth Company . . .

Once you prove you have a business, there is a product, and clients paying for your company, but you are not yet profitable, you are entering venture capital (VC) country. Venture capital is usually money invested in private companies by way of equity (giving shares or some ownership) not secured by assets. This is different from the banks, who do not want ownership at all but rather have their money in the form of a loan secured by tangible assets, so-called "asset-backed loans."

Venture capital invests in most industries (common exclusions are retail, real estate, and natural resource extraction) and across the life cycle of your business with different stages of investment. Venture capital is also known as "patient capital" because the "ventures" are young and growing businesses, but they need time to evolve into profitable

---

[3] Yasmin Glanville, "The challenges of growth," *CA Magazine* Web site, 2007.

Figure 4.4: Sources of Capital (non-bank)

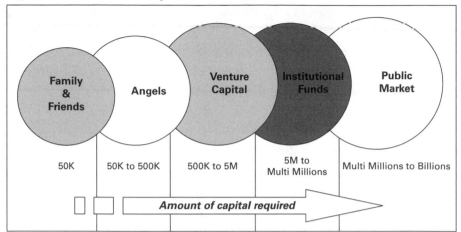

businesses. Get a quick snapshot of the Sources of Capital in Figure 4.4 and you can see that, in general, VC focuses on start-up and early stage companies needing $1M to $5M. However, large sums of capital in venture investing may, under certain circumstances, also be appropriate for companies that are in development, such as Porter Airlines, which got over $100M in start-up capital. In the Canadian VC investment space, the capital raised varies from year to year with 2006 at a level of $1.6B raised, down from $2.2B in 2005, and a high of $4.5B in 2001.

There are two key criteria that differentiate VC from more conventional sources of capital. A VC investment typically:

1. involves minority equity or quasi-equity participation (owning common shares outright or having the right to convert other financial instruments into common shares) in a private company; and

2. is expected to be a long-term investment (generally within three to eight years) and requires active involvement by the investors in the companies which they finance until they are sufficiently developed for disposition (exit via a sale or VC shares or Initial Public Offering [IPO]).

It is critical to realize that VC investments are an involved rather than a passive form of financing. The bar has been raised and most venture capitalists strive to add value, beyond capital, to their investments in an effort to help them grow and to achieve a superior return. Doing this requires active involvement and most venture capitalists will, at a minimum, claim a seat on your board of directors.

Although a venture capitalist invests for the long haul, that does not mean forever. The primary objective of VC investors is to achieve a superior rate of return through the "liquidity event"—selling to a competitor or an IPO or anything that pays back the investments. The exit strategy will help you decide where to focus your time and money.

First-Stage Financing: Expansion

Your company has proven, repeat customers and now needs to grow, hence the name "expansion capital" or "growth capital." The VCs will overlap with institutional fund managers who manage privately-held pools of capital given to them by pension funds and large banks to invest in companies. These sophisticated fund managers put capital into all sorts of companies, including traditional manufacturing and construction, not only the technology darlings.

Private equity money ranges from wealthy entrepreneurs with their own money set up in a fund to the professional fund managers who go hat-in-hand to the big institutions to ask for money to build up their fund. These VCs and institutional investors need to give back that money in five years with a good profit. The Technology Industries Association surveyed entrepreneurs and found that this Series A round, first-round asking for $750,000 to $3M was the toughest to raise.[4]

During your first round of financing, VCs will be looking for "skin in the game" or that you need success more than they do. Are you up to your eyeballs in getting money from any and every other source? Have you squeezed out every government loan or give-back such as SREDs? Your business is now at a stage where traditional banks say no and your future is risky. The VCs want you to be leveraged, house mortgage, and all, because their logic is that if the fund loses, you too will

---

[4] Michael Volker, Technology Futures at www.bctechnology.com/statics/mvolker-feb1403.html, February 14, 2003.

crash and burn. If you are not leveraged, it makes sense that if things go sour, you could pick up sticks and move over to Apple, leaving the fund holding the bag.

Corporate Strategic Investors, such as Rogers or Bell, are increasing and taking the wind out of VC sales. Companies like Google, Intel, Pfizer, or Motorola realized that if they finance startups, they can then have first rights to buy out the owners earlier in the market development for $5M rather than when they cost $50M. In-house VC groups are looking for companies with complimentary products or technologies that fit into their market space. Bell Canada absorbs many fledgling technology companies as the executives believe it is better to have the technology in their special vault rather than in the market.

Venture capital is also increasingly going into companies that are reasonably established but with room to grow. "It's critical to know the difference between venture capital and private equity's long-term direction," Alan McMillan, serial entrepreneur, says. "With seed startups, the VC invests in ideas, but the bigger private equity funds invest in a mature company with consistent revenues."

McMillan says it is an important distinction because, "The tech growth story is not going to be throwing off cash. That sweat equity goes back into the business. Also, the exit Nirvana is the IPO on the stock market, but in reality, tech companies will get sold to larger tech companies. These are venture capitalists' expectations."

Disney took into its house the Canadian-designed social community called Club Penguin, developed by three parents in Kelowna, British Columbia, who were concerned about their children's Internet travels. They bootstrapped their finances until they sold, going without an investor partner. Disney ended up paying $300M for the business (see Figure 4.5).

"If these early stage companies who sell direct to a big corporation had partnered with knowledgeable VCs and with private equity investors, though," says Rick Segal of J.A. Albright, "they may have grown the business and then developed themselves that much more and gone

Figure 4.5: Acquisitions Are Appealing

Industry	Acquisition	Price*
Disney	Club Penguin, Kelowna	$300M
Cisco	Pixstream, Waterloo	$554M
Redback	Abatis, Burnaby	$636M
Boeing	AeroInfo, Vancouver	$ -
Telus	Assurent, Toronto	$ -
Yahoo!	Flickr, Vancouver	$40M
Nortel	Architel Systems, Torornto	$400M
The Shopping Channel	Mix Promotions, Montreal	$ -

* The prices for Boeing, Telus, and The Shopping Channel were private transactions and not public knowledge.

to Yahoo!, Google, or Disney for a far higher multiple."[5] PayPal, for example, burned through $180M of private equity partners' money and skills before being sold to eBay for $1.6B. It's worth doing a few years with the private equity partner and then selling. However, a bird in the hand . . .

Types of Companies VC Investors Like or Don't Like

Venture capitalists don't provide a niche service like retailers. They don't focus on narrow products such as bags for horse riders, or distributing scarves from France, as these businesses will not grow or scale up quickly enough. They are also not attracted to service companies for the same reasons as it takes a great deal more time to grow a Deloitte Accounting business model to a profitable size than a PayPal. A technology company with a new software program ready to sell over the Internet to the global market is easier to grow. There is also more opportunity to sell it up to an eBay or Google.

---

[5] Speech by Rick Segal, Toronto Venture Group, Toronto, March 2006.

If You Want to Consolidate . . .

If your company has been going for a few years and has revenues (does not need to be profitable) and you want to expand even further, maybe increase production or enter new markets, the bigger funds are interested in contributing larger amounts of investment, say $5M and upward.

Growth Capital

The private equity fund wants to finance an established business that needs to restructure and capitalize. In particular, these professionally managed funds seek the business owner interested in pursuing two options.

Option 1: Need for liquidity
Option 2: Want growth, but can't get it on their own

For example, a company may take 25% equity and some debt to buy out Dad from the family business. As in Somerset Entertainment's situation, Andy Burgess, the CEO, wanted to grow the business and needed the cash to capitalize, but without being crippled by covenants offered by the banks.

Some company owners with businesses eligible for private equity discover that their lifestyle business will need to be more professional. One CEO was draining out a $500,000 salary for herself, in addition to her shareholding. In a professional partnership, this sort of cost cannot be justified. Having the discipline of private equity investors will benefit the bottom line more. Over the long haul, this CEO would have found her bank balance swelled far more in five years with share growth than with taking such a large salary. Indeed, it is astounding how companies can save millions by challenging current management team's assumptions; having a third party with a fresh viewpoint can be very beneficial.

Once you come to this natural point at which you are confronted with a decision to grow or remain content, you can look at Stage 2 Growth private equity. As the CEO draining the company for her salary found out, in order to be taken to the next level, changes must often be introduced with the investor:

- management techniques,
- mode of governance (the way decisions are made), and
- structure.

If You Are Established with Revenues . . .

You are a mature company with liquid markets. You are ready to meet the fund managers investing for institutional money. Fund managers are the same as VCs, in that they are judging you, but their needs will be more sophisticated and detailed, focusing on how you are managing your company. The big difference between VCs and fund managers is that VCs take higher risks while private equity fund managers want a mature company with regular cash flow. They are not going to bet on an idea and your dynamic personality.

Mezzanine Financing

Perhaps you are heading for the stock market listing or wanting a buyout and you need money to "bridge" over the gap to that large financial pay-out. If your company has run out of money and you need to get a bit more runway space before you take off, you can get what is called bridge financing. It's more expensive, but it's quick and there's no need for valuations and other due diligence since it is pure debt.

This means that there is some money that is just on loan to you and must be paid back according to a regular timetable and with interest. The investor gets some ownership in the business so as to influence how the money gets spent.

Mezzanine is available through institutional investors, such as Roynat Capital, who will want established earnings and an ongoing business that needs to expand. Fund managers, such as Argosy Partners and Wellington Capital, and the merchant banks, like HSBC and BMO, look for these larger deals and management buy-out situations to provide mezzanine financing which is the mix of debt and equity.

Your Friendly Bank

Take note where your bank sits on the food chain. Look at how far along the life of a company must be before banks kick in with a serious loan. Banks come in last. Yet banks are often the first place entrepreneurs mistakenly think they should visit. It's not that bankers are mean, but they are the most risk adverse and only kick in once you have suffered many sleepless nights wondering how on earth you are going to survive without losing your house and life savings. Only when you have proven, regular customers, are getting new business, and have a positive cash flow are the banks are willing to finance. At this stage, banks are happy to get involved and are helpful as a senior lender. They are like the big brother who's first in line for dinner and who can take all the goodies he wants before the others even get a look at what's there. If things go wrong, they get first pick at your business assets to cover their costs. Not to pick on banks—they do have to protect their customers' money, so it's quite right that they have to be more prudent in practice.

"I would like to borrow some money," you say. At this point, how many times did you imagine your bank manager's smile at this point to resemble a stuffed, preserved crocodile displayed in the Royal Ontario Museum? Indeed, it does seem that banks are a lightening conductor attracting criticism from business owners but, in all fairness, it's a result of people not understanding the bank's role.

Even Robert Frost got in on the criticism saying, "A bank is a place where they lend you an umbrella in fair weather and ask for it back when it begins to rain." True, but at the risk of harping on this point, for good reason. Do understand that banks are for senior debt financing, which means they get first dibs on any assets if your company should have the misfortune of going south. If you want to get smart with your money, you need to be clear about what a bank can and cannot do. You may be surprised. The main point is that bank financing is an excellent way to go so long as your business has little or no risk.

Bankers Can Be Proactive Partners

Are bankers really the remora feeding on the hull of the company? (See Figure 4.6.) "First determine what type of capital is appropriate for

Figure 4.6: Banking

Pros	Cons
• No dilution	• Banks usually require substantial security.
• Relatively low rate of interest (hopefully!)	• Banks have tough terms and conditions, which are likely to be enforced.
	• If in default your loan will be called.
	• Bankruptcy is tiresome and expensive.
	• Too much debt weakens the balance sheet.

your business," suggests Suzanne Mar, senior account manager for Royal Bank Technology Banking Group. She says, "Will sharing monthly reports with your banker be a burden?"

Four Differences Between Private Equity and Conventional Banks

With discussions on how to tax private equity at the same rates as banks, it is worth understanding how private equity and banks work and why the private equity investor is actually an entrepreneur rather than a cog in the big corporate machine (see Figure 4.7).

1. **Risk.** Equity investors are willing to risk their entire investment but exchange that risk with the belief that the business will grow and multiply like rabbits breeding with equally enthusiastic rabbits. "When you put your own capital at risk, you are an entrepreneur too. If you don't put your own capital at risk, you don't work as hard at it," says Peter Plows, the manufacturing expert with Cobalt Capital. Banks loan against real estate, cars, and equipment because they are first in line to take these to sell off and make back the money they loaned.

2. **Long Term.** Venture capital money is a long-term investment ranging from three to seven years. Bank repayments begin within months, while the VC repayment can happen far later.

3. **Grow Together.** The VCs and the fund managers do expect to be active in the business and its strategy to grow. The VC involvement

Figure 4.7: Range of Financial Choices

PURE DEBT   **PURE EQUITY**

		Mezzanine	Warrants	
	Debentures			Common Shares
Loan		Convertible Debentures		
			Convertible Preference Shares	

More expensive   *Dilutes Shareholders*
Reduces profit   *Low Valuation*
Hurts the balance sheet   *More Complicated*
Source: Loewen & Partners

varies by fund, but they will be sticking in the oar until the business has evolved enough to take public or sell or for the owner to earn back the business. Usually, private equity investors will want a board seat. Banks may take a board seat too and tell you where they want the money spent or not spent. The difference is that there is no unlimited upside for the bank. The loan and repayments are set and never change no matter how well you do.

4. ***Partners Not Lenders.*** The money comes with the requirement that the investor has minority or equity participation (owning common shares outright or having the right to convert other financial instruments into common shares). Psychologically, banks lend while equity partners want you to grow the business and will help you to do so. Banks just want that regular repayment and if you grow, well good for you.

Can you now understand why you have to find money elsewhere? Many people go to their bank first and get disappointed and upset when turned away, and then depressed without realizing it is not a criticism of their company. Banks have to be risk averse as they are preserving the capital of their investors. It is why they are far up the food chain. When you stand on the stage after winning your Deal of the Year award, do resist the urge to berate the banks for not taking a risk on your company. Your company was not a "mathematical fit" at that time.

Know Your Way Around the Funds

As already mentioned, the VCs and fund managers you approach are part of the food chain of begging. Pension funds and endowments give money to venture funds. A VC fund is in the early part of the food chain. They themselves have already begged to get money into their fund from the big banks, business pension plans, and union pension plans, such as HOOPP (Hospitals of Ontario Pension Plan) and the Ontario Teachers' Pension Plan funds, by promising a set rate of return.

The VC and institutional funds are not people flush with money, wanting to give it away to better their fellow man. They need to make a decent return because they have to pay back the money they borrowed. There are financial expectations set by the people who put money into the fund. People who will give them money have expectations for a higher return than the average stock market return.

The traditional source of money for VC funds is from the institutional investors. The VC is a small fish in the pond fighting for a piece of the funding pie. The government and the Business Development Bank of Canada (BDC) is also a fund. Their money comes from the government. There are labour funds made up of thousands of investors who have each put in $5,000 with typical investors being grannies. Corporate funds are those such as the Dow Venture Capital Fund. These tend to come in enthusiastically and then realize that it's a long-term investment and withdraw.

If You Want the Public Market . . .

Owners want to get money for their hard work and sell ownership to another company or go public with the IPO. The IPO is where you move from the private money to public money. The TSX-V has worked hard to give a range of options for smaller companies as well as the big IPOs:

- capital pool,
- Reserve take over (RTO), and
- IPO.

Sources of Funds

You will need to give some thought to the form of your next round of financing. It could either be a public issue or a private equity placement. In the public marketplace, size definitely counts. What one achieves by going public is to raise capital and to get one's shares listed and to create a market for them.

There are two sources of financing.

1. **Public.** You go through a prospectus. It is expensive and beyond the budget of all small businesses.
2. **Private.** There are still rules that govern how you do this and who are the legal stakeholders allowed to participate.

Incidentally, quite a number of companies go public prematurely and then wish they hadn't. The problem is that if a company is small, the stock rarely trades and, in fact, there isn't a real market. See Figure 4.8 for a summary of the advantages and disadvantages of going public. Roger Dent of Mavrix Fund Management says, "While a company is still small, and that can be under $50 million, analysts see no purpose or profitability in writing it up, and brokers don't follow it because stocks that only trade rarely don't give them much commission."[6]

Figure 4.8: Going Public (IPO)

Advantages	Disadvantages
Premium valuation ("public multiple")	High legal, accounting, & professional fees
	Annual listing fees
Freely traded stock	Disclosure requirements onerous
	Need a free float and market following
Access to capital	Non-alignment of interests (capital pools)

[6] Speech by Roger Dent, CEO Roundtable, Canadian Innovator's Forum, March 2006.

Going public is expensive; besides the brokers' commissions, there are remarkably high legal expenses and auditors' fees. Private placements are much less expensive. Furthermore, one has far greater flexibility in deal structure. On top of the financing cost of going public, there are the ongoing annual costs. These include listing fees, the cost of preparing and disseminating quarterly reports, annual meetings, investor relations advice, and so on, and they will run you at least $120,000 a year and probably more. On top of that, if, merely because of lack of market following, your stock does not perform as your new shareholders anticipated, you will constantly be getting calls from disappointed and irate investors asking for information.

If your next round of financing is to be $10M or so, it will be of a size to be of interest to institutional investors and you may find that it is simpler and less expensive to take the private equity financing route. Roger Dent says, "I am all for public issues so long as the timing is right."

Why Private Equity Takes Public to Private

The big private equity firms who do the mega-deals take companies off the public market in order to do the things that would encourage investors to push down the stock or sell. Once they clean house, they throw the company back to the public market. The debate rages about whether private equity does any good using this tactic in comparison to public companies; research is proving the improved value. A recent study by Josh Lerner, Harvard Business School, and Jerry Cao, Boston College, looked at over 500 companies brought back to the public market by private equity companies and discovered that not only did these companies rise in value faster than the overall indexes, but also faster than companies not partnered with private equity. The statistic shows that the long-term impact of private equity firms is that if held three years or longer, they outperform public companies by 18%.[7]

The blindfolds are being lifted, though, and activist shareholders of public companies are beginning to ask managers of public companies to do what public equity partners would do. Carrefour, a French company and the second largest retailer in the world, had their big shareholders

---

[7] Private equity is roiling the economy, CNN Money, March 5, 2007.

make the request to behave as if they had a private equity partner, like Blackstone or Onex, for example. They sold off real estate and invested in other long-term activities as a result.

Buy-Out Financing

The IPO used to be like reaching the top of Mount Everest for entrepreneurs, but even finance has its fashions. The company would be listed on the stock exchange and then have a good supply of capital from all the happy investors. The VCs, fund managers, and management would all get their investment returned and then some. In real life, it doesn't always work that way, which is why getting bought out by a U.S. company is attractive. When the Canadian company is in the same line of business, it often attracts a premium sales price and the parent company is motivated to pump in more capital ensuring continued success. Going public can get quick cash but then interest by investors may drop, especially for smaller stocks, leaving the stock "orphaned." The CEO may struggle to raise capital and also pay the accounting fees required.

Choose Your Type of Investment and Investor

Now you have learned about angel, seed, venture capital, institutional funds, and banking, you can understand the different roles each plays. It is a bit like a Sudoku puzzle, but once you fill in key information, the rest falls into place.

You can see there is a path for every company with required steps that your investors today and your future investors will want to see. No one can predict your future, but they can get a gut feel from the milestones behind you.

Dig for Detail

Before we turn to the question of what we need to do to get funded, it might be worth a fast cruise past all the potential investors out there again and what exactly they need before they give you a single dollar. There are proper roles for bank financing and private equity to help you along your path. These next few chapters will teach you when to use each type of capital and how to work with each investor. First up are the angels. Let's learn how to get a little bit of heaven! Just as in everything, there are right and wrong angels and you need to recognize the right ones. Then we will visit the VCs and, last but not least, the private equity fund managers.

TAKE AWAYS

There are many sources of funding out there, all wanting to put their money into growing businesses. Your opportunity to get some of that money just increased because you now know where to narrow your search. Pick your size of business and amount of capital required, then match yourself to the correct type of fund. The "fit" between your business stage and the private equity fund's investment criteria matters.

CHAPTER 5

WHAT ANGELS AND SEED FUNDS NEED

Business you know may bring money, but friendship hardly ever does.

Jane Austen, *Emma*, Chapter 1, 34, 1813

To mix metaphors, angels are the white knights of the economy. Without angels, many businesses would just not get past that seed stage. You already know the eight stages of company development and where angel investors tend to invest. They are positioned at the early stages of your venture, once you have a bit of a track record and want to get away from using ten credit cards to grow the business.

"Angels are private investors," says Dan Mothersill, founder of the National Angel Organization. "They come from a wide variety of backgrounds and careers. They love business and want to share this passion for information technology, manufacturing, alternative energy, finance, services areas or whatever they do." Angels will bring $250,000 to $500,000 in capital, their skills and the sheer joy of helping your company. In addition, at the early stages, so much of business is who you know: angels can introduce you to their large networks, getting you in front of the right people to grow your company.

Use Other People's Money for Early Investing

Angels will assume financial risk that would send your average banker screaming for cover. At the toughest time of the business, angels usually get involved, often before there are even a few clients. They are the gardeners of the early growth businesses when they are little seeds beginning to sprout. Angels want to share their knowledge to get the business growing faster and stronger.

Four Types of Angel Investors and Why They Do It

The closer you get to the professional investor, the higher the incentive to invest will be. "What is my money going to make?" and "What return will my money provide?" The money at this stage is unsecured, which means there is no building to sell or mortgage to claim. The angel is lucky if there is anything to recoup. There is also no registered claim on assets, which leaves the assets unencumbered in case the owner needs to get debt from the bank. In other words, your company has a positive bank balance and no debt owed because the angel is part owner of the business by putting in capital. The more equity you have, the higher your ability to get loans, sometimes up to three times the amount of equity. Banks are comforted that you have $500,000 in the company and will lend you much more. This use of debt is the cornerstone of private equity.

Be prepared to release a good chunk of ownership at this early stage. Angels need a worthwhile block of ownership because, as your company grows, you will move up in size of investor from angel to venture capital (VC) and the angel's equity interest in your company will be diluted (made smaller). As an example, the Maple Leaf Angels explain, "If our Angel group members invest $500,000 at a pre-money valuation of $1M (and thus end up owning 33% of the company), and then a venture capital firm invests $5M the following year at $5M pre-money valuation, the original angel group investors will now own only half as much of the company, even though the company value has increased more than three-fold."[1] To make money for their efforts, angels expect 25–50% of fully diluted equity in your company.

---

[1] Entrepreneur page, Maple Leaf Web site, 2008.

```
MACHINE ID                              3E2I
CARD NUMBER              4506**********286

MAY30 12 AT 17:28                  REF # 6664
WITHDRAWAL                            $100.00
FROM CHEQUING             00042    ****632
ACCOUNT BALANCE                       $515.12
DAILY CANADIAN CASH LIMIT
REMAINING                             $600.00

        Thank you for banking with CIBC
```

1 800 465-CIBC (2422)
www.cibc.com

Le logo CIBC est une marque
déposée de la Banque CIBC.

1601653
1896BIL-2009/12
C-2004247

1 800 465-CIBC (2422)
www.cibc.com

Le logo CIBC est une marque
déposée de la Banque CIBC.

1601653
1896BIL-2009/12
C-2004247

There are four types of angel investors.

1. Family Members

The first angel or individual willing to invest is probably your mother or other family member. Your parents may give you the money as they think, "This will be good for our boy, Billy." This early equity—perhaps an inheritance and then family and friends—allows a bit of track record.

2. Corporate Angels

The professional angel investor will like to see that an owner is serious and getting enough traction to become something. The corporate angel is a successful entrepreneur in his own business with approximately $200,000 excess cash. This category of investor is typically successful and is running companies making $50M revenue. They have probably sold their business to the likes of IBM and now have money to burn. The one thing to know about these angels is that they are not ready to retire. They will want to be part of the action. They want to act as a consultant. These sources of capital may have to be converted over to the idea of putting their money into something riskier than their investment portfolio.

Some corporate angels may be more interested in what you can do for them than what they can do for your business. They may be thinking about how to get your business sold off to the first interested buyer so that they can get back their cash and a whole lot more. This type of angel is risky and may at first seem like a saviour, but turn into an Agent Smith in dark glasses, shoving you down a Matrix highway where you don't want to go. Google potential angels' past company investments. Are the companies still around and are the founders happy?

There are the less obvious angels all around your business right now. Look up and down your business chain and talk to suppliers and customers and see how you can optimize your cash flows. You can delay payments (with suppliers knowing or not) using them as your float.

3. The Retired Executive Angels

The retired executive angel is an attractive angel. They have time and networks for you to tap but perhaps will not want to be as involved in the day-to-day business. You may have expectations that they will pick up the slack and help out with building the customer base or future investors. In reality, they might be lonely and looking for friendship. Pay attention to how much they talk about themselves compared to finding out about your business in order to avoid becoming someone they use to visit memory lane rather than grow your business. They love the challenge of business and are old warhorses—give them a whiff of the battle of getting a business up and running; it stirs up their blood to get back in the game but without the day-to-day responsibility.

4. The Old Money Angels

Finally, there are the old money angels. These are wealthy families looking to fund companies. They sometimes give away money to achieve something philanthropic at the same time. They may want to support environmental causes, inner-city education, or pet interests of their own. Social Capital Partners, founded and run by Bill Young (family member of founder of Red Hat, Bob Young), has funded a number of social enterprises which are businesses that employ disadvantaged populations such as new immigrants, single mothers, etc. A good example is Turnaround Couriers, which is a bicycle courier company that hires at-risk youths and services some of the cities largest law firms and banks. SCP is both commercial and philanthropic; if you want to improve the world through teaching people how to fish rather than giving them one philosophy, they can help with both funding and HR help.

How to Recognize the Angel Investor

Besides the fact that they have loads of cash, the characteristics of angel investors may surprise you. They are often not the ones at the exclusive clubs or living the champagne lifestyle. They can be the most understated people in middle-income neighbourhoods. Most are men, although a few women are getting involved too. Texas is boasting a Women's Angel Club for the state.

Angels will cluster around industries, such as biotech, technology, or medical devices. Look at industry associations. Angels will be members of clubs and organizations focused on their area of expertise. They will be giving presentations or be quoted in the newspapers. Google your industry topic, read the articles, and call the people interviewed. Go to industry conferences and make sure you introduce yourself to every presenter and take their business cards. Call them later and ask them for people who are investing in your area. These are also the people to approach as possible investors in your business. In most big cities, there are angel groups that you can find with a quick Google search and their Web sites will explain how to approach them.

You will find angels close to your market area. Angels like proximity to their home. Most angel investors invest funds to businesses less than 100 km from their homes. They do not want to drive too far and definitely do not wish to fly. Many angels meet company owners at social events, such as watching their wives play in a tennis tournament. Be aware that your opportunity could be the person sitting right next to you at a business breakfast, so do share your business story with others.

All of the angel investors are attracted to deals they understand. If they have been involved in agriculture ventures, there is very little chance they will flip over to oil and gas. They rarely wish to venture into unknown territory. They have worked in your industry but they will be analytical too. Since they know your industry, they can bring a bird's eye view and use that to make shrewd investments.

Look for someone high up in the industry. Look for someone you respect and are a little intimidated to approach. Your company will be of interest. Angels like investments that are the type of deal where they know they can bring value. If you can already see clearly how the angel could bring tangible value-add, you are already improving your chances of attracting funding.

Key Factors That Attract the Attention of Angels

Know the key factors angels look for in an investment and sprinkle these points into your conversation with them when chatting about your business.

- *Location, Location, Location.* The first priority tends to be distance. The business cannot be more than two hours away from the home of the angel investor. There are exceptions to the rule, of course, but these are exceptions.

- **Sector Interest.** The IT, biotech, and manufacturing sectors tend to be popular, but there are other areas too such as companies for the Web. Bryan Watson, executive director of the Toronto-based National Angel Organization, says, "Web 2.0 companies use open-source tools, so they require a lot less capital to build their service. Anywhere from $50,000 to $250,000 will get a Web 2.0 company to market, whereas in the past, Internet firms would have needed $1M to $2M."[2]
- **Cool Deals.** Your company must be easy to understand. A medical device is a good sell as it is tangible and simple to understand. Technology tends to be more complicated and you need to know which big companies will eventually be your target clients and see if you can network with senior executives within.
- **The Hockey Stick Revenues Curve.** Angels are in early, at the riskiest stage of the deal and they want to see 200% growth, not just 20%. Since angels are high-risk characters themselves, these growth rates will get them excited if you demonstrate you are able to justify the financial figures in great detail.
- **Vision to Grow.** If you want to be the biggest thing in Richmond, British Columbia, good for you, but the angel will not give you any money. You need to know that most companies have to do the bulk of their business outside of their comfort zone and, nowadays, outside of their country's borders.
- **Experience.** Angels want to see entrepreneurs who have taken a company from $0 to $10M. That practical knowledge will be more attractive to an angel. They want to see that you have that experience and, if you personally do not have it, you need to get in with someone who does. You need that expertise on your advisory board.
- **Good Investment Proposition.** Your technology can be the best, but that's not what matters. Remember Beta and VHS. Beta was far superior but they quickly lost out to VHS. Having the best technology does not make you a stand-out winner. You need the investment proposal. Someone has to pay money for your

---

[2] Kara Aaserud, "A match made in heaven: angel investors and Web 2.0 firm," *PROFIT* magazine, May 2007.

product. Smug engineers can suffer from myopia over the commercialization of their designs.

- *Staying Power.* First to market is no longer attractive. After all, Google was a late entrant to the search engine industry. Sustainability is what is required. If someone comes into your competitive space with a lot of money, will you stand up to the competition? You need to think about how to build barriers to new entrants into the market. Can you lock in your customers somehow? VHS had the machines to play their tapes and these cost less than the BETA version. Price point made the market tip over to the VHS side, even though the product was of a comparatively inferior quality.

- *Competitive Advantage.* Defining what gives you the edge over your competitors is tantamount. This means having an advanced pocket calculator while everyone else is still using a slide rule. What can make your offering tip the market in your favour? What will make your product unique if not exclusive? What will make it hard for competitors to come in, catch up, and blot out your name?

- *The Written Plan.* A thorough and understandable business plan at the early stage is appreciated. Angel investors will spend their time conducting their own due diligence. If you have already done the competitor analysis and all the elements of looking at your business, you can help shorten the process. This translates into getting money sooner.

- *Return on Investment.* Angels will want ten to fifty times their money back. They want to see an exit strategy that shows you can afford to buy them out from ownership. You will never be able to do this from your revenues, which requires you to have a plan to find someone to buy you. Have future companies in mind who might buy your business.

Enter the Dragons

Instead of calling a VC reality show *Angels' Cloud*, CBC chose the title *Dragons' Den* which is probably a far more realistic description of the trial-by-fire process entrepreneurs go through to find angel investors. Trent Kitsch was one of the people pitching an equity share in his sports underwear company called Saxx Apparel Ltd.

> ## WHAT TO PUT IN YOUR BUSINESS PLAN
>
> **Management team** description of track records of performance.
>
> **Market opportunity** is large (i.e., a $100+ million market). Show your strategy to claim significant share of this market (i.e., 20%+).
>
> **Use of Funds** and list of key milestones such as research and product development, building a sales and marketing infrastructure and hiring executives.
>
> **Growth Potential** to show that you can manage the scale necessary to succeed. Plan to generate significant profits beyond the initial product idea and achieve multiple sources of revenue. Financial projections can be based on assumptions to demonstrate consistent profits and cash flow growth. Show you have thought about managing your competitors.
>
> **Competitive Advantage** around intellectual property protection, exclusive licenses, exclusive marketing and distribution relationships, strong brands, scarce human resources (i.e., knowledge and skills), or access to scarce raw materials.
>
> **Technology** investment usually goes to first-of-a-kind new ideas. The concept behind the technology must be proven and verifiable.

He says, "When I began looking for angel equity investment for Saxx, I wasn't looking for only money as investment, but smart money as investors. I have turned down thousands of dollars' of offers for equity from family, friends, and overly rich passive investors who wouldn't add anything other than money to my business. I felt the best way to pursue my seed round of investment was to only solicit people from the industry with experience and connections to match. This strategy has definitely made my job in raising funds more difficult due to the smaller group of potential investors, but as I found great smart money angels from the industry, it has made my seed round so much more valuable than just the dollars raised."

Angels Compared to Venture Capitalists

Both angels and venture capitalists like to be involved in decision making, but keep in mind that the former wants to invest; the latter *has* to invest. This will bring a different approach to their involvement in the management of the business.

Work out the valuation of the investment carefully and have your heated discussion early on so as to minimize the pain after closing the deal. Look for how realistic the angel is on partnership percentage. How much of the business will you have to give up for your investment? Valuation expectations need to be managed. The angel group, Maple Leaf, says, "If you offer 20% of the company for $500K then divide the proposed financing ($500K) by the offered percentage (20%) to get the post-money valuation ($2.5 million), and subtract the money ($500K) from the post-money ($2.5 million) to get the pre-money valuation ($2 million)." Angels caution that it takes a unique business to get a higher valuation than $2M at the early stages.

Experts can (and should) be contracted to come up with valuations, but remember, it's also whatever the investor is willing to pay. Trent Kitsch of Saxx agrees, "I was way off on my early valuations of Saxx. Angel investors are no different than you and I when we are shopping for a car. Investors weren't interested in Saxx at a $3,000,000 post-money valuation and asking $300,000 for 10% equity, but the interest skyrocketed when I just said to myself, 'This is a million dollar idea!' and priced a post money valuation for $1,000,000 and 10% for $100,000. Then what happened? We had oversubscribed interest at that price which drove the price of our first round of investment money of $2,000,000 or 10% for $200,000."

Kitsch suggests, "The moral of the story is use an initial offering price of the value for the company in the realm of reality or even a bit low and angels seem to come out of their shells. To the car analogy, I might not be interested in buying a Porsche for a premium price but I for sure will listen to the salesman if he is realistic on price or seeming to offer me a deal."

Kitsch is running Saxx from Kelowna, British Columbia. And his visit to the *Dragons' Den* was well worth the public relations. The CBC online competition for best plan voted Saxx the top business, netting $50,000 for Kitsch—worth putting up with some dragons' breath.

Three Don'ts When Dealing with Angels

First, do not ask for a non-disclosure agreement—this shows you to be a rookie. Angels have been where you are now and don't want to be there again—they would much rather be an overseer compared to stealing your idea and starting from scratch.

Second, do not be overly eager to agree to their terms right up front. Do you give away your product this easily? The angel would hope you would fight to get the price point on your product and not expect to get what they want from you straight up. They love a bit of a challenge! Trent Kitsch says, "Never get too excited until the ink is dry. I have pitched a number of angels and let my emotions get too high and believed I had a deal. Also to the point of letting not confirmed deals alter my strategies with other potential investors. Don't let the angels run you around too much both physically and emotionally until some documentation of a deal or expressions of interest subject to some points is signed."

Third, do not believe that the angel will magically infuse the business with revenues—you are still going to have to do all the hard work. Indeed, some entrepreneurs are disappointed the angel only goes to board meetings and does not make phone calls to potential customers. Define both of your roles and how it will look on a monthly basis. It does help to write down your expectations for the relationship and ask the angel to read it and see if it matches expectations. "I run a business building Web sites for rock stars and I have learned to sift through angel investors who are there for the cool factor rather than helping me grow the revenues," says Kevin Leflar, CEO of Official Community, manager of Web sites such as Blue Rodeo. You are too busy to be hijacked by rambling, random meetings, and board get-togethers. Set a timetable for the year ahead and establish set meetings. Categorize the topics for those meetings—strategy or operations? My board and I know our roles and I value their deep skills in my industry and help in opening doors but I still have to do the sales calls."

Types of Seed Stage Investors

Following the first angel investment, it is time to pass the hat again. Now you are ready for the seed fund investors. This is the first set of financing rounds and it is fiercely challenging. You cannot expect to be structuring the deal or managing the downsides. The seed investor knows that if things go bad, they will be left with IKEA furniture and a few computers—that's it. Zip! Even patents for proprietary technology are worth very little. If seed investors have forty pages of downsize structure in the term sheet, they know they have the wrong deal. Rather, focus on the growth of the business and the opportunities.

In Canada, about 10%–15% of total venture capital goes into seed startups, which is not too bad when compared to the U.S. In 2006, 51,000 U.S. companies got angel funding, with the average raise of US$500,000. Healthcare services and medical devices and equipment attracted the lion's share (21%), followed by software (18%) and biotech (18%).

Remember, VCs have seen hundreds of entrepreneurs and categorize them into the following:

- *University Spin Offs.* Perhaps you won the business plan award for best new business idea. Now you want to make it happen in the real world. Your issues will be a green management team and little market validation of your idea. If you can get letters of approval of your idea from big buyers or even do a test run of the idea, you will get far more initial interest.
- *1st Timers.* These are the guys laid off from Nortel. Typically, they are engineers or product experts and like working with a board of directors and may find that a challenge.
- *2nd Timers.* These entrepreneurs have done the first round of getting funded and are back for a top-up and refuelling. They are less work than the fresher categories. Investors will take a harder look at this stage because business is a tough deal, just like Hollywood; yesterday's heroes are not necessarily today's stars.

Quick Test for VC Money

How ready are you to leave the angels and go for a higher level of funding, asking for $2M and up? See the "Am I Ready for VC?: The Checklist" (Figure 5.1) and use it to make sure you are ready for the VC stage of investors. These are the exact questions most VCs will ask you when you approach them for capital; answer them all with confidence.

Figure 5.1: Am I Ready for VC?: The Checklist

• Do you have a management team?	› Yes, but certain key management portfolios require strengthening.
• Are you a registered company with registered Web site trademarks and business names?	→ All company and trademark registrations have been duly finalized.
• Are you incorporated and aware that there are different types according to ownership of equity? If you plan to solicit investment, C-corporations are appropriate vehicles for medium to large entities firms but taxation may be higher.	→ The company is duly incorporated and permitted to solicit investment.
• Do you and/or any other owners have "skin in the game?"	→ Total commitment is shown by putting own capital at risk, including mortgaging own house 100%.
• Have you a clearly defined competitive advantage?	→ Unique product with limited likelihood of replication. Watertight and realistic marketing plan is in place.
• Are your revenues increasing steadily to demonstrate demand?	→ Positive revenue trend growth.
• Is your revenue growth sustainable?	→ Sales contracts are signed with several key customers.
• Have you done your financial projections for the next few years? Are your cash flow projections accurate and realistic?	→ Breakeven is defined. Financial projections are completed with supporting financial models.
• Is your intellectual property protected?	→ Patent and copyrights are registered or are in the registration pipeline.
• Have you squeezed out all government grants?	→ Two IRAPs are done and applied to SR & EDs. See Glossary.
• Do you have an advisory board?	→ Strong advisory board is populated with several respected captains of industry.
• Have you set out a clear "exit strategy" for your investor?	→ List of three potential suitor companies.

Since the dot.com bubble, VCs are understandably grumpy and they write tough term sheets, probably wanting 40% ownership. (You can earn back shares.) They want to see that the company has traction with customers. They wonder, "Will this company run out of time and money before they reach their break-even point?" In the Canadian finance industry, the dot.com bubble burst and the U.S. tourists limped home. When foreigners come in, they go back to the U.S. early. Realistically, there are fewer people to talk to and fewer people to make investment decisions.

Valuations are more important at a later stage. But why choose a seed or early-stage company when an investor can get money for a company validated by the market? The VC is attracted to funding your business as there is the strong possibility, if you pass all their due diligence, that your company will give far higher growth than the more mature companies.

Put yourself in the VCs shoes and how they need to be reassured that you will make them look good to their investors. Let's move on to the next chapter and see how VCs tick.

TAKE AWAYS

Angels will take your company from an idea scrambling to survive all the way up to a going concern. Angels will push up your professionalism and train you to ask, "Where do I take the company? What drives my revenue up? What is my cost management strategy—do costs rise proportionately as I sell more?"

CHAPTER 6

WHAT YOU SHOULD KNOW ABOUT VENTURE CAPITALISTS

My biggest motivation? Just to keep challenging myself. I see life almost like one long university education that I never had—every day I'm learning something new.

Richard Branson, Founder and CEO of Virgin

In the mining business, when prospectors or geologists find something that looks like gold, they'll rub a touchstone across the ore. This ceramic stone helps distinguish whether the rock is real or just fool's gold and is an invaluable tool for assessing the worth of a mineral sample. Investors, too, have their personal touchstones that they use for testing your abilities.

"I am often asked what Secret VC Toolkit helps us decide where to invest," venture capitalist Rick Segal of JLA Ventures, says with a smile. "Some people say the Ouija-board approach works well." If you know what the investor will be assessing, you can prepare. To get inside the headspace of a hyper-intellectual and selective venture capitalist (VC) investor, let's find out who they are, what their issues are, and what motivates them to invest their cash in your business.

What You Need to Know about Venture Capitalists

"Private equity firms regard themselves not as asset-flipping gigolos but, rather, as sophisticated, serial monogamists, always on the prowl for profitable long-term relationships,"[1] says Daniel Gross, *Slate* magazine's business journalist. It's true that a private equity investor wants long-term relationships as does a VC. The big difference is where these two types of investors are to be found on the growth curve of a business—the fund managers are at the mature end while VCs are between the startup and established stages.

Although VCs may consider themselves similar to private equity fund managers, they have a far higher appetite for risk and are usually more entrepreneurial, that is, mercurial, outspoken, and able to sum up your abilities in a second. They need to be sharp because they are investing in you and your business, which is not an assured home run. It's very different for the fund manager who has the business's long-term history to judge; success does not rely solely on the people in the business or on the potential for technology growth.

If you are an early stage business, your first step is to present your business plan to the appropriate VC. However, before we do that, let's learn why they are drawn to risky people like you.

It Always Goes Back to the Relationship

"The professional investor's base personality is not as trusting as the business owner's," says VC Ilse Treurnicht, President and CEO of Toronto-based Primaxis Technology Ventures Inc. and now The MaRS Centre. "He is thinking, 'How can this business go wrong? If the business starts to go south, how will this business owner treat me? Will this end with lawyers?'"[2]

Where the business owner sees a glass half full, the VC sees it disappointingly half empty; instead of seeing opportunity, he or she only worries about what could go wrong. Such a naysayer focus can leave

---

[1] Daniel Gross, "It's Not You, It's the Deal," *Slate* Web site, posted Tuesday, November 27, 2007.
[2] Ilse Treurnicht, Investing Conference, Toronto Venture Group, May 2004.

entrepreneurs uncomprehending and resentful. Just remember, owners, that when it comes to attitude and you are asked the question, "Is the glass half full or half empty?" the answer is, "It depends on whether you're pouring or drinking!"

Indeed, the fact that the VC is the Doubting Thomas of the business world can be infuriating to the entrepreneur, particularly when this downer dude is the one deciding to invest in the business idea. It's better for you—the CEO—to understand from the beginning that the type of character attracted to investing is an analytical beast. Few entrepreneurs would use the word "analytical" to describe their skills—they'd prefer something like "rapid developer of idea to market," or "throw something out there and see if it sticks," while you prefer the "Ready, Fire, Aim," approach of Tom Peters, author of *In Search of Excellence* and uber-guru of management.

Here's the crux of the relationship: creative tension. It will make the business stronger. The angel investor may be a mixture of nit-picky analytical and entrepreneurial enthusiasm, but the VC and institutional fund manager lean more toward the nit-picky side—like the Tower of Pisa. The VC accepts your vibrant personality but you also need to use your emotional quotient (EQ) and come to grips with the Excel-dominated brain of the VC.

A start-up VC sees himself partnering with an entrepreneur to build a company. Venture capital, whether at an early stage or prior to initial public offering (IPO), is a bold business. Great entrepreneurs believe they will change the world. That's powerful, intoxicating stuff. You, the business owner, must have this big vision because you will need it. Getting rich takes a long time. Progressive entrepreneurs cannot be afraid of failure. Fund managers know this, but they also need to make sure you're not just drinking Kool-Aid and sharing a sugar rush of false ideas.

What Do Professional Investors Expect?

Imagine a nest. It has room for ten eggs and the mother goose watches patiently for each of them to crack open and hatch. She is hoping her goslings will grow into healthy geese and eventually fly off to make their own nests. Hopefully, a few of the eggs will be golden and bring exceptional wealth.

Fund managers also have room for five to ten investments and want them to grow for five years until they can exit the fund. The big funds that put money into a VC fund expect to earn more than they would from the general market or anywhere else, thus creating pressure for the VC to find potentially highly profitable companies. You may think, "Oh, my business has revenues but not at the 25% level." Do you think you have to be profitable and, if not, do you think the VC route is closed? Good news. If you have money coming in the door, then it is very likely some VC out there will be interested.

Your Full Dedication

Venture capitalists need to be highly particular about the type of company they choose to put into their fund. When you consider that each fund may invest in ten companies, there's not a lot of room to buy into a business that's not going to do what it claims. As your company grows, there are a variety of professional investors out there interested in partnering with you, even with all the hairy risks.

As we mentioned earlier, nothing comes for free, and if you want capital, then VCs will want to acquire an equity stake in your company. The size of their investment will be in proportion to the value of your business. Once your "skin in the game" is clear, the VCs will want smart management, product validation, channel build-up, a rounding-out of your products, and an established sales force. As your business grows and you move on from the research and development (R&D) stage, the valuation of your business will increase. The VCs like to do roll-outs of the product, not just remain in the R&D stage. They will want to stay around and invest in second rounds.

What Venture Capitalists Need to See Before They Trust You

There are two jobs that VCs need to do very well. First, they need to understand how big your potential market could be if things went swimmingly. Second, they must assess the team's talent and ambition. Imagine meeting a young Richard Branson. Would you have glimpsed beyond his hippy ways and seen the iron glint of his sheer tenacity?

Job 1: Identify the Killer Weapon for Success

Ultimately, the VC wants to assess how big the pie can get. This is the true market size and VCs want mega-markets. Facebook saw its original market as college students and that size of market was lucrative enough to chase.

"VCs do like to pull out the pie chart," smiles Alan McMillan, serial entrepreneur. "There are embittered entrepreneurs because their story did not turn out to be a bigger pie but, ultimately, private equity cash can give you your best shot at growth." The pie chart also shows that ownership is worth giving up, because if your company is provided with money to carry out all the programs you need in order to grab a bigger market share, well then, your smaller piece of pie will be worth more. This point is graphically illustrated in Figure 6.1.

Figure 6.1: The Challenge

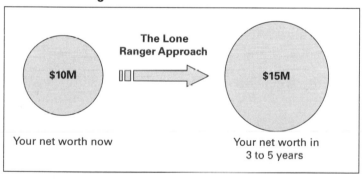

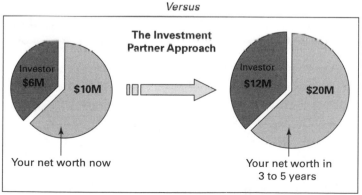

A piece of the larger pie is worth more than the whole of the smaller pie!

Many business owners don't realize that they will have to give up some control if they borrow money to grow the pie. Instead of refusing to accept this fact and getting angry about the greed factor, remember that it's better to have a small per cent of a large pie than one hundred per cent of a crumb. Even more intriguing is recent research that demonstrates that an entrepreneur who gives up more equity to attract investors grows a wealthier company than one who parts with less, and that even what may seem to be a smaller slice at the beginning of the VC investment time period ends up being worth more.

"Most entrepreneurs want to make a lot of money and run the show," says the researcher Noam Wasserman. "New research shows that it is tough to do both." On top of that, Wasserman warns founders, "If you don't figure out which matters more to you, you could end up being neither rich nor king."[3] Parting with some pie looks more appetizing when you decide you do want to be rich.

What Are the Risks to Achieving Market Size?

Facing uncertainties helps to lower the fear that you are a myopic entrepreneur with a huge blind spot and no contingency plans.

- **Technology.** The worst pitches that make equity investors close their cheque books faster than school boys closing their books on a Friday afternoon are those based on technology. "People have blinders about their work when they sit in the basement and think they are saving the world with their new software," says Mark McQueen of Wellington Financial. "From the VC's perspective, if people can steal your idea at a cocktail party then it is not worth much."[4]
- **Industry Intensity Risk.** VCs invest in growing industries and in teams with the Machiavellian efficiency to exploit their niche. If three large incumbents already dominate the business, will you be noticed? What are the regulation barriers? If one company controls

---

[3] Noam Wasserman, "The Founder's Dilemma," hbr.org, February 2008, page 103.
[4] Mark McQueen, Toronto Venture Group Conference, March 2006.

the entire industry, this will not be seen as a good opportunity. Other people should be at the rock face too if it's attractive.

- **Paths to Exit.** List the paths for your exit. Have you thought about five years from now and how the fund will get back its investment with a kicker of a return? Have you made a list of potential buyers who could pay? Can you perhaps include a competitor or a foreign company wanting a foothold in the North American market? Also, which competitors could you buy in order to grow?

Job 2: VCs Must Identify a Team of Tigers

The second challenge for VCs (after identifying that the pie has the potential to become big enough) is to find the right team. "The key to VC valuation is management," VenGrowth Management's Peter Carrescia says. "Until you have your first company blow up, you will say that it's all about the management, but you don't really know what that means. However, once your investment does go south, you will then understand just how much it is about the management."

Perhaps the highest praise is to win the "Deal of the Year" from the investment community. In 2007 the winning business was Sandvine, a company that develops equipment to help broadband service providers manage the heavy demand of traffic on networks. It was financed by BDC Venture Capital, Celtic House, Tech Capital Partners, and Ven-Growth, and the $600M market capitalization highlighted that the deal was a major success in the VC world, making it well worth looking at how the VCs hooked and landed this fish.[5]

Looking back at how he chose Sandvine, Michael Waitman of Celtic House tells a story of early VC investing by George Washington, who was approached with a proposal by a twenty-one-year-old named Henry Knox, back in the fall of 1775.

Henry Knox pointed out to Washington that the British forces were lodged firmly in Boston with no signs of leaving and Washington needed to change the battle odds. Knox proposed taking his men to

---

[5] Mark McQueen, Wellington Financial, Sandvine CEO named CEO of the Year, blog, May 30, 2007.

Fort Ticonderoga where a recent military battle had chased away the British, leaving a large haul of cannons. Knox wanted to lug back to Boston all fifty-nine pieces of weaponry (equal to sixty tons of artillery) across three hundred miles of frozen lakes and rivers. All this was back in the days when there was neither a fork lift nor a Mack truck handy. Bringing the big guns back to Boston seemed impossible, but Washington gave Knox the go ahead. "I believe in you, Henry Knox. You have led your men well and I trust you to figure it out. Here's the money."

Washington would later marvel at the tenacity of Knox to wait until the winter ice set in while keeping his men occupied and happy—perhaps the biggest challenge for military leaders. As Henry Knox's men finally moved the cannons across the ice, the biggest one fell through. Most people would say, "Oh gosh, just leave it behind." But the team refused to let it go. They dove into the icy water, minus wetsuits, tied a rope around the cannon, got it back up to the surface, and carried on to Boston.

By now Washington was convinced that Knox had died of dysentery or had his scalp removed and, as is the unpleasant requirement of every VC, had written off his investment. To Washington's delight, Knox arrived in time to position the cannons on the hill above Boston. In the light of day, the British saw the deadly weapons aimed at them. Their leader, General Howe, is reported to have said, "The rebels did more in one night than my whole army would have done in one month." Finding themselves vulnerable to a devastating attack, the Brits forfeited Boston without a fight and sailed away.

Why did Washington believe in Henry Knox and his big vision over the advice of his other generals? This is the big question of the VC world. Who are the Henry Knoxes of the technology world today? How big is the scope of their dreams and where is the gold over the hills? Can they muster up their troops to drag that gold back, even with the potential disaster of it falling through the ice?

The core character trait of taking on the responsibility of getting the work done is the key reason why Henry Knox succeeded where so many fail. "As soon as a CEO entrepreneur says things like, 'We missed our target because our suppliers let us down,' or 'I couldn't find the right people,' then I know for sure that this is not an entrepreneur I'd invest in," says Mike Volker of WUTIF Capital, director at Simon Fraser University and an angel investor with RIM. "They just don't have it."[6]

People Risk

Ideas are easy. Execution is hard. On the battlefield of business, we don't kill people anymore, but we do kill businesses. The team must be able to shift strategy, change the leader, if necessary, but have the tenacity to keep at it. "Acceptance of mediocrity is the death knell," says Peter Carrescia of VenGrowth Capital Management Inc. "You cannot accept to be good enough. You must win at all costs. When I worked at Microsoft, every division had that philosophy and they crushed the competition."[7]

Ask yourself these questions.

- Is there big vision?
- What do you want out of your business?
- What do the founders want to do?
- Are there cordial relationships between the team and partners?
- Are you mentored? Who is giving you advice?
- Have you executed a strategy in the past?
- How will you behave with a board of directors breathing down your neck?

VCs Like Repeat Teams

Every VC drools over the team that finishes one company's launch and then starts another company that goes on to even more success. This is known as the "alumni phenomenon" and probably the story of PayPal is the most famous. PayPal was a scary ride for the private equity partners as the company founders signed up millions of subscribers but burned

---

[6] Mike Volker, Web site, 2007.

[7] Peter Carrescia of VenGrowth Capital Management Inc., ACG Conference, Toronto, November 2006.

through $180M of VC funding before they broke even and achieved their exit strategy of being acquired by a big corporation. PayPal was bought by eBay during the nuclear winter of dot.coms in 2002, for $1.5 billion. At this point, the two founders of PayPal could have retired and produced their own movie entitled *My Excellent Exit from My Start-Up Company*, but instead they went on to far bigger successes. These are the management teams that can get VC funding with their eyes closed. In fact, the entire original PayPal team reads like a Who's Who of private equity deals such as Facebook, YouTube, Linkedin, Slide, Sequoia (a top VC firm), and philanthropy.

VCs know that tough times teach the best lessons, one of which is that the first idea may not be the right one. As with the many ideas of PayPal alumni (YouTube began as a dating site), Sandvine's first market was wrong and there were a few nail-biting years of flat-lined revenue and calls for more cash. Those brave VCs who were able to pump in capital pushed through for success.

"You never think it can happen to you," says Chad Hurley, alumni of PayPal and co-founder of YouTube, which was sold to Google for $1.6B. "But seeing Peter and Max and the guys (back in PayPal) come up with ideas, and understanding how to make things work gave me a lot of insight. You may not have a business degree, but you see how to put the process into effect. The experience helped me realize the payoff of being involved in a start up."

The Sandvine team built Pixstream and sold it to Cisco for $450M. Within the same month, 9/11 struck and economic disaster followed. Cisco, being the brilliantly managed company it is, counteracted against the downturn by cutting hard and fast; the former Pixstream team found itself shut down and free.

Recognizing the rare chance to finance a credible team, Andrew Waitman of Celtic House said to Kaputo, "Dave, you're coming off a huge success of selling to Cisco. Right now you have the opportunity to raise money for your team." Waitman advised Kaputo to raise enough capital to get across the nasty desert ahead. They took in $20M on the strength of their team alone, although they did not yet have an idea or, needless to say, a PowerPoint or business plan. On the sole strength of the team's previous track record competence, VCs invested. The team then got down to figuring out which markets to attack, and their first pick was not the beachhead that broke through to their big market success. Sandvine needed to stop and change direction. They did not reach their predicted targets and many VCs did decide to stay away.

This is where many entrepreneurs get bitter with the VC community for perhaps stepping back when an abyss opens in front of them.

This is the nature of free enterprise and there's a great deal of broken glass from smashed businesses that did not make it and from the investors who backed them. People get hurt and scarred. Once burned, VCs do not forget and often take it out on the next entrepreneurs. Moreover, there are those VCs who behave like quasi-bankers, forgetting that there are human dynamics at play when you sit on a pile of gold. People will laugh at your VC jokes in order to get the investment money they need.

As a company builds in revenues, it must fight to secure financing. Funny thing, once the company starts making enough money to be able to step back, the tables flip rapidly and the VCs want to give them money. It is at that point that the entrepreneur remembers just which VCs were generous with their time and which attended the board meetings, yet added nothing to the business. Your time will come. When you do make it big, have the grace to get inside investors' heads. Would you have given yourself more money when you had not yet achieved your targets and things were looking bleak?

What Companies Do VCs Like?

When VCs return to dig through the archaeology of a success such as CVCA's Deal of the Year, Sandvine, do they discover it was the excellent due diligence on the facts that did it? More likely, it was the quality of the team that stands out from the debris—not the founder alone but a team able to work together at the required high-stress pace.

How do you define value? Your conversation may begin with the investor asking for a quick snapshot of your financial picture, but a weak earnings before interest, taxes, depreciation, and amortization (EBITDA) will by no means end the chat. Valuation of a business comes from the fund itself and the type of companies they already have in their portfolio.

"Often companies we like do not have EBIDTA or revenues, so we cannot use these tools as value markers." Instead, Peter Carrescia of VenGrowth Capital Management Inc. says, his team values businesses with the following:

- high barriers to entry;
- the capability of rapid revenue growth;
- an analysis of what will happen in the market over the next three years;
- identification of the number one issue to overcome; and
- the perfect intersection of company, services/products, and cycle in the market.

The whole business of investing is complex and wrought with chaos. A very big difference when investing in IT compared to other businesses is that the VCs know that eventually it all comes down to the team involved. Tech VCs can perform the complex science of due diligence, research the market, and call past clients, but the only valid metadata worth drilling into is the people. The art of predicting winning people is much harder. Investing in a practiced team is a good indicator of success but it is still an art.

How to Get the VC to Call

There are certain things, such as resumes, that catch the eye of seasoned pros and get them to pick up the phone and call you. VCs don't invest in technology or markets; they invest in people. If the people stuff goes wrong, it's hell. They put you through due diligence, while at the same time trying to find out what kind of person you are. When you pitch in, it's a sociological experiment to see what makes you tick and whether you will be co-operative or will crack.

Probably the most powerful action you can take is to find a referral to a partner in the business. It's a bit like dating. If someone they trust refers you to a VC, they will take your call. Bad phone manners are an immediate red flag. The VC knows they are entering into a seven-year relationship and they will not waste time with someone who rankles. If they can't see themselves married to you, it's a quick, "Thank you but no thanks."

Plan Well

Expect to spend at least a few weeks preparing to visit a sophisticated investor. Otherwise, you are dead before you even begin. Without the work, you might just as well climb into a coffin, hand a stake to the investor and say, "Drive it in, please."

Your business plan is much like a resume and it's the ticket that will get you to the next stage: a face-to-face meeting. Attracting money to your business will be easier if you show your vision of the business and how you plan to execute it. You can make yourself far more attractive to investors if you have a merger possibility on the radar that you can name.

"It's the people, not the product, that investors are most interested in," says Treurnicht. "And first impressions are important. Be active and interested without being arrogant. A banking or VC relationship typically lasts four to eight years, so investors [tend to] look for people they like and believe they'll get along with."

The VC Screening Process

VCs have to screen deals that come through their doors. They see thousands of proposals and you have to break through to get their attention. Your business plan can help you stand out from the crowd, or not. If you do not have a decent plan, forget it.

Where Does Your Deal Fit?

Ask your VC where your company investment would be placed in their fund horizon. If your company is first in, then you have more time (five years) to make money before being required to pay back the full amount. If you are last in, the time for the VC to get out will be closer.

It also depends upon when you meet with the VCs and at which stage they are with their fund. If they have already filled up most of their fund, they will be very choosy about the last two companies. If they have just obtained the cash, then they will be feeling more generous. After the investment, find out who will handle your file. Will it be the same person who did the due diligence and who spent time getting to know your business? That person will have an emotional attachment. If a new guy is handling your file, there will be far less commitment.

The VC is a high-risk, high-return animal. Three out of ten companies in their fund will drive their fund's return. If you are in that portfolio and your business is struggling, expect some pressure from the VCs. They want winners as these are their bread and butter. VCs make money for people who make them money. There are usually ten years in their life cycle: the first five years are used to seed your business and the remaining five are used to harvest the investment. The VCs must get out. They are not there to fund you into retirement.

The VCs know they will have to invest their own time in carrying out due diligence. They need to check out your company and see if what you claim is in fact the truth. Have you tried to represent your business and its risks or have you concealed a few problems that could cause a five-lane pile-up in the future?

Figure 6.2: Rough Guide to VC's Path to Investing

❑ **Screening**
  Quick flip of investment proposal
❑ **Evaluation**
  Detailed interrogation of your concept, your people, returns you are offering and company visit
❑ **First Round**
  Negotiation of terms of investment
❑ **Full Due Diligence**
  Check up on your business, talk to your customers
❑ **Negotiation**
  Discussion of terms and acceptable deal
❑ **Legal Review and Documentation**
  Filing of finance deal
❑ **Funding**
  Provision of funding

VCs will have many questions, but Adam Breslin of Pender Management says, "Part of the process is to get to grips with the risks and reach a level of agreement between the entrepreneur and the investor [as to] what the risks are and how to try and avoid the holes."

Risks to Watch For

"The risks business owners face today are so much more complicated than the basic challenges you envisioned at the outset to sell your product to the market," says Breslin. "In fact, the risk list is so daunting that many entrepreneurs respond by ignoring most of these risks altogether. CEOs agree that most entrepreneurs have an automatic dislike for risk management. It seems to be just another set of authoritarian rules taking them away from their most pressing goal—generating revenue. Breslin notes that, "The more CEOs discuss the problems they face, the more they realize that an active, integrated approach to risk management will actually pay off and, usually, sooner rather than later."[8]

Here are some of the risks identified by investors and CEOs and a look at some of their solutions.

- **Strategic Risk.** These are potential losses that stem from poor decision-making regarding strategic resources. Your choice of products and services delivered to carefully selected markets creates your risk profile. For example, the biggest risk for Toronto book publisher Shore Publishing, and its CEO Penny Shore, is selling the books it publishes. Recognizing that vulnerability, Shore says, encouraged her company to reduce its risks by switching from fickle consumers to the more stable business-to-business publishing market.

- **Operational Risk.** Failed internal processes, people, systems, or external events results in operational risks. Often, it's only when things go wrong that entrepreneurs recognize the importance of seemingly routine activities. Toronto's 2003 SARS outbreak made news around the world. Peter VanderPlaat, CEO of Mississauga-based Desert Spring Products, has customers in Asia and Europe. Selling its flagship product, an innovative indoor humidifier, depends on a

[8] Speech by Adam Breslin, Canadian Innovators Forum, Mansfield, Ontario, June 2005.

crucial training program for their sales reps and distributors. When SARS hit the headlines, British marketing staff refused to work with Canadians. "It nearly shut us down," says VanderPlaat. "The fallout lasted over a year. Next time, we will be well prepared because we recognize that this is a key part of our sales process."

- **Information Security Risk.** This involves the risk of losing control of your confidential customer data in an era of growing privacy legislation. Although he does most of his business in Canada, Sam Dennis, CEO of Toronto-based Rydium Canada, a digital advertising company, noted that he has to keep on top of ever-changing U.S. regulations—because although his clients are American, the privacy law will apply in Canada. His risk is not being able to observe U.S. law in Canada.

- **Outsourcing Risk.** This term refers to losses stemming from interruption of services provided by suppliers. The risks arise from outsourcing parts of a medical device, for example, to manufacturers who do not adhere to your company's quality and behavioural standards, says Arun Menawat, CEO of Novadaq Technologies, a publicly–traded, Mississauga-based producer of medical devices. Menawat says he is relentless in assessing suppliers and the risk they pose. "With medical devices, you are dealing with safety issues and regulations that have enormous impact."

- **Security Risk.** The loss of an organization's assets, cash, or accounting information involves security risk. This is a clear-cut example of how paying attention to risk can help your bottom line, not hurt it. Jack Hoang, CEO of i3DVR, says his company has developed software that can count how many customers are lined up in front of a restaurant counter. The program can then estimate revenues on a real-time basis and flag any anomalies—discouraging counter staff from attempting to intercept any of that cash.

- **Legal Risk.** This type of risk involves losses from violations of the law or uncertainty regarding a company's legal position, rights, and duties. Many private companies address this risk by establishing high behavioural and cultural standards. They state something along the lines of "ethical standards in our company surpass regulatory requirements. We do not wish to be 'clever' and push the boundaries."

- **Reputation Risk.** When your business's reputation among various stakeholder groups deteriorates, you are risking your reputation. Companies that offer advice, for instance, must be prepared to take responsibility for the quality of that advice. Your liability here could be growing as U.S.–style litigiousness spreads north. Toronto publisher Penny Shore notes that a few years ago bad advice in a book might result in a negative letter from a disappointed reader. Today it could just as easily result in a lawsuit. Even if the case is thrown out, she warns, it could seriously damage your image.

When private companies actively manage risk, they gain a better understanding of their business, its weak points, and the best opportunities for expansion. Risk and governance become less about compliance and more about managing for growth and efficiency.

Common Mistakes by Entrepreneurs

VCs say they are always surprised by the number of investors who seem oblivious to the mistakes that can tip the decision to invest or not to invest.

Lack of Personal Risk

Do not expect others to put money in your business if you don't put any money in yourself. You need "skin in the game" or else investors sense you could bail out and get a job at Google when the going gets tough—which it inevitably does.

Poor Presentation of Financial Information

"Another big mistake," says Mark McQueen of Wellington Financial, "Is handing over a spreadsheet with every item listed, including stationary and envelopes. You do not need to provide that information to the investors." If they ask, you can pull out your details but they do not need to see every line of the P&L; otherwise, they may end up banging their heads on the table. Moreover, the investors will want their information quarterly, no matter when your year-end falls, so give it to them based on the common tax schedule.

Not Knowing the Fund

You're not the only ones trying to "spin." VCs spin just as much and they want you to take a big chance on them too. It's a quiet little secret that fund managers and VCs want to be known and admired too. If you take the trouble to research them, it demonstrates that you are genuinely excited about them coming on board. By now, you recognize there are as many varieties of funds as animals in a zoo; Google the funds and read their Web sites in detail. There will be a list of the companies they have in their fund portfolio that will make it very clear which industries they like. There are funds at this stage for most types of businesses, from mining, manufacturing through to technology, but you will have to read their investment criteria. Check out the CVCA's Web site, which gives you a good number of Canadian private equity investors. Remember that your industry needs to fit their skills. Do your research. Who have they backed before and what do you have in common with those companies?

- Ask the other entrepreneurs running companies in the portfolio what their VC did for them lately.
- Is this fund patient? You want to be comfortable that they are not going to do a quick flip of your business but, rather, that they care about your vision.
- Will the fund be there for the next round of financing?
- Do they have a network of contacts?
- What is the reputation of the VC? When you go for your next round of money (as you grow), the next investors will want to know who went in the first time. If your investors are headquartered in Las Vegas and resemble the cast of *The Sopranos*, maybe take a pass. If you choose to take the easy route and get your business financed by some heavy in the 'waste disposal' business who wears big knuckle rings, know that this short cut will one day be brought out into the harsh light of day and may cost you blue chip funding years down the road.

Lack of Standing in the Community

You are going to very few private investors and you are selling an extremely expensive item. Put yourself in your investor's shoes. This person is spending $1M to $5M of his own money on your company. Is he going to hand over cash to someone who calls up and says, "Hey Joe, I hear you've got some extra money kicking around and I have a terrific company for you." Absolutely not. The investment community is like six degrees of separation and they will find out everything about you.

Jan Carlezon, CEO of a failing Scandinavian airline, turned it around by teaching his employees that each of them counts in the customer experience. When travellers receive a smile at the check-in counter, when they sit on a spotless seat, when they reach for a clean blanket—each of these little elements is a moment of truth, a moment when the brand is reinforced. Imagine if the washroom were dirty. That moment of truth would tarnish the other positive parts of the customers' experience. The customers would feel that your maintenance of the aircraft was shoddy and that your whole business was like that one carelessly kept washroom. Attracting investors is about each and every experience the investor has with you—from conversations to setting up the meeting, to the paper you use for your investment proposal. It's all providing a message about how you operate your business.

If you write a blog or chat in Facebook, know that your friends are not the only people reading your words of wisdom. Do not divulge details about your private equity partners—"These VC bozos made me write a sixty-page plan they didn't even read." Rick Segal of J.A. Albright, obviously a well-read VC, blogged about this entrepreneur's blog gaff on his blog!

If you have something difficult in your background, a lawsuit, for example, be upfront. As Dr. House in the Emmy winning TV series *House*, says, "Everyone lies." A fund manager who had just won a top businessman of the year award said, "Being a cynic and never believing in anyone these past twenty years finally paid off." Google makes it easy enough for a monkey to do a surface background check and fund managers have lawyers to do more detailed sweeps. In 110 B.C., Publilius Syrus wrote, "A good reputation is more valuable than money."

A Word for Women

It has been suggested that limited access to "old boy" networks and a male-dominated financial industry has posed challenges for women seeking growth capital. "Those conditions partially explain why women gain just 6% of the $69B of venture capital available in the U.S.," says Ilse Treurnicht. "Still, women don't make it easy on themselves, either. A passive style, conservative attitude and inability to 'talk the language' are just some of the factors holding women back."[9]

The good news: perceptions are slowly changing and there is money available for solid, high-growth firms that can adequately communicate their promise to investors. If you are female, grow some thick skin and deal with the stereotypes early on in your conversations. Here are a few:

- Woman entrepreneurs do not want to grow their business as quickly as men do.
- Female entrepreneurs just don't "get" how to source funding.
- Lack of networks is one reason for women's challenges. When women were asked about their networks, they listed various men's names. When those men were asked about their networks, they did not mention the women.

Before you write to your local newspaper to complain, take a breath. What is true are the statistics on male- versus female-run businesses which illustrate that female companies may grow at a slower clip, but they tend to have a higher survival rate. Understand that, when it comes to accessing private equity, fund managers favour the growth versus survival factor. It's only logical that when you go about raising capital, your pitch must be at growing the business; otherwise, leave private equity to the more aggressive CEOs. Barbara Orser, professor at Carlton University, reiterates that critical point, "Here's the bottom line for women: only entrepreneurs who start robust, high-potential businesses—and communicate that promise—will get the money they need." Smart women

---

[9] Rebecca Gardiner, "How Women Can Get Funded by Banks and Venture Capitalists," PROFITguide.com, June 24, 2004.

understand that thinking and reassure investors by spending more time on illustrating their ambition when reaching out to the VCs.

Do Your Homework

Written by the Scribes of Delphi and then by Plato are the words "Know Thyself," and this wisdom resonates today when it comes to getting to know the stakeholders of private equity—venture capitalists.

"Entrepreneurs must know what their limitations are," advises Markus Luft, serial high-tech entrepreneur and now executive-in-residence expert for his former financial partners, Roynat, who helps with their portfolio of companies. "Owners must come to terms with their weaknesses and know what they don't know," Markus says. You know you are ready to put together a management team when every major decision has to come through you. He says, "If owners do not build teams, they will find themselves out on the road selling while still being needed back at the office. There is a serious bottleneck to growth." Markus knows what he is talking about, as at the age of fifty he entered entrepreneurial life and took two companies up a growth path and sold with Roynat at his side. "By the time I sold it this past September, Headwater had 85 staff and $11.5-million in sales."[10]

In order to move the business forward, Luft suggests considering the questions below.

- What makes you competitive?
- What is your market?
- When did you update your business plan?
- What kind of cash flows are required?
- What is the exit or IPO timing (if any) and what's the roadmap?
- How will you create your board? How will it run the company? What kind of people are needed on the board?
- What is your exit strategy (multiples? EBITDA? [types of valuation])? You must know what factors come into play, and understand them all.

---

[10] "Entrepreneur," *Financial Post,* January 8, 2007, at www.financialpost.com/story.html?id=cb62a4d1-fb4d-48ad-9994-a70cc8d20c57&p=3.

"If you can't position your business," Markus warns, "Your value will be undermined. The bottom line is: DO YOUR HOMEWORK!"

You Understand Controlled Greed

"There's nothing in this world more demoralizing than money," said Sophocles, someone who apparently went through fund raising. If VCs say no to your investment proposal, don't take it personally. Ask them what they think you could do or who else you should approach and you may get an excellent tip.

If you understand the VCs' double-sided sword of fear and greed, you will be able to handle deal making. VCs are not in the business of charity. It is their money and they need to please their clients too. Behind the so-called greed is a far greater emotion—the fear factor. VCs fear losing money on a deal (you) and being the laughing stock of Wall Street, Bay Street, or Silicon Valley; they are also afraid of losing their fund and never working again. Their job is very public. Private equity financing, besides being the riskiest part of the business world, is also quite open to scrutiny. If you believe the business textbooks, the risk ought to drop as your business grows, but in reality the risk stays high for much longer.

"I tell entrepreneurs in government programs that when they get financing, it is never what they wanted or expected," says Rolf Eichfuss who helps small and medium enterprises (SMEs) at the National Research Council Canada. "It's not a great deal, but it's today's deal."

TAKE AWAYS

Investors each have their preferred target investment size and type of business. Research their Web sites to learn where they have invested and what types of companies they see as a "fit."

Watch your aggression levels . . . step away from the coffee. Be aware that it is a small community and financing is a tough business for both you and the investors.

CHAPTER 7

THE VALUATION: CREATE THE FRAMEWORK FOR FUND MANAGERS

It is not the employer who pays the wages. Employers only handle the money. It is the customer who pays the wages.

Henry Ford

On a cloudless morning in June, I join a group of CEOs at the National Club downtown on Bay Street for a buffet of muffins and fresh fruit. The speaker for the roundtable is Elliot Knox, managing director of Bedford Capital, which invests in companies with steady revenues over $5M. Knox runs a hand through his hair and surveys the group.

Today's discussion is for owner-CEOs interested in learning more about private equity and the topic is, "What I Wish Every CEO Knew When They Receive Funding."

Many owner-CEOs believe it's critical to understand that single defining moment, the point where an investor signs over capital. For investors at the more mature end of private equity—the fund manager—the critical time is actually the five-year mark, when typically they like to exit their ownership in a business. Their focus is on taking the company to a professional level. "Definitely, there's a template I wish every owner-CEO knew at the start of the five-year investment period," says Knox.

So, What Should Every CEO Know?

Moving the group of CEOs to the boardroom, Knox begins the discussion of how fund managers value the potential of a business. Knox says, "I judge the CEO within the first fifteen minutes of a meeting. Once the team has passed the personality test, I will move quickly to finding out how strategic they are as this will impact their ability to grow."

One CEO asks Knox to explain which characteristics appearing within those first fifteen minutes he feels show good leadership. Knox says, "The fund manager invests in a wide range of companies and may have to turn around companies along the way which subsequently gives them a tough view of CEOs. I have no idea how to make you successful as a leader. I have never found that one element. I can tell you what I have observed with successful CEOs and it may surprise you." According to Knox, most CEOs who were successful were wrong. "These CEOs were told they could not do what they wanted to achieve, because no one had ever done it that way before. They ignored the critics and naysayers and forced their ideas through. In hindsight, these CEOs changed the way business was done in their industry." From these observations, Elliot Knox says, "I could say that if you are pushing to change the way your industry looks and works, you will be a very successful CEO."

The best entrepreneurs do want to change the world. They may even see something that makes them mad and go and change it. Then they change it for everyone else. Anita Broderick started The Body Shop because she was furious with the big beauty product companies. The top, top entrepreneurs have that Don Quixote tilting at windmills ability to take on markets that seem saturated such as Hotmail shooting holes in the postal system; MySpace changing the meaning of community; Skype hammering the big boys of telecommunications.

Value Defined

The first question for owners is how will the value of their business be defined? At the mature end of company life, Sandra Bosela of Edgestone Capital, says, "We define value as a company with a strong market position, growing finances, growing revenues and long-term cash flow from year-in and year-out customers."

The fund manager will want to see your company's operating matrices—drivers of growth. What are the long-term performance drivers for the industry? Can the fund manager improve the company's performance? Attractive fundamentals, such as being cyclical on the upturn, add to its value. Also of interest are undermanaged companies where opportunity has not been focused on growth and where there is room to make growth a strategic focus. You have great products but how can you grow your markets? Is your company underfunded and not reinvesting in the business but paying out dividends or payments? You have a great business model, but it is untapped. These are the sort of situations fund managers value and like to mine with management to improve the set-up.

What is the biggest value destroyer? "Without a doubt, it is poor leadership," says Nathalie Townsend of Northrock Capital. "Someone who has grown a business may not want to make the leap to a more complex organization. Early on in our initial discussions, the CEO must align company interests with the private equity investors and devise a value-creation plan together with the management team, discussing the opportunities to create wealth. We do this before putting in money because it prevents any nasty surprises."

Do You Set Clear Objectives?

Elliott Knox looks around the room at the CEOs sitting sipping their coffees and finishing their muffins and asks, "Do you have a mission statement? Right. Now, can you recite it?"

The CEOs in the room murmur to each other. None of them passes the test except for one who mutters about being a Top 100 company on the stock exchange with world-class manufacturing capability. Elliot then asks, "Now, why do you want to be on the list of Top 100 companies? Is that the level where the gravy starts coming? Why do you want world-class manufacturing and what does that mean? Does it mean you strive for the best practices or are you just a copy cat?"[1] The CEO just smiles sheepishly and everyone laughs.

Now, if the mission statement and objectives have motherhood and apple-pie jargon, this signals trouble. When the fund manager digs deeper and asks why, if the owner again says it's because of survival or to make money, these are disappointing answers. According to him this is not the objective required in order to take the business to the next level.

Begin with the Exit

Sherlock Holmes is an enduring character enjoyed by readers worldwide. What makes his stories still surprising more than one hundred years after they were first penned? Scottish author Arthur Conan Doyle said he always concentrated on his conclusion. How can you know the road to follow if you don't first establish your destination? Getting financing has its end point too—the exit or liquidity event.

The biggest mistake made by business owners is being preoccupied by the moment at which they receive the cheque. They presume that the end in mind is the moment the cash goes into their bank account. "Not so," says Knox.

You must understand, and this is critical, that the investor's destination is five years further down the road. To the person new to the world of finance, this end seems murky and unfathomable. How can you see five years into the future? Yet, if you want to attract money, this is exactly the challenge ahead.

A logistics business owner wanted to retire. The business had good margins and customer loyalty, and the owner wanted to exit. He thought he had a world-class business. He had a vision of being a Top 100 company and he had built a system for a world-class business, but he had

---

[1] Elliott Knox, CEO Retreat, Canadian Innovators Forum, Toronto, May 2006.

spent $1M annually building that world-class system. Now he wanted that money back.

'Ihe fund manager asked, "Who's buying your business?"

It could not be a small guy. It had to be a major company. But would they already have a system?

"Yes," says the logistics owner, "They would." So why would they buy this retiring owner's business with its over-investment in the same system? When you look at your objectives, you should start with who is buying your business five years down the road. Whether you sell or not, it is a great private exercise to think about.

Had he had a clearer strategic objective, it would have been more logical for the owner not to have bought the business system. Obviously, it would have been foolish for the owner to tell his employees, "I don't want to put in a system because I want to exit in five years." However, if you plan toward keeping more irons in the fire, if you make decisions with that long-term objective in mind, you will be more successful. Don't leave your options closed, for example, by deciding to hand your business over to one child or to one competitor. As it turns out, the logistics guy sold his business for a decent sum, but he could have been richer.

Make Your Own Plans

A good plan is a plan of action and not a dream, a hope, or a fanciful thought of being a Top 100 company. A fund manager will want to see a CEO who spends some time planning strategies but more time acting on opportunities.

A company was losing money and when the fund manager probed the CEO about his concerns he said, "I can't sleep because I'm thinking about the people I will lay off." That's nice, but as the fund manager commented, he might not have to axe those jobs if instead he thought about opportunities and a way forward. When your fund manager asks you what keeps you up at night, the expectation is that you worry about the money. The fund manager wants to hear you are worried. If the fund manager senses you are not worried about the money, things get ugly.

Figure 7.1: Your "Willed Future"

Objectives	Planning	Implementation
Begin with the end in mind	*Beyond the budget to the possible:*	*Know Your Actions:*
Describe the end game in five years. Your Exit Plan:	Market definition and vision	Plan the little things
Who is buying you?	Products and services	Plan the big initiatives
Why are they buying you?	Financial projections	Communicate the plan
What would give you extra appeal?	Marketing, sales, and business development	List milestones to hit
What would be overkill?	Operations, quality, and product development	Work on positive management style
What should be the key use of money?	Human resources	Link feedback to pay
What will be your revenues and EBITDA?	Finance and systems, management, and organization	

Source: Adapted from Elliott Knox, Bedford Capital

The Doable Plan and the Stretch Plan

People like to provide plans with milestones that are obviously achievable, that provide for bonuses or lead to the return of part of the company, but that is not motivating for investors. Fund managers want to see their CEOs take risks that stretch them, such as moving into a new market like China or shifting manufacturing to El Salvador. Figure 7.1 is a good example of planning that will impress fund managers.

See It, Own It, Do It

"Hello, Mark."

"Hi."

"Let's get together for lunch next week."

"OK. Do you have anything in mind?"

"Italian?"

"I prefer Chinese."

"What about a burger instead?"

"Great. Can you give me a place and time?"

"Sure! On Robson Street there's this great little spot. I'll call to book and send an e-mail with directions. How about if we meet next Wednesday at noon."

"Terrific!"

We have just spent more time planning a lunch than most CEOs spend planning the implementation of their strategy. Most strategy stops at the seven pages in point form of the business mission and the big picture. The next step is the plan. Think of it as arranging that lunch date. Figure out what is to be done within the next month, followed by what is to be achieved within the year. Get your strategy past sitting around the table talking about the Mission Statement.

Your Communication Ability

Fund managers have learned from their investment failures that a CEO's ability to get people excited about the company's vision must be extraordinary. When the fund manager walks into an office, the CEO's communication skills will become obvious from her level of energy and ability to engage everyone around the boardroom table. If the CEO's attitude about sharing the vision is "why do the factory floor guys need to know," then chances are the company is not tapping into the full company brainpower and there is not enough strategic depth down through the ranks of staff.

To Whom Do You Communicate Your Plan?

When Bell Helicopters built a long-term plan, they brought in their suppliers to share their strategy. Always share your plan—even if you're stuck in a bad patch. It's a funny thing about humans—they will want to help you achieve your goals.

Another big destroyer of value is when the few people running the show fail to get together regularly and keep the company's vision and strategy aligned. In growth companies, there are not a lot of people on the team and horsepower is spread thinly. They all need to agree on what it takes to be successful and then say it and say it again and then again.

Do Your Staff Know the Plan?

Your fund manager will want a meeting with your staff to talk about strategy. One CEO thought he had the best plan and explained it to the fund manager. When the team was asked, "How big will we be in three years time?" no one seemed to know. The sales manager did not know his numbers beyond last year's sales. The production guy did not realize it was growing quickly but did realize he didn't have the skills. Everyone should be made aware of the growth plan. "If the CEO does not involve the staff in company strategy frequently, this is a big mistake as it will mean that the staff will not be motivated to get out of bed and get on with building the business," says Sandra Bosela of Edgestone. "Management teams get excited if there is a leader with a clear vision, one who discusses goals with the team and asks for their input. This way they all get to understand the vision." This is strategic depth and it is very important if you want value added to your business.

Your Management Style: Delegation, Co-ordination, and Control

Setting Milestones

Get used to setting objectives and milestones and see how you do. It is possible to measure—get used to doing it before you meet with a fund manager.

Elliott Knox says, "If a CEO from a portfolio company comes in and tells us about a missed deadline, what does the fund do? Will we fire the CEO? Probably not. We appreciate candour."

When the company misses a milestone, get everyone involved. Why was it not done? Is the plan achievable? If this problem keeps recurring and more deadlines are missed, the fund manager is sure to say, "Houston, we have a problem."

Positive Management Style

Listen to your investors, make up your own mind, but do respect their outsider view. The CEO of Domino's pizza stresses the importance of your attitude to the private equity partnership: "The ability to work with the partners in a spirit of trust and fairness is what it's all about."[2]

Fund managers pay attention to your leadership style. If you are a hard task master, you tend to put people off. During a team building workshop, a manager blindfolded an employee and then helped the person navigate an obstacle course to the other side of the room. The manager would ring a bell whenever the blindfolded person began moving in the correct direction. By the end of the course, the person would respond quickly, almost running. The exercise was then repeated with one difference. This time the manager was given a small, rubber hammer to tap the blindfolded person gently whenever he went in the wrong direction. It is extraordinary how much the whole journey slows down—the employee, not wanting to receive that tiny tap, froze in his movements.

Make your staff successful and use incentives such as a simple verbal thank you at the weekly meeting, dinner coupons, or tickets to the hockey game. Or you can become more structured with cash bonuses and opportunities to earn stock. Sales teams may be more motivated if you set up objectives for sales where they can earn points and at the end of a quarter, receive a bonus.

The Importance of Feedback and Pay

What gets measured and rewarded gets done. This seems simple, yet a fund manager shares a story of how he judged an investment in a store franchise.

---

[2] Scenes from a Private Equity Roundtable, Knowledge@Wharton, 22 February, 2007, posted 11:38 A.M. ET.

He recalled visiting a problem retailer in his portfolio. "I went into the store and was initially impressed as the staff had cleaned up the shelves since my previous visit. I asked the first staff person I saw about the cleaner shelves."

She replied, "The order came down for us to do that."

The fund manager asked, "What was the incentive to do your job well?"

She said, "I don't know. I have no idea what my priorities should be or whether I am doing the right thing."

This young woman did not know if her focus should be on cleanliness, on customer service or on keeping the shelves stocked. It did not matter if she kept the shelves clean or dirty because either way her pay appeared like manna from Heaven.

Did it change her performance? No.

The beauty of private equity is how it ties pay to the performance of the senior team. Everyone's got "skin in the game," from top managers to the private equity partners. It's serious stuff. Since private equity gives cash without claiming assets if the whole thing blows up, they are psychologically invested to ensure that they give you their best. Public company pay is supposed to be tied to performance but there is less incentive to make that link. Dunkin' Donuts' CEO, Jon Luther, partnered with Bain Capital, Carlyle, and Thomas Lee Partners. Luther says, "I insisted that the officers invest personally. Management has a substantial amount of personal money in this venture. It makes a huge difference to the 40 officers of the company when they show up for work. There's now a different discipline regarding how they spend money. If it doesn't grow the business, why do it?"[3]

How Do Funds Add Value?

Entrepreneurs looking to sell their business in five years' time will benefit from bringing in partners in order to juice up business performance. For example, funds have portfolios with many similar companies. VenGrowth

---

[3] "What do private equity firms have that public firms don't," CNNMoney Web site, November 27, 2006.

looks at technology companies with a common thread. In their fund, they have thirty companies in the tech space. This bird's eye-view gives an enormous advantage toward learning trends and can enable them to see what will happen over the next three years.

"Many funds give lip service about adding value along the way, but input is vital for growth," says Sandra Bosela when asked how to grow the company and the steps to take when looking at investing in the business. You cannot start this after you have the company. She adds, "As we assess a business for investment purposes, we look at how we could grow the business."

You may remember a TV advertisement where a man dives into a pool, lifts weights, and then gets a hair cut, followed by the phrase "Hair Club." Bosela's team developed the value of this company as it had a strong retail network but room to expand regarding the product and service range offered to clients coming to the stores. As a result of seeing this value-added possibility, Bosela jumped at the opportunity. She advises, "Once you have the company, you should not be starting to analyze growth strategies."

Bosela says, "We must be careful not to fall in love with the product or service. We must look for a potential exit and how to position the company. After four years with the business, we help prepare it for the capital market and make sure it is Sarbanes-Oxley compliant."

It is the end of the morning roundtable and Elliott Knox closes the meeting with the CEOs and everyone heads for the spring sunshine beckoning from outside. One of the CEOs, who had discussed his mission statement earlier, came up to shake Knox's hand. "You know," he began, "I always thought you bankers were slick and just wanting to get a piece of my business to pay for your champagne and Porsche lifestyle."

Knox smiled painfully and the CEO continued, "But I realized something today. In fact, you could almost say I had an epiphany."

We waited . . .

"I see that private equity is not a banking or finance structure. Private equity is a *way* of doing business."

Elliott broke out into a huge grin and hugged the man. Indeed, that is the value of private equity—doing business in the best way possible.

Venture capital's grown-up brother is the institutional investor: the fund manager. Private equity fund managers are very different in how they view their role and how they add value. Private equity fund managers invest in established businesses usually with $10M in revenue and up. The value of a company is set by the depth of the management team and their strategic depth. Essentially, strong operations will be the goal of the fund manager.

Summary Points: Achieving Mutual Understanding

1. Companies who attract investors know about the mathematical "fit" required by investors: your position on the business growth curve from startup to maturity and the dollar amount of money you wish to raise.

2. There are two key differences from a bank loan for the venture capital investment. First, private equity involves minority equity or quasi-equity participation (owning common shares outright, or having the right to convert other financial instruments into common shares) in a private company. Second, private equity is a long-term investment (generally from three to eight years); and requires active involvement by the investors in the companies, which they finance until they are sufficiently developed for the fund to exit from the business.

3. Private equity is an involved rather than a passive form of financing.

4. Growth capital can be matched to the company that wants to grow to the next level. The changes most often introduced by the fund manager are:

   - management techniques,
   - mode of governance (the way decisions are made), and
   - structure.

5. An entrepreneur who gives up more equity to attract investors grows a wealthier company than one who parts with less. What seems to be a smaller slice at the front of the venture capital (VC) investment time period, usually ends up being worth more.
6. The value of a business at the mature end of company life is defined as a company with a strong market position, growing finances, growing revenues, and long-term cash flow from year-in and year-out customers.
7. Build a five-year strategy with your team and discuss it constantly with everyone.

It is critical to understand that the private equity investor's destination is five years down the road and then they will want to exit from your business. In order to recoup their investment plus 25%, you must look for a potential exit and how to position the company for a buyer, an initial public offering (IPO), or another idea in order to generate the liquidity to release the capital.

You can now match your company and size of capital investment to the right angel, VC, or fund manager. You know what each level of investor will value in a company and by truly understanding the investor's needs, you will be able to encourage them to invest capital in your company.

With that in mind, we can now move on to crafting your plan, getting prepared for your face time with potential investors, and, once you have a signed letter from the investor saying they wish to proceed to negotiations, making sure you get a signed investment deal. But before you get too excited, we need to visit a private equity investor at your first meeting, just as you are about to present the story of your precious baby—your business.

PART III
GETTING "INVESTOR READY"

CHAPTER 8

FOUR BRUTAL QUESTIONS AND WHY YOU NEED TO ANSWER THEM

The principle driving force behind economically successful societies is trust. Strangers have to trust each other to work together with one another.[1]

Clem Sunter, Anglo American Corporation, plc.

*H*ere's a little test for you. Most business owners don't like to plan, or any of that "wussey" stuff, because they've got along by the sheer force of their personalities (and some string and chewing gum). Planning hampers them, weighs them down, slows the flow of their work. The problem comes when they want to take their business to the next level. Then they discover the growth curve is alarming and the cash is not forthcoming. Bill Gates said growing from a startup to the first 400 employees was the toughest part. What if I told you that if business owners took the trouble to answer a few questions—four exactly—their business would get the money to grow?

---

[1] Clem Sunter, *What it Really Takes to Be World Class* (South Africa: Human & Rousseau, 1997), page 98.

Remember Walt Disney's the little engine that could and how it forced itself up the hill because it repeated, "I think I can, I think I can." Sure enough, it makes one last shudder and to our enormous relief, heaves up all those carriages onto a flat track to the final destination. This extra effort is what it takes to get your business up that terrifying slope of growth, which leaves so many companies exhausted, discouraged, and spent.

Did Walt Disney borrow Virgil's (the Greek philosopher) pithy saying "I can, because I think I can," give it a fresh coat of paint and—for all those dads out there in the movie theatre—and use the hot technology of the fifties—the train? Maybe, but Walt was smart in taking an ancient wisdom that still resonated thousands of years later and re-working it.

What if I told you that when it comes to money, there are four ancient questions rooted in the past that could shovel the coal onto your steam engine faster than frat boys loading up their beer fridge on a Friday afternoon? What if I told you these four questions are the fuel to power your train up the track—the key to getting money invested in your business?

To get you into the right frame of mind, let's step back and breathe deeply. The CIO of eBay confided that he was able to get so much done—achieving truly astounding growth—due to the concepts in one book: Steven Covey's, *The 7 Habits of Highly Effective People*. Apparently, this eBay technocrat discovered how to inspire his team using one of Covey's habits: Begin with the end in mind. Covey's wisdom is also rooted in ancient ideas. Let's take a leaf out of Covey's book too; apply this habit to you and your financing situation. What is the end we have in mind for you?

Simple. It is getting the $500,000, $1M, $5M, $10M, or the amount you need.

Imagine standing in front of the venture capitalist (VC) or fund manager. It is the moment when you finish your presentation. You look at him expectantly. You know he's read your proposal and listened to your presentation. You know how much it has taken to get you to this point—nurturing your idea, forcing it into a business, working weekends to pull together the plan and your presentation. This is it—trussed up into this one stressful minute where you stand captive at the front of this boardroom. Your system floods with fight-or-flight adrenalin. You eye the door, agonizing, craving to rip it off its hinges and bust through to the other side, back to the safety of your world, chest heaving and panting in relief. It's a horrible moment. Call it judgement time.

Presenting to the money guy brings you to this awful point and if it's any consolation, know that many, many people have gone through that exact moment.

Here you are—will your ego get crushed? There he sits in front of you—tough-assed money guy. He leans back in his chair, steeples his fingers and stares at you with steely eyes, like an eagle spotting a field mouse.

Now—imagine if you had the answer memorandum to all forthcoming questions. How would you feel? If you knew you had answered his concerns to the best of your ability, that your plan and presentation had covered all the bases, that he's thinking—"Gee whiz, this guy is well prepared. He's capable of taking my money and growing it into something worthwhile"—wouldn't that be easier? You might have a chance of not ending up rocking back and forth at the bottom of the closet.

To learn more about where fund managers are coming from, I visit the top private equity fund manager in his offices. The place has honey wood floors, gleaming with polish and blanketed with Persian rugs. Buffed chrome and glass sparkle reassuringly while I examine the expensive art with tasteful scenes of lakes. I'm even offered hot chocolate with mini marshmallows while sitting in one of the deep, suede sofas. Very Zen.

When I comment on the interior decorating, my host, the fund manager, tells me, "We like to make clients feel at home." My fund manager, let's call him Mr. Deep Pockets, ushers me out to the elevator. We head for lunch at Canoe Restaurant to even more polished wood and a spectacular view of Bay Street skyscrapers and Lake Ontario.

I get to the point quickly, "What does the business owner or CEO need to know about the guys with the investment dollars? Why do you, the fund manager, want to get into an investment with the entrepreneur? How does this private equity stuff work?"

I am not reassured as Mr. Deep Pockets grimaces and sighs. He shakes his head, "The truth is that investors are in the game of saying no! It is easier to reject than take some more time and effort to see if this business is worth the effort. Now that the nuclear winter of finance is over and the dot.com bubble is fading, it means you do have a good chance of getting heard. This is where it gets tricky to understand, but permit me to explain my reasoning."

I shift my attention from the delicious vichyssoise soup to Mr. Deep Pockets who is looking like a kindly uncle bestowing the favourite toy of his youth to his niece.

"Here's the deal," he says with a shrug. "Any business owner asking for investment has five minutes. Yup! That is all that we take in reviewing an opportunity."

I am shocked by this and am about to scold Mr. Deep Pockets and tell him this is not fair. Abruptly, I remember my own mother's mantra, "Life's not fair!" I sit back and take in this hot potato of information. There you go. That's the deal and if you want money, you need to know the playing field along with the cruel rules. Might not be fair, but now you know—five minutes."

Mr. Deep Pockets is on a roll, "When we're really not interested, we're nice about it. We let the owner down carefully because we do know this is his life and everything is riding on the money. If we say, 'Next quarter show us your plan,' we mean get out of our sight."

I try out a line, "My partners turned it down but I liked it."

"That means I want you to think I'm a nice guy but scram!"

I use another, "Looks interesting . . ."

"Translation—ciao!"

"Nice little business?"

"Read between the lines—it stinks!"

Mr. Deep Pockets explains that funds will quietly drop your business plan into the garbage can and move onto the next deal. You have to look at the odds. Mr. Deep Pockets is seeking five deals—five golden eggs—to nurse over the next four years. He is eyeing you and weighing up whether your business is that golden egg. From his many years of pain in handing over money, only to see some idiot lease a lavish office and fill it with furniture straight from *Architectural Digest* instead of investing in sales, Mr. Deep Pockets has toughened up the hard way.

He assures me his back is criss-crossed in scars from all the lashings imposed on him by business owners using the fund money in reckless ways, and I almost wince with his agony. Gone are the days when any dot.com got money from the back of the serviette diagram. Investors need proof you have an authentic business, not just an idea.

This is why when Mr. Deep Pockets has you in his boardroom and is interested, within minutes, he morphs from nice guy into seek-and-destroy mode. Think Yul Brunner in *Westworld* as the crazed robot chasing you down in a cold fury that only an automaton can do. He's coming at you with all that aggression, pumping bullets into your beloved business, and you think, "what the heck, I don't need this!" As a founder or owner, yours is not to ask why; yours is just to be ultra-prepared for the challenge. This is it. Be glad he is paying attention because it means he is interested. This is the test—you've signed on—and you are going to show this cynical, angry man that you will not abuse his money; that you will take it and multiply it with all the efficiency of an iron knived sous chef slicing, dicing, and whipping all those onions (revenues) into the wok the way you said you would.

Mr. Deep Pockets leans over his coffee and confides, "It all comes down to four brutal questions." In almost a whisper, he says, "Any investor worth his or her salt runs through them in the first few minutes of judgement time."

Mr. Deep Pockets assures me that he's used these four brutal questions back when he was a freshly minted, rookie MBA with an idealistic gleam in his eye and he uses them today with his slightly cynical (his words) insight.

Getting "Investor Ready"

Later, I learn from Internet articles, Harvard Business School books, and research that Mr. Deep Pockets' questions are not so original—they are ancient wisdom for all professional investors. No matter the amount of capital you are seeking, the money-seeking process is similar and the questions will indeed fall under four brutal categories.

I also learn that, just like Walt Disney, Mr. Deep Pockets lifted his four questions from a higher source, the über-investor himself—Warren

Buffett. Just in case you are unaware, Buffett is one of the world's wealthiest and most astute investors. He started with a few dollars and built a jaw-dropping empire based on his investment acumen.

Buffett says that no matter the size of investment you need, you can see there are common questions seasoned investors will want answered, whether it's an angel investor interested in investing $50,000, your friendly VC willing to put in $2M or your fund manager, who is keen as get-out to hand over $10M to your business. Warren Buffett, the top investor who chose to live in a place far from the New York madding crowds of your usual blue-shirt-and-braces investment types and whose ability to pick companies is better than a pig snuffling for truffles, has a four-question test.

Before you approach investors, I'm sure you can now see the sense in ensuring all of your investment proposal materials answer these four questions.

1. Are you the right people to make this happen?
2. What is the business opportunity?
3. Is it sustainable?
4. What is the return on investment for investors?

So far, so good. Seems easy enough. Mr. Deep Pockets chuckles as if I've just said I'm going to try sky diving and that it can't be that difficult to jump out of a plane. He draws on his cigar and begins to unpack a more revealing meaning for each question.

1. Are You the Right People to Make This Happen?

"Back a quality individual before backing a sure fire idea," goes the folksy saying. When pressed, most investors say they first evaluate the management team for evidence of their thirst for achievement because it is known that a weak management team with a terrific "A" Plan is a crumbling keystone in a beautiful building. Eric Morse, a professor in Entrepreneurship and Family-Owned Business with Ivey Business School, says that if you have a mediocre product but a great team, it is well worth backing because energetic people will find better products and markets. If the product is great but the management lacklustre, the investor will pass on the deal.

Mr. Deep Pockets says before he even hears about your ideas, what he wants to know is have you ever run a company this size before. Is "hustle" evident? Do you see the opportunity and drive a big bus at it really, really hard? The great entrepreneurs get close to their customers, close enough to smell the need before the customers can even *think* of it themselves. At this stage, do not rely on your investment proposal doing the fundraising work for you. The books and theory on growing companies rarely mention the power of that "hustle and sheer energy." Mr. Deep Pockets is looking for that crackling, high-voltage spark in you and your team at your presentation.

Many high priests of funding boot camps insist that financing is about the big plan that shows the sustainable difference and market size. While there is a place for planning, successful businesses rely on the execution. The teams most likely to attract money will be those that demonstrate they will roll up their sleeves, get on with the unglamorous grunt work of operating plans and do things just a little bit better. Anyone new to running a company—such as McKinsey & Co refugees—who have a good idea and now want funding, probably will not get the money, no matter how smooth they appear. No one, except your mom, is going to fund your learning curve.

Investors know the quality of management ratchets up (or down) the profits and research supports it. A Silicon Valley fund went through their first five-year investment cycle and decided to do 20/20 hindsight research on past deals and levels of financial growth. Their most important finding was that the businesses that threw out the highest returns were the ones where the CEO took the helm and steered with a firm grip right to the end. Investors will be ruthless in weighing up your CEO gravitas. What are the chances that you will be the CEO capable of guiding your company from start to finish—going public with an initial public offering (IPO) or the buy-out event where the investors get their money back and then some? Are you CEO material or are you a marketing guy? A CEO sees the big picture five years out, can run through the cash flow, balance sheet and key financial ratios with ease, and is not fixated on the product only.

Perhaps the thought that someone else could do this business makes you break into uncontrollable laughter? Your confidence is commendable—now's the time to build your case and help your investors race to the same conclusion. How are you going to get the fund manager nodding his head in agreement that you are the one to lead this company? Spell it out!

- How did you get into this business? Show your passion for why you live and breathe the long-distance freight business. If you're running a medical business, are you a doctor? Have you had exposure to the medical industry? Do you at least have medical people on your advisory board who are (or were) attached to useful organizations? Get these names into your plan and presentation.
- Build your track record with company names where you have worked. If it was Boeing and you now make paint for jets, that is a terrific link.
- List past activities in your industry you have achieved to show you can translate ideas into quantifiable results. Use dollar amounts of sales revenues you achieved, only if they are in the tens of millions.
- If possible, show you have achieved mega sales to the same target market you are about to chase.
- Show big-name companies, big dollar amounts, big results achieved. It's only a few lines, but have something.

What sends investors screaming from the room is the owner who says, "We can flip this baby, sell it to Google, YouTube, or IPO it and increase the worth by a multiple of ten," which translates into, "We can all buy Porsches and country homes in Muskoka." The owner with this "to infinity and beyond" leadership style may be the next Richard Branson or Donald Trump, but probably not. Successful people who win are those who make things or create services that they are passionate about, not to make a quick buck. Whether it is making organic compost from worm poop (really!) or creating the next Dell—financially strong owners want to make a difference and are up early every day making it a reality.

Do an Audit of Your Team

There are many ways to display the management talent to capital investors. Write out resume-building activities carefully and be clear that when you go for financing, there will be archaeologically intense digging about your past. Better to be upfront about problems as this works better than investors uncovering it.

When the fund manager asks, "How did your team get together?" do not go into problems you had with partners or that the team consists of your buddies. The fund manager is expecting you to list the record of accomplishments of your team. In the past, when and how did your essential people learn their skills and develop their talents? Emphasize your team's marketing, operations, and finance experience, not just college degrees.

The investor will want to see who is going to be doing what to make how much money. Demonstrate the organization of team roles and accountabilities. If there are more than two partners, who is the CEO that makes the final decisions?

In the present, what are the skill inventories you have in place and how do these people give you a competitive position in the market place? Is it one person or more? Naturally, investors want to see the passionate entrepreneur, but they also want to see that there is evidence of a balance of operational know-how and domain experience. If there is only the techie dreamer, you can forget about it.

Who is the CFO and does she handle the accounting and administering of the business, or is it your mom? Don't laugh, in many family businesses the seventy-year-old mother is running the books, and often very well! Investors are familiar with these scenarios and know that businesses have to run lean; they are not surprised by small management teams, with finance being the most common weakness. Investors know that their own core skill of financial knowledge will boost your company, but they do want to know who will do the back-up administration, the marketing, and the product improvement as you grow the business. Coming up in the future, are you already anticipating the skill gaps and identifying who to hire?

How prepared are you for a position of growth? What actions are you going to take?

KEY PEOPLE QUESTIONS

- How did you get into this business?
- Who is working with you now?
- Why expand the team?
- How are you doing marketing?
- Would you hire more sales people or market through trade shows, magazines, and the Internet?
- Is your lifestyle and geographic location important to you?

You may be quizzed on what you would do if you couldn't run the company once it grew to a certain size. This could signal that the investor does not have enough confidence in your leadership skills. It could be a test to check the size of your ego or perhaps the fund manager has another big company he may want to merge with yours. Whatever the reason, there has to be management capability to grow or a recognition that you may need to step aside as CEO. Check your ego at the door. Be realistic about your competence and preferred size of business to run. Perhaps you may have to hand over the reins in the near future but instead of seeing this as a failure, recognize the opportunity to turn around and start another business. There is nothing wrong with being a serial entrepreneur who builds up a business and then sells it to start up the next idea. The second time around, you will find investors lining up to partner with you.

If you do not have a strong team, don't despair. Be aware there are creative ways to do this without hiring expensive people on a full-time basis. First, can you upgrade your own team's management skills? Set up your own advisory board. Invite industry experts to be part of it. Would they let you list their name and experience on your investment proposal? This shows investors that you can attract networked people to your team once the money arrives. Advisory boards with recognizable industry names can add strength to your bench of talent even if you only meet twice a year.

Can You Carry the Ball?

Mr. Deep Pockets says, "I look for the guy who gets in the game, runs full blast, and takes the ball down the field. If there's a bump—which there always is—will you be stricken with terror and freeze?"

It's an interesting question that is at the core of strategy: the ability to get the big dream done. Your goal is to score a goal! How are you going to move your team down the playing field? What are the milestones towards the goal? There are tried-and-true methods to make sure your team sets checks and balances so that the business does not go off half-cocked.

Prepare your own report cards. Do you have the last few years' budget and plans? Can you use these to demonstrate that you have already set clear goals and achieved them? This is a very big clue to your character and whether you do what you say you will do. The proposal you will be presenting says you will do many things. How confident can the investor be that you will keep your word? Past plans with results will give the investor comfort.

Can you organize a team? Many owners have not set up basic communication systems and routines, such as scheduled meetings for marketing or even for the board, nor have they drawn out the activities that make up the business model or shared the company strategy. These management activities enable staff to take on decision-making activities. Without them—you will draw a big negative. If your CEO is still writing all your press releases, you need a plan to delegate. Effective owners know that the business can speed up and grow because there are systems and management to handle the increasingly complex webs of work.

Can you communicate complex ideas? The investor knows that how you present your investment proposal demonstrates exactly the way you will sell your product. Ouch! Get a one-or-two sentence catch phrase that rolls off your tongue to explain what your business or widget does. What need in the market does your company fill? Can you get it into two lines? Wordsmithing those few sentences will be worth it, as you will use it in your next trade show presentation, your executive summary of your business plan, the first page of your sales presentation, and it will be the first communication with your investors. How about if you simply communicate? Seriously. An extraordinary number of deals get done by chance chats watching a tennis match, for example. Be open to new people. Go to industry events and schmooze. Don't hang around the back of the room; get in front of the people you want to know. Invite them out and send them your business plan. The investor game is so much about the luck of being in the same place as the right person, but it's more. Luck favours the people who take that extra effort to communicate—funny that. Remember, too, that fortune favours the fearless.

I quiz Mr. Deep Pockets: "Does the size of company affect the type of management team?"

"Ah … in this case, size does matter." He smiles, "The larger your revenues, the more I worry if you do strategy with your team and get goals into their heads. Or is the company direction a mysterious secret? One trick I use is to visit offices and factories to quiz the next level down about the strategy. That tells me more about the management and if it matches what they are telling me."

I say, "Wow! Standing in front of critical investors giving you a look-over is worse than the ninth grade dance."

Mr. Deep Pockets grimaces, "Actually, it's more like your ninth grade dance and you're not wearing any clothes."

2. What Is the Business Opportunity?

Next up, once you have jumped the people hurdle, it's the investment opportunity. Is there a real business? Are there people digging into their wallets to pay for what you produce? What is going to bring in *beaucoup* cash?

The VCs in Silicon Valley and the big fund managers in marble-floored offices have all been through Death Valley and those who survived the scalping parties have tough criteria for this question. Market size is where all the technology investors aim their questions in particular, not on the schmaltzy and heart-warming niceness of the team. Tech investors want to know the potential market size. In the IT world, it's like the movie business—one *Shrek* can pay for all the *Barnyard Animals* duds.

To illustrate the business, begin by defining your company around the customers and their "pain." Then position your company to solve that problem.

Mr. Deep Pockets sketches a company idea. "We improve energy use in private homes. Now that's an attractive market—I'm imagining cities of customers wanting to reduce their energy bills. Now you've awoken my greed—that's good."

Where business owners fall flat is putting a dollar value to the problem. In this case, the product, X, lowers customers' electricity bills, but the savings is only $10 a month, while the unit costs $240. It will take two years for a consumer to break even and that's not enough to get people to take money out of their wallets and buy.

"Now my fear kicks in and it's no to this deal," says Mr. Deep Pockets.

Figure out the absolute driving reasons to solve a painful problem. Is it painful enough to make people use your product? Perhaps if product X's unit cost could be reduced to $24, if housing energy costs continue to go through the roof, and it is $60 per month you could save, then this business could be worthwhile. Do the math because your investors will.

Fund managers want to know if this is a niche market or a mega market. Are you selling tires for tractors in Saskatchewan or tires for snow conditions across the country? Could you apply this patented tire in the airline industry? In other words, how much money could the investors stand to make if you got the entire market? It has got to be big. Is the overall market big enough for the business to make $100M annual revenues in perhaps five to ten years? They must see the big opportunity and know that they could potentially make a lot of dough. Snow tires for tractors in Saskatchewan is just not going to cut it. To demonstrate your market answer these questions.

- How long have you been working on this?
- How much have you sold?
- How much could you sell?
- What size, in dollars, are the entire market sales in one year?
- How could you define the market so that it could be a billion-dollar industry?

3. Is It Sustainable?

Do you have a unique and sustainable competitive advantage? If your intellectual property or technology is similar to what's already in the market, that will pop the profit balloon.

What makes you get ahead of your competitors? Demonstrate that customers will reach out to your basket of goodies, pushing aside the competitor's basket each and every time. Your competitive advantage is the cornerstone of your presentation but do not make your management team part of the advantage. Do you have a viable business or is it a white elephant? Remember the ill-fated Concorde? Great idea, great technology, but not financially viable.

Are you in an established market? Analysis of your company and where it fits into the business environment is crucial. When your industry is clearly laid out along with the strength of your position, it should prove your potential for rapid growth. Fund managers want to see a $1B market or the potential to grow to that size. Projections that were pulled out of the air of potential markets fuelled the whole dot.com insanity. Get data to back every one of your claims, as investors are still cynical from their last roasting. They will be suspicious of a sort of *Farmer's Almanac* of generalizations and rambling statistics.

How competitive will your industry be? Remember Chapters racing against Indigo to get real estate to open new stores? Please, don't say your competition is Microsoft, Google, Rogers, or Telus. Even worse, don't say you don't have any competitors because, if you are good, you will quickly attract attention from established players to price you to death. Every idea, every concept has a competitor out there.

What will be your barriers to entry? In other words, how can you make it expensive for new companies to start up after seeing your idea? What is your competitive advantage? For example, the record industry has held onto their stars by being able to organize mega concerts where the real money gets made. It is more difficult for a small Indie music label to be able to offer the smashing European tour organized by, say, a Sony Music, which gets attended by fans actually paying cash for tickets.

Solid copyright, patent protection, and long-term client contracts all make entry of new companies into your industry that much more difficult. Does your business model, intellectual property, or brand name create a barrier to competitors wanting your customers, like those zombies lurching after living people in *Dawn of the Dead*? How can you bolster the fences around your market? For example, get your brand name associated with a bigger brand. Intel inside branding has been formidable. A small part of the computer managed to become a critical part that customers believed meant quality. Hard to beat. A niche product done well invariably ends up in the mainstream markets, but they are easier to start and defend. Steve Jobs defined the desktop computer market niche as a child's toy.

Can your product be easily substituted for another? If you are developing software for processing client requests, make it specific to the insurance industry, for instance. Customize it more and add free training. Make it that much more costly for customers to switch to a competitor.

What are the risks? What could be the worst thing competitors could do over the next two years? If you are vague on the answers, do not start the conversation.

4. What Is the Return on Investment for Investors?

If you've got through the first three questions, investors are ready to get serious and decide if they are going to give you the money. Do not make the mistake of going with your story and expecting them to figure out the amount of money you need and how you are going to pay them back. To get the cheque books flipping open, you will have to prove three things.

1. What is the growth rate to make the business worth backing?
2. What is the return on investment? This depends on company size, but can range from 8% to 25% to 40% plus.
3. How will your investor get out his money (exit) within his desired time frame? Demonstrate that you understand the importance of an exit plan for the investor.

What Is Your Financial Growth?

The investor needs a financial model that is built with real numbers from the past and detailed numbers going into the future. This is where many businesses fail. They do not understand the financial funding models built by business analysts. A soundly constructed model separates the wheat from the chaff, the growth businesses from the plodders.

There are drivers that make the money come into the piggy bank. For example, one of Tim Hortons' drivers would be the number of customers per day. How would you increase that number? How much would it cost to increase that number? What is in the plan to show that the customer numbers will keep going up? Opening new coffee locations? Specifically, state what you will do with the money. Have clear action plans to demonstrate you know what to do once the money gets you on the runway. What's the destination and who's doing which job? The investors can play with the model and increase or reduce the drivers. For example, they could see what the returns would be if you only opened half the number of franchises you said you would. The investor will use your model to test your assumptions of what grows the revenue.

How to Value Your Business

Mr. Deep Pockets ends our lunch with cups of rich Kenyan tea and I decide now is the time to bring up the tricky subject of valuation. Fund managers think this is their sole territory, but it's a huge controversy for owners. Valuation is the huge sticking point for all concerned. Some business owners accuse finance people of throwing the bones to come up with a number, while finance people argue that owners have too much emotional investment in the business and see it through rose-coloured glasses.

Mr. Deep Pockets pays the bill and mulls over my question. As we stride back to the elevators, he finally speaks. "Value is in the eye of the beholder. It is that mix of art and science. Albert Einstein said that after a level of skill was achieved, science and art tended to blend. He believed the greatest scientists were artists too."

I nod.

He was on a roll. "Then throw in the incredible importance of timing because values are cyclical; you need to catch the peaks."

"I suppose the Baby Boomers getting ready to bail will drive down values soon?" I reply.

"Absolutely! Also, different buyers use different valuation methods. A business is worth what a buyer will pay. It all depends on the type of buyer."

Curious now, I ask, "What are the different types of buyers?"

"Broadly speaking, they can be loosely grouped into two camps. There's the "financial" versus "strategic" buyer. Come into my office and I will show you the difference."

He sketches a diagram. At a glance, I see that valuation is driven by two simple concepts: finances and synergy. The latter is the strategic fit with the company valuing your business. For example, if they build fuel tanks in British Columbia, they will value a fuel tank company in Ontario to take their company to national standing. That synergy is worth more money.

Financial valuation is determined by laying out expected profitability or future earnings. This valuation is used by professional fund managers and VCs. A strategic valuation is decided by competitors, suppliers, or customers who could buy your company to fit into their business and value it more. Figure 8.1 presents this concept in graphic form.

Figure 8.1: Valuation of Your Business

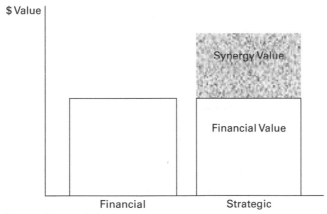

Source: Loewen & Partners

In the short term, a strategic valuation will give you the most cash for your business. The greater the "fit," the bigger the premium. All this means is that you need to plan your exit for years by knowing competitors and suppliers who might buy you.

Valuation by Future Earnings

Here's where you show how much your investors can make on their investment: what is the value today and what will it be in the future? Value boils down to the future earnings. The best way to see future earnings is to look at the present and make some projections. This is called "discounted cash flow"; you can find details on this concept in any introduction to finance text book. Investors get quite huffy about who sets the valuation, as they believe it to be their prerogative. Nothing sets them off in a tailspin faster than a presentation or plan with a value attached. Wait for the investor to throw the first valuation shot, but you can have your own valuation estimate.

The Exit

We leave the building and Mr. Deep Pockets jokes, "That brings me to my final point. I want to see the exit strategy defined. How are you going to get a liquidity event?"

I shrug, not sure what he means.

"You know, this is really important to know when looking for investment money from private equity. Within five to seven years (or less), the typical investor wants to exit. The entrepreneur will need a major cash infusion event to pay us off. This exit could be done by going public with an IPO. That was the favourite from the 90s, but today the favourite is management buy-outs. You could target a competitor company that might like to buy your business."

This was the exit plan for a coffee shop entrepreneur in London— Big Ben and the Queen and all that. The Seattle Coffee Company owner designed his coffee shops to be bought by Starbucks. He even made his signs the same size and round shape. All the new owner from across the Atlantic needed to do was pop out the Seattle sign and snap in the Starbucks.

With Baby Boomers about to start leaving the business world, investors are acutely aware that five years from now there may not be easy exits. That's why it's important to help out and have a solid list of buyers.

What Exactly Is "Investor Ready?"

With the long-term view, you can work on how to affect the value of your business. That is the application of Covey's very good habit: begin with the end in mind. Figure out the answers to the four questions. To summarize how to get investors ready, review the investors' hot buttons.

- Your Team
- Proof of Concept: The investor wants to see that you have designed a light bulb, have made it, turned it on, and sold it to a happy customer.
- Competitive Strength: Patents, barriers, partners, and alliances. If Sony has offered to give you some chips to use in your technology, this is newsworthy. Alliances can be a deal maker.
- ROI: Are you going to be able to grow the business sufficiently?

We will go into more detail but there's the big view. As I take leave of Mr. Deep Pockets, I see nervous-looking people fidgeting in the waiting area and smile. Mr. Deep Pockets has given me the inside scoop on the questions your plan and presentation must address. As Leonardo da Vinci said, "Simplicity is the ultimate sophistication." You need to work at refining your business to a simple, but sophisticated concept. You will need the following:

1. the initial two-sentence pitch—the infamous elevator pitch,
2. a written investment proposal document—the financial plan, and
3. a practiced verbal presentation and PowerPoint presentation.

Each investor you are going to approach will judge why they should give you money. Your job is to make that process as simple as possible—you must show them that you are beyond the string-and-chewing-gum stage. You are ready to maintain a mature partnership. Let's carry on reading and you will learn how to show future value and to put together a financial opportunity that gets investors shouting, "Yes—go straight to GO!"

TAKE AWAYS

The cardinal rule is to get "investor ready" before you see any potential investors. Be prepared to answer the four brutal questions.

1. People—why are you the right team?
2. Business—what does the company do to make money?
3. Sustainable—will customers keep paying?
4. Money—how much could the investor make?

CHAPTER 9

CREATING PLANS THAT GET YOU FUNDED

Money will never make you happy and happy will never make you money.

Groucho Marx, The Coconuts
Morrie Ryskind, U.S. screenwriter,
Robert Florey, and Joseph Santley, 1929

If you found a glass Coke bottle on the desert sand, even if you had never seen such an object before, you would perceive that it had been made by an intelligent entity. So it is with business: its complexity is proof of its design.

The Coke bottle surrounds the actual product—carbonated, dark fluid. Yet, that bottle has become ubiquitous as a global brand. Making money is a result of all the little actions that get the strategy done: the brilliant management of cash flows, the production expansion, the supply chain's meticulous design, and prompt delivery to the world market of customers.

Your investment proposal is that Coke bottle.

You want your potential investor to have that *moment of truth*, that the simplicity of your document demonstrates your clear vision. When they hold your investment proposal, you want them to have an epiphany that here is a worthy business.

In reality, there is a great deal of money out there looking for the right opportunity to rear its head. Investors are dying for that Coke bottle on the desert sand moment. They want to come across a business owner who has put deep management competency and time into their business, who can explain its worth in elegant terms.

Help your investor judge your proposal to be Coke bottle attractive with your well-designed investment proposal.

Getting to Your Coke Bottle Plan

If you have a budget, get an expert; otherwise, this chapter applies to the early-stage business founder. Know that the hardest part of writing an investment proposal is getting started. We are lucky to have the beauty of technology to help; you can even find plan outlines available on the Internet.

There are software packages available to build business plans and these can be useful when beginning. You will be able to create a solid foundation. But for heaven's sake, do not hand out these paint-by-numbers plans to the financial community. Use them as a base and whatever you do, build the investment proposal into your own design and language. Make sure your grandmother could understand it, which means leave the jargon for your presentation at the next conference.

The objective of the full business plan is to be able to show fund managers that you are a professional business. This plan can then be used to create the investment proposal required to obtain financing.

Why the Investment Proposal Is Important

There's a saying, "Good businesses get funded, not good plans. But good businesses write good plans." All investors will assume you have a business plan for raising capital but in actual fact, they want more. They want an investment proposal which is built using the business plan and then they will punch it up with a financial story.

In the early stages of financing, a business plan is more than adequate, but the higher up the food chain you go, the more complex your investment proposal will be required to be. Expert help is recommended (see Figure 9.1).

Figure 9.1: Levels of Business Plans

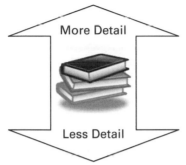

More Detail

- Operating Plan
- Strategic Plan
- Bank Loan Funding Plan
- Investment Proposal
- Idea/Feasibility Plan

Less Detail

This might seem obvious, but read the plan and know it inside and out. It is fine to have an expert help you and your team work through your ideas and tussle with your priorities. They can get you a plan, but don't hand it over to a consultant and never look at it again until you're sitting across from Mr. Deep Pockets asking for money. If you ask the finance person sitting on your right if the sensitivity analysis the fund manager just requested is in the package, or if you don't know your key ratios, you will look inept and ill-informed. All will be lost with that one slip.

It sounds painful but expect to put in at least three hundred hours of time into your plan. Six to eight weeks of hard slog will be essential. You need at least one hundred pages of external research. Know that you will be asked to hand over your plan to a top-notch analyst who will take a big stick and poke holes in it. If you have put in the time, you will be able to validate and uncover all the flaws before the analyst unearths them.

The purpose of the plan is to spark interest. You want to tell where you are going, as this indicates if you have shared interests. Reading the average business plan can be perceived to be fantastically mundane: customers, product, service, market, competitors, a dash of financial plans, a sprinkling of marketing—nothing you wouldn't find in any plan—yours will have all the grindingly familiar bits. The only thing that makes it special is *you*. That is, of course, the miracle of being an entrepreneur. You put all these bits together in a way that makes it all come alive. It takes incredible energy, lonely, dark hours sweating it out, and some very hard times. You are the person who has chosen to believe and who puts shoulder to the wagon wheel to get it moving. It is why fund managers choose to make you the most important part of their decision to invest.

As with anything, there are fashions in business management. Last season's delights can look really lame this year, but there do seem to be the basics from even twenty years ago that endure, such as the basic white shirt. In plans, there are the basics too. These are what we will focus on, so even if you don't get the money (be ready for that) you will be better off for having dedicated some thinking to your direction.

First Decide How Much Money You Need

Your first decision is how much money you really need. No one is going to give you money to sit in the bank account and earn interest, which is why you need to spell out your needs very clearly. Carefully determine your cash requirements ("the purpose of issue"). Do not make it more than required so that you can avoid unnecessary dilution.

The type of private equity investment you could attract depends on many factors, such as size of company, cash flow, industry, your personal history, revenues, and many more. Your objective is to get financing in a way that fits your personal needs too.

Types of financing fall into three buckets.

- Equity—ownership into your company.
- Mezzanine—quasi-debt, quasi-equity.
- Debt—usually higher cost than bank debt and often subordinated debt, which means it is secondary and behind senior bank debt.

Mezzanine money, if you are eligible to get it and if it fits your ownership needs, is often preferred to equity as it is a mix of equity ownership and plain debt. You do not have to give away too many shares, thus avoiding dilution of your ownership. Historically, mezzanine is a preferred structure for fund managers too as it is subordinated debt, meaning it gets paid back right after the senior debt from the bank, which lowers the risk.

Focus on the mentality of the investor. He wants to make a good return on his investment and with the least possible risk. He looks for a good risk-return ratio and an element of debt structure provided by "mezz debt" helps minimize risk. If you run your business to plan, he will get his money back—the interest rate gives a stated amount for part of the return he wants.

Mezzanine financing is open only to those companies with a well substantiated projection of cash flow for the next three years. Your anticipated clients who can be expected to produce revenues must be detailed. Optimistic guesses with no evidence will turn off potential investors who otherwise would be interested.

Just to add more complexity, different funds have different criteria around debt, equity, and mezzanine financing.

All fund managers want some equity that they hope will bring the return up to the level they seek. Investors in early-stage companies want an anticipated rate of return of 20% to 25% over three to five years with the hope of some blue sky. Venture capitals (VCs) want higher rates of return, but again it depends on the business and your industry.

What Is Important in the Investment Proposal?

You may have a business plan already, but you'll need a formal investment proposal in writing. Your management team can help in discussing and getting the key points. A pertinent and realistic financial model of your past and projections for your future are critical.

In the investment proposal, there are essentially four elements.

1. Executive Summary.
2. Story about the Opportunity. What makes the deal unique? What is the opportunity in clear terms? Be sure to include the features of the markets and implementation plan along with the talents of the people on the team.
3. Detailed Financial Model.
4. Brief Summary. Tell the investors how much money they are going to make and how they are going to get their money out in a few years. Discuss the terms of the deal.

Authenticity over Exaggeration

While writing your investment proposal, you may feel a tendency to sell rather than offer. Rather than offer the facts as they are, sales language may creep into the document that will not be well received by investors. Surely you feel that you have the next best widget that will solve an immeasurable amount of problems; otherwise, you wouldn't feel so passionate about your venture, but be certain to use facts to prove this. Investors are savvy and successful, they have heard it all and possibly said most of it themselves when it comes to selling a product or people. It is best to keep sales jargon out of the document. It will show that you respect your audience if you sell them on the facts rather than doing a sales pitch.

Why an Executive Summary Is Crucial

The fund manager sees a pile of opportunities and you can not expect them to read through your whole document unless you catch their attention in the executive summary. Once the fund manager is intrigued, then the fund team will take the time to review it in more detail. The executive summary is your prime chance to appeal to the investor's appetite. Generally, investors will focus on less than five pages of an entrepreneur's forty-page investment proposal, so it is important to know what they are looking for and make it succinct. The last thing that you write should be the executive summary since it's the one thing you can be sure the investors will read. Piece it together by lifting information from each of your key topics.

If it is your first time to get investment funds, the executive summary can be one to two pages with a fifteen-page plan backing up your pitch. An early entrepreneurial business seeking funding can have two to three pages of executive summary and a thirty-page plan. Larger companies (over $20M) need three pages with a forty-page analysis.

Investors expect to see the following in the executive summary:

- how much money they could potentially earn;
- evidence your team has the know-how and guts to do what they say they will do;

- how the investors can protect their interest; and
- how they can exit their investment to get their money back and then some.

The Opening Page Gets Their Attention

Your first page should be brimming with enticing information about you that uses energetic phrasing and bounds along with enthusiasm. In the first paragraph, above all else, you must succinctly describe what it is your company does. Leave the superlatives and adjectives at home and keep it to a concise description. If your business makes banana bread from multi-grain out of three locations in Montreal, you are not a national distributor of the finest baked good products in the country that promotes a healthy, balanced lifestyle; this is marketing and investors can smell it. To them it smells bad in an investment proposal. In fact, you are a producer of multi-grain banana bread with three locations in urban Montreal. If you need to spice up what your company does, you tread dangerously on the brink of appearing to overcompensate for a bad business.

In the next paragraph you must demonstrate the "pain" in the market. What is missing out there? The answer to this question should be, emphatically, your business. After having described what the pain is, follow up with what you do to fix this "pain" and introduce your target market.

In a following paragraph show why your target market is attractive. If you can get market research to illustrate the size of the market, now is the time to show this data and how you are attractive to them. Are they big, niche, growing, retiring, or coming of age? How big are they now and how big will they be? If you only had this one paragraph to explain the most important point about your market, what would it be?

As with all the information you are introducing in the investment proposal (and your business plan), illustrating the details with pie charts, tables, or graphs is a great way to let an investor's discriminating eye scan your documents for pertinent information. These tools create emphasis for important information that should not be overlooked. The size and growth potential of your target market is just this kind

Figure 9.2: Use of Proceeds

Purpose	Amount
Acquisition	$600,000
New Equipment	$350,000
Marketing program	$250,000
Operations	$400,000
Working Capital	$200,000
Total	$1,800,000

of important information that would benefit from the illustration of charts or graphs.

If you have any signed contracts, deals, or agreements on the horizon, it is important to include them. Talk about your past successes with humility by describing their merits with the facts.

Show your balance sheet and explain some of the highlights within its accounts (the kind of analysis that is needed is explained in the steps below). You must have a forecasted income statement. What is important to remember when including financial information in the executive summary is the emphasis that you are making. It is critical to be upfront and honest, but if there has been no cash flow to date, because the company is still in its nascence, then there is no reason to add one at this time.

It is important to include the amount of capital being raised. If you are raising $250,000 or $5M, say that and show how the money will be used, as shown in Figure 9.2.

Write the executive summary last. This will allow you to understand the big picture first and make things easier when tackling this important portion of your document.

The Four Steps to Growth

For the fund manager to look carefully past the first page, your written proposal needs to contain language and numbers that fit his criteria. In other words, you need to include substantial numbers to validate every point you make.

Figure 9.3: Four Steps to Outstanding Growth

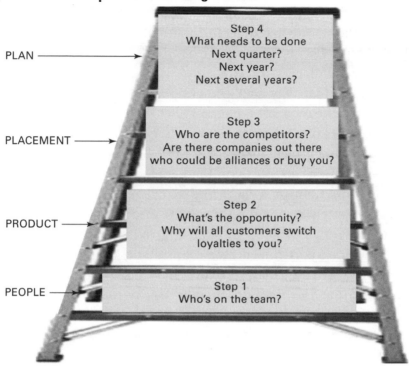

PLAN → Step 4
What needs to be done
Next quarter?
Next year?
Next several years?

PLACEMENT → Step 3
Who are the competitors?
Are there companies out there
who could be alliances or buy you?

PRODUCT → Step 2
What's the opportunity?
Why will all customers switch
loyalties to you?

PEOPLE → Step 1
Who's on the team?

These can be summarized into the four pillars that hold up terrific cash flow. The Four Steps will help the investor evaluate your investment potential (see Figure 9.3).

1. People
2. Product or Service
3. Placement or Position in Market
4. Plan to Go to Market

1. People

Demonstrate long-term people planning by directly tackling the tough issues on investors' minds. They will appreciate the CEO having a succession plan for her role in case she gets hit by a bus—stranger things do happen. Try to demonstrate how the business has the strength to continue if something should happen. Investors have also been through company growth and often the founder needs to step away from the helm; the skills that get a company up the growth curve may not suit the more mature company. If the CEO can have the humbleness to acknowledge she's aware that different stages of business require a different leadership style, investors will be happy.

Who are the officers, directors, and management? Set these out in table form. Are there any management people worth mentioning? For instance, do you have a sales manager? Set them out in table form and give the résumés of all the people mentioned. Above all else, investors focus on the management of a company.

No-go decisions are made on the people—you and your management. Investors want to see a record of accomplishment. They want to know if there is a person on the team who has operated a startup before there is any possibility of financing. With unseasoned management, try to add a part-time person (consultant) who can pump up the talent level. Since you are short of cash, make use of equity as compensation. Your investment proposal could clarify the time dedicated by the part-timers.

People who have succeeded before can also be on your advisory board; that will impress.

Detailed résumés add cachet. If you do not have someone for one of the high-level positions, sketch out how the company will operate and when you will fill the position.

2. Product or Service

You need to demonstrate what it is exactly your company will do. Use images to simplify what you make or do. Now don't get into a long-winded love fest over the technological brilliance of your device or what ever it is. That is the classic mistake. The key questions to answer are:

- What do you do?
- Be able to define the problem someone is having and how your company can solve that problem. For example, a woman with mouse problems hates using mousetraps as they snap at her fingers and she doesn't like taking that dead mouse out of the contraption to retrieve the trap for the next mouse. Your company has tasty pellets laced with a mild poison. That mouse will eat the poison and die on

the spot. You can then sweep the mouse into the garbage without having to touch it; plus you may get more than one mouse. How do you phrase that?

> "Kill more than one mouse at a time and never have to touch the rodents. Use Mouse Pellet—the hygienic way to catch a lot more mice."

- What are the existing opportunities, not the dreams? Is this a viable business?
- What is your current system? What is the new system you are launching? Are you utilizing technology you have developed? If so, that is a major plus. Investors want to know what a company's competitive advantage is and they love something that is technological as it is harder for competitors to copy.

Proof of Growth

- **The WOW Factor.** This is the proof of the concept. The fund manager is looking for a large possible market to provide the 25% growth per year. How is your business going to grow? How can you prove it?
- **Scalable.** Software is an attractive product because it is scalable at an extraordinary rate. Once you have your first copy, you can run off thousands. The least scalable business model is services. Deloitte accountants are not easy to expand across the market because it is such a deeply human business. "Big markets look sexy. Big markets are also a problem. Sitting at the vet today, I saw a brochure for an injectable chip that makes it easier to identify a lost dog. No doubt, the investor meetings all started with, 'Well, there's a hundred million dogs in the United States, and if we just make a dollar annual profit on each one. . . ,'"[1] says Seth Godin, author of *Purple Cow*.

   Mr. Godin specializes in marketing and recalls the problems of marketing too wide, too soon. "The problem with huge markets is the same problem you'd have playing squash or racquetball on a court that's too big. The ball doesn't have a wall to bounce off of.

---

[1] Seth Godin, Web blog at www.sethgodin.com, March 2, 2007.

Huge horizontal markets have no echo chamber, no niches, no easy entry points. To make a system like this work, everyone has to agree on the technology and then there has to be a huge push to get millions of people to make the same decision at about the same time. It might work, but it's awfully expensive."

- **Stick to the Numbers.** Most fund managers are financial creatures preferring to stick with the numbers that they know such as projected cash flows or Returns on Investment (ROIs). You need to stay in their habitat and not veer off into your favourite place, which will be your product. Get that back-up file for validation of your product and that it will do what you say it will do. The fund manager may be an expert in finance, but he will understand your market too. You want to be talking finance to this person. If you embrace that one point, you will write a better investment proposal. Fund managers will understand your product, but will not want to go into the nitty-gritty too soon. Once they are very interested, probably during the due diligence stage, they will invest the time to do research on what you are claiming.

- **Use Relative Figures When Discussing Your Product.** Fund managers need relative prices. For example, do not say "We will sell this gadget for $99." So what? This means jack to someone not in your industry. If you say, "We sell for 10% less than our competitor without compromising on margins," the fund manager will sit up and pay attention.

3. Placement or Position in Market

Saying that you have no competitors is the kiss of death to a deal. You are not unique. Everyone has competition; on the other hand, don't say your competition is Microsoft. That is an eight-hundred-pound gorilla coming to crush you. It also makes you look dumb. Show that you are savvy about your level of industry and you know who the other players are. They may be potential merger or acquisition opportunities down the road. List the types of organizations, not the names, unless they are very well-known companies. Explain why competition is less in the small- to mid-sized business.

Figure 9.4: Competitor Positioning Analysis

	CIRCUIT SWITCH	PACKET SWITCH
TWO-WAY WIRELESS UNIFICATION	**Voice** *Cellular*	**Data communication** *Fax* *Computer to computer*
ONE-WAY WIRELESS UNIFICATION	**Content** *AM, FM radio*	**One-way paging** *Pagers*

Source: Jim Balsillie

Describe who the competitors are in your line of business and there are always substitutes. If you are Cadbury making chocolate boxes, you know that the problem your box solves is what to give a hostess as a gift. A substitute could be flowers or candles.

Your sales contracts will be a big interest. Who are your clients and long-term customers? What contracts did you have? These are of major importance, big time.

When Research In Motion (RIM) wanted to position themselves, they used a very simple table that can have very powerful results. The table in Figure 9.4 is an illustration of a competitor's analysis used by RIM. By using two key criteria on the X and Y axis, the analysis makes clear where RIM would position themselves.

4. Plan to Go to Market

Outline your expansion plans. Say what the costs will be and the anticipated schedule. The worst thing to do is to try to hide your weaknesses. You must have a strategy with clear milestones for what needs to get done during the next quarter, next year, and beyond. How can you build a business aggressively if you are not clear on what needs to be done? Your plan needs the train, the tracks, the conductor, the driver, the map, and the fuel to get going. Show that you have thought about all of this.

Finance Numbers Tell an Exciting Story

In putting together the investment proposal, you not only need the financial model, you need the story. Once you describe the product, the market, and the management team, lead into the financial model and how much money you are going to make. Key forecast basics are:

- revenue model,
- expense model,
- income statement,
- balance sheet, and
- cash flows.

Current and projected earnings and cash flow are important to all levels of investors. Current revenue and future revenue substantiated by signed contracts are important to some. Revenue gains will boost earnings and cash flow if there is reasonable certainty about profit margins.

The critical success factors (CSF) of forecast success are to be conservative, reasonable, and:

- demonstrate you will spend wisely,
- defend the first few years down to each and every dollar,
- cash is indeed king so know your breakeven point and how quickly you eat up the money (burn rate), and
- know the metrics.

Building a financial model is quite complex. You need to pull in an advisor or accountant to help you get it right. This model is the keystone to any investing financial presentation. What you are saying really is, "This is my story and here are the numbers to show how things are and will unfold."

Revenue Model

This is a critical component to any financial summary. However, many entrepreneurs, especially ones with startups, will insert the revenue model into the "company" portion of their document. This is perfectly allowable and should be encouraged, in most cases, when a business is still quite young and the model from which revenue is expected to be generated is still in its nascence. Creating a visual model will allow investors to quickly understand how you expect to get money from the customer's pocket and into your hands.

Summary of Financials

Once you have decided to raise money from the private equity market, be prepared to provide an extensive amount of financial information. They may want to see everything from revenue growth rates to earnings before investment, taxes, depreciation and amortization (EBITDA), margins, capital expenditures, working capital, and cash-tax rates, as well as, monthly and even weekly cash flow analysis—depending on your company's maturity. You are, essentially, acquiring a potential shareholder who will be your biggest advocate, as well as your greatest critic. He wants to know from the outset where you and your business stand. He will push you because his success depends on the performance of your company, which means you and your performance. He wants to make sure that you are going to treat his money as if it were your own.

Income Statement

The income statement should be dated from when your business started, in table form. Below the income statement for each year, add, in tabular form, the ratios, such as for gross profit and the family of ratios. An example of an income statement for fiscal year 2007 and 2006 is shown in Figure 9.5 for the software developer InventoTex Inc.

To give an example of some of the vernacular expected and some of the questions that will need to be addressed, we can see here that InventoTex has been doing quite well, with strong revenue growth for a software developer over the last year. Gross margins (gross profit/sales) have dropped slightly from 2006, something that the company will need to answer as it represents an irregularity in comparison to the sales

Figure 9.5: Income Statement (in thousands)

Fiscal year Mar. – Feb.	2007	2006
Sales	4,005	3,507
Cost of Goods Sold	**2,122**	**1,718**
Gross Profit	1,883	1,789
Total salaries	**320**	**265**
General & Administrative	**653**	**546**
EBITDA	910	978
Amortization	110	98
Pre-tax Profit	**800**	**880**
Taxation	**288**	**317**
Net Income	512	563
Gross Profit margin	47%	51%
Operating Profit margin	24%	23%
EBITDA margin	23%	28%
Net Profit margin	13%	16%

growth. Possibly, clients have changed and the company is forced to source materials from more expensive contractors, but the company would need to know the answer to this and present sound, factual data for why this has happened.

EBITDA is an important concept that investors use a great deal. It is used as a proxy for the operating cash flow of a company, in other words, how much your company is making.

In addition, a common valuation parameter of EBITDA times an industry multiple (such as six less debt). The EBITDA margin (EBITDA/sales) tells an investor how much profit is being generated from the operations of a business. This concept is something that investors use as a benchmark to compare businesses.

Finally, net profit margin (net income/sales) simply illustrates how well a company can generate profit.

Balance Sheet

The balance sheet shows what assets the firm has and how it has financed these assets. An important thing to note: saving receipts of all business expenses will prove an invaluable habit to get into when it comes down to knowing how much you have spent in the business. Do it; your future self will thank you. Every receipt represents capital you have put into your business and each one raises the value. InventoTex's balance sheet is presented in Figure 9.6.

Figure 9.6: Balance Sheet (in thousands)

Assets	2007	2006
Cash	550	53
Inventory	1,301	1,123
Current Assets	**1,851**	**1,146**
Property & equipment	245	112
Startup & other costs	36	45
Total Assets	**2,132**	**1,303**
Liabilities		
Bank Indebtedness	112	220
Current Liabilities	**112**	**220**
Notes payable	90	75
Total Liabilities	**292**	**295**
Shareholders' Equity		
Retained earnings	1,930	1,008
Shareholders' Equity	**1,840**	**1,008**
Total Liabilities & Shareholders' Equity	**2,132**	**1,303**
Current Ratio	16.5	5.2
Debt-to-Equity Ratio	0.1	0.3
Total Debt Ratio	0.1	0.2

We can see here that current assets have grown substantially over the last year, which is consistent with the increase in profits and higher cost of goods sold. The company has a very healthy balance sheet with strong asset coverage over its liabilities; we can see this clearly in the current ratio (current assets/current liabilities). This is particularly important for this company because of the uncertain nature of the industry in which it operates. Always keep in mind the industry that you are in when giving your analysis.

InventoTex is not highly leveraged as noted by the debt-to-equity ratio (total debt/total equity). It so happens that InventoTex was heavily indebted, but because of disciplined management and positive cash flow, that indebtedness was responsibly paid off before it was due.

Finally, the total debt ratio illustrates how much of the company is financed by debt.

Capital Structure

The equity structure has to be clearly explained. Questions that need to be answered include: who are the shareholders in the company? How many shares do you have outstanding and is it common equity (the investor wants to know how much of the company has already been divested). This information is very important to an investor because she wants to know how much of your company her money will buy.

An explanation of the debt structure is also important. Investors need to know the extent and nature of the company's debt commitments because it represents a potential conflict with their capital. Investors need to know the type of debt (bank loans or other creditors), the cost (interest payments), the term (long or short), and the amount.

Cash Flow Statement

By now, you have your strategy that answers where you want to go in the next five years, but do you have the cash to get there? Once your growth strategy gets going, it's awing just how much cash is needed. Cash flow management will become your biggest challenge. When your growth rate is going to be above 30% (200% is normal for high tech), you have to ramp up, and just because you've got customer orders flying through the door, doesn't mean you'll be able to get out enough product. Ironically, as sales volumes trend upwards, you will need more cash, not less. Customer payments usually will not fill the gap.

The less mature your business is, the more detail you will need to include in your cash flow statement. Startups, with no cash flow, will be expected to generate even weekly projections because investors want to keep a tight rein on where the money is and where it is going. We turn again to InventoTex, our fairly mature software developer, for illustration (see Figure 9.7).

It would seem InventoTex is going to be fine for the next few years; however, the industry is volatile and needs quite a lot of margin for security. Questions may arise for the company, such as, "what property was disposed of under investing activities?" Actually, what happened was that InventoTex had dreams of creating its own hardware too and bought a piece of land with a small factory on it. Unfortunately, this never became feasible and they sold the derelict property.

Figure 9.7: Cash Flow Statement (in thousands)

	2007	2006
Net Income	563	163
Add back non-cash items:		
Depreciation & amortization	48	30
Cash from Operations	611	193
Financing Activities		
Increase (decrease) long-term debt	(100)	100
Cash from Financing Operations	(100)	100)
Investing Activities		
Proceeds from disposal of property	198	0
Cash from Investing Operations	198	0
Change in Cash	709	93
Cash at beginning of year	149	56
Cash at end of period	858	149

Using ratios to analyze the cash flow statement is only part of how the fund manager sees a company because there will be analysis overlap from the income statement and balance sheet. Essentially, the cash flow statement speaks for itself along with the quality of your future revenue planning. Get ready. If you are asking for $4M, investors will challenge you. They will ask if you can do it for less. Your financial data will give you the backup to justify the capital you want.

Key Consideration: Cost of Capital

The cost of capital is not just a financial calculation based on EBITDA and interest. It also takes into account other factors and each adds value.

- Shareholding Dilution
- Balance Sheet Implications
- Any Impact on Future Cash Flows
- Management/Board of Directors
- Operations/Strategic Partnerships
- Longer-Term Issues/Exit Strategies

Why You Need Projections for Five Years

Projected income statements for three years will show the projected earnings. This is important to demonstrate that you grasp the future revenue growth that is organic and based on acquisition sales growth. Your projections signal whether your business will generate a good return on investment within the time frame. This projection will show how the proceeds of financing will be used for the term of the capital, plus give an idea of how the company will run during that time.

In some cases, a business will not have had any revenue to speak of when going out to raise capital. In these start-up cases it does not make much sense to include an income statement if there is, in fact, none or include a cash flow statement if there is no cash flowing. However, these two statements along with the balance sheet must be included in your projections.

The discounted cash flow sets value by using revenue forecasts and adjusting this to take into account the risk the investor takes and the opportunity cost of using the money. Your deal is based on the valuation of your company.

- How much will be invested?
- How much of the company can be expected to be shared?
- What could the ROI be?
- What will the depreciation and write-offs be—earnings and non-cash?

Detail working capital projections, such as salaries, office rentals and computer costs, cell phones, and the lot. Match increases in staffing to your predictions of the climb in market demand. Keep in mind production increases and other less obvious costs.

Establish your fixed costs, such as office furniture, equipment, trucks, office building, manufacturing plant, and so on. Put in your extra costs, like marketing and product promotion. Build in a bit of fat for those difficult times you are sure to hit.

It seems very dull and time consuming to collect all of this data, but keep in mind that investors do not want to see your full spreadsheet either, as these change. That is the sign of a real rookie if you bring in the Excel spreadsheet in full.

Make It Tie Up

The worst flaw in an investment proposal, worse than fingernails along a blackboard for fund managers, is when the numbers in one table do not add up to numbers given elsewhere in the report. Check, check, check.

Check for these common mistakes.

- Expenses $\neq$ Cash Out
- Revenues $\neq$ Cash In
- Assets = Liabilities and Equity
- Balance Sheet and Cash Flow

Have Sensitivity Analysis Ready

Often overlooked is the capital expenditure and number of people required. These are your cash cycles and are where investors really focus. Your numbers must tell a compelling story to justify your market returns, and potential investors are going to be more skeptical than buyers on eBay inspecting a Picasso.

Can you show you've planned for changing market conditions and that the growth rate is attainable? Can you construct a sensitivity analysis? In this case, investors will get an idea of your valuation. In the industry, it's a multiple of revenue. Investors want to see what the return on invested equity can be.

The Meeting

You do not get the keys to enter the kingdom of the finance guys unless you have passed the other tests first. It is a process. When you demonstrate ROI and competitive advantage; when you can give solid evidence to support projected growth over the next few years; when you can talk about what is so special about your company that will get you ahead of the pack—now that is the Coke bottle moment.

SEVEN QUESTIONS TO KICK-START YOUR FINANCING

Ask yourself these questions to see if you are ready to approach potential investors.

1.   **What Do You Have to Show?**
    a. I can talk about the product. Once they understand the concept, they will know how much this could make.
    b. Here's a three-page plan and I've got some diagrams of how the business works.
    c. I have a written business plan and a PowerPoint ready to go.
    d. We have a detailed investment proposal that has an analysis of our business plan and all the supporting research filed, ready for investors' investigation. We have detailed financial cash flows and projections.

2.   **What Level of Financing Do You Need?**
    a. I need to get any capital I can. $50,000 would be good.
    b. The product is a winner. If we could get $300,000 to finish the prototype, this will take off and earn millions.
    c. We are surviving quite well. We need to buy new equipment to take us to the next level, though, and we need $1M.

d. Our vision is ambitious and we need capital to take us there. This is our third time getting funds and we are asking for $5M.

3. Can You Prove Your Growth Potential?
    a. If you Google this company, you will see that this company will be bought in four years for gazillions.
    b. We have a business plan laying out the competition and the market with numbers to prove our projections. My kid nephew and all his friends used us so much, their school bought a prototype and then a couple more schools signed long-term contracts.
    c. A professional analyst checked out the business and we have an investment proposal with a thorough look at our external environment and how this matches our internal skills and our key business functions. Our revenues are $3M but our costs eat the profits.
    d. Our revenues are $10M plus.

4. Do You Have Anything to Give?
    a. What do you suggest?
    b. Previous history of paying down debt rapidly and reaching break-even when predicted.
    c. Part ownership and a payback of their investment in four years . . . maybe.
    d. Part ownership and a great exit by being bought by our main competitor. We can give part of the business, as we know it's better to have some part of a pie than no pie at all.

5. What Is the State of Your Company Finances?
    a. A shoebox stuffed with receipts is my accounts payable.
    b. We manage. My staff get paid on time and we pay our bills.
    c. We have a good idea of our revenues and monthly costs, and we have it well documented. We really don't spend a tonne so our accounts are pretty simple. We pay our taxes.
    d. We have taxes paid and financial statements done. We have a finance report done every month with financial targets. We have a bookkeeper but need a CFO.

6. Are You Comfortable Asking for Capital?
    a. Sure. I've asked my uncle for money and I have been able to get the bank to give me loans, so I've had experience.
    b. I've had an Angel investor on my board.

c. I would prefer to have professional help at this stage as we are complicated.

d. We have a good track record to show our future will be solid. I think any fund manager will be pleased to have us in their portfolio.

7. **How Are Your Own Finances?**
   a. I need to pay my taxes from last year. My own situation is not a reflection on how I conduct myself in business.
   b. We are stretched on the home front.
   c. We have basic accounting covered but my mum does the books.
   d. Everything is computerized and on Quicken, complete with budget and investment plans for the next three years.

Your Financing Profile

If your answers were . . .

Mostly (a)	You are not ready. Do not mess up your reputation and jump the gun at this stage. You need to get your house in order first. You probably still need to ask your mom for money as she is the only one who will fund you at this stage. Get organized!
Mostly (b)	You are getting the idea. You may be ready for seed funds or angel investors. See an expert to start talking about what your focus needs to be.
Mostly (c)	You are in the starting blocks for a strong take-off down the track, but be careful. Get your investment proposal written and consult an expert to do the financial modelling. You can stand up to first-round and second-round investing with VCs and institutional fund managers with smaller funds.
Mostly (d)	If you are telling the truth about your revenues and if you have outsiders agreeing with your assessment, then you are investor hot! You are ready to meet fund managers of private equity.

TAKE AWAYS

The business plan is revisited but with the focus on what the private equity investor is thinking while reading your business story. The investment proposal is different from the business plan.

Most business plans do not contain that spark of interest that the growth equity investor or institutional investor likes to see. Take care to write an investment proposal, not a classic business plan.

It will be worth your while to have a proper analyst build sophisticated and relevant financial models and conduct a due diligence prior to approaching this level of investor. After all, if you were handing $5M of your own money to someone, wouldn't you want them to make the investment in their future?

CHAPTER 10

THE SMART PRESENTATION: RAISING CAPITAL FACE TO FACE

A feast is made for laughter, and wine maketh merry: but money answereth all things.

10:19 Ecclesiastes

"Come in for a chat. No harm done," announces venture capitalist (VC) Rick at the How to Get Funded conference held every year at Silicon Valley's plush golf club. What he really means, if he's honest, is, "Let me scoop your deal before any other investor sees you. That is— if you are any good." Worse still, if he does not like your business, can you guess what he says about you over lunch with his investor pals? It doesn't stop there either. Assuming his fund runs in the same industry as yours, he sits on the board of companies that could use knowledge of your strategy for their benefit. In fact, VC Rick, is obligated by law to disclose all information that he knows, and forget about asking him to sign a non-disclosure agreement (NDA); it rings the alarm bells that you're a rookie and besides, you risk annoying him.

By now, you know the investment community is globally small and, gee whiz, if you treat the visit with the same forethought as a chat with a business buddy in Future Shop's parking lot—well, put it this way, you don't deserve the money. What's the moral of this story? Do something that is against your entrepreneurial DNA—get a carefully planned presentation and stick like crazy glue to your script.

Looking for Capital

After the conference ends, I snag a meeting with VC Rick, who is an investor at the high-risk end of venture capital and when I visit his office I have time to look over his impressive list of deals completed and awards gleaned. There are framed photographs of VC Rick signing over his original company to Microsoft along with recognizable company names, logos, and impressive amounts of money raised. VC Rick is a rarity of the species, as his picks of emerging company deals—mostly raising $2M for early-stage companies—have not been the usual lottery tickets where one out of six duds is a screamer. VC Rick enters the boardroom looking like he's coming straight off the set of *CSI Miami* and I wonder if the stubble is for careful effect.

He removes his sunglasses and we sit. I start by asking if he has key advice—a mantra—for the entrepreneur visiting his office for the first time, hoping to get funded. I give an example along the lines of Jedi Master Yoda's, "Luke, use the Force."

"Absolutely," he says, "Imagine I am your brand new salesman. Now, instruct me."

I shake my head in confusion and with all the patience of that little green guru in *Star Wars*, he tries again. "Tell me about the client—who are they, what do they need, where do I find them, how would they use the product, and what are the reasons this client would cough up money to buy your company's world-changing product?"

It is a great exercise because company success does boil down to revenue—clients paying money for your work. He smiles wearily and shakes his head. "Do you know how many business owners stand in this room and fifteen minutes into the meeting, I still don't know who the customer would be or what the product would do for them?"

"Is it the jargon that you don't like?"

"It's the lack of a big, driving goal. Imagine if General Montgomery spent all his time discussing how war ships and planes were built and their fire power instead of getting on with the big picture and desired results of D-Day. It's the same for entrepreneurs. They must show they know the goal and vision of D-Day and could organize their own Normandy landing with the left side of their brain, manage a team of Microsoft geeks with the right, and steer their earnings before interest, taxes, depreciation, and amortization (EBITDA) with the rest."

VC Rick takes a breath and continues. "It's never the technology alone that gets money out of the customer's wallet. Ask Beta, Eight Track tapes, Lotus Notes, and all those companies with the way-cool technology that overshot the customer's need. If you spend your twenty minutes telling me about your technology, I can't stand it! It means you're just not CEO material."

"Crikey! You can tell all of this in twenty minutes or less? Must be psychic."

"Nope, just bored out of my skull by people who have not taken the time to expand their skill set. Guys bogged down in their product are like fingernails down a blackboard."

The Mothership PowerPoint

Your pitch should very much follow the flow of the executive summary of your written plan, but be personalized. You do not want to repeat it verbatim. Elaborate where deemed necessary. Let your personality and character seep in. *To thine own self, be true.* In other words, be frank and honest and, most importantly, be yourself.

VC Rick drops to a whisper that reminds me of *The Godfather*, "Let me be clear. This is not a marketing presentation; you are not pitching your clients. It's a financial proposal and it's about the future earnings of your company. If I see another demo, I will *scream*."

"Investors do want to be told a story. They want to be slowly cajoled into the tale, not slammed with inflated facts. Start low key and pace yourself. Take us along a logical route. Build up to the crescendo of your next five years of market growth. Then switch over to how we, the investors, can get our original investment back plus how much more profit I might make. The end."

I ask, "Is there a template to design a standard fifteen-minute presentation?"

"Absolutely, and it applies whether you are a small- or mid-sized company. Owners with more than $10M in revenue would expand out these topics. Obviously, customize the slides to emphasize your strengths. Since you only have fifteen minutes, you can't possibly include everything. If your marketing is your strength, dwell on that. You want to tell the investor something good. If your marketing is weak, leave it as one sentence."

Figure 10.1 below outlines what you should include in your presentation.

Figure 10.1: Quick Business Pitch

Slide	Content	Purpose
Front Cover	Name of company, logo, and tag line describing your business. Your contact details.	First impressions and quick idea of what your company does and how they can get hold of you.
The Team	Business acumen, domain knowledge, operational expertise. Quick bullet points focused on the connection to your company and past success.	What have you accomplished in your life? Do your skills match this opportunity?
The Need	What is happening in your clients' situation to cause them dissatisfaction?	Is there enough of a burning need for your solution?
Your Proposition	What is it that you do, and how are you different from what's out there already?	How you can fill the need? Key selling points of your business that apply to the problems. Is there the WOW factor?

Slide	Content	Purpose
Product	Technology, science, or business drawn in a model.	How much have you sold? Are the propietary and intellectual properties protected? Can customers substitute another product out there for yours?
Revenue Model	Where does the money get made?	Are the future cash flow projections fair?
The Market	What is the dollar value of the entire market?	Can this business scale up? (It had better be beyond a niche market.) Are there many smaller guys doing well or a few big gorillas? What are the barriers to entry? Should you take your product to a big company and license it instead?
Competition	Why are you better and who can kill your business?	Is there anyone out there you can buy or who could buy you? Why would clients pick you?
Barriers or Risks	Industry analysis of the risks and how you plan to get over them. Your competitive advantage and why you are difficult to copy.	Are you savvy enough to know the problems and do you have specific strategy to face these or does the fund manager have to raise them?
Go-to-Market Strategy	Will you sell directly or use a channel such as a distributor or trade show?	How quickly can you reach the market? How will you get clients to switch to your product?

(Continued)

Figure 10.1: (Continued)

Slide	Content	Purpose
Milestones Met	What have you done with funds in the past?	Are you someone who does what you say you can do? What's your track record?
Target Milestones	What will you do with the money?	You have forward-planning capabilities with key checkpoints.
Financial Slides	Provide historical data and forecast three- to five-year projections. Income statement and balance sheet. Cash flow statement.	Is it a nice business but not a good investment? Investors want to see past performance. What will be their payback?
Investment Highlights	Key points for investors to remember (e.g., 25% IRR, five patents).	What three points do you want investors to remember?

First Impressions

VC Rick says, "At the face-to-face meeting, the investor will be assessing your grasp of the business and your confidence in running it successfully."

But you know that, already.

"I see hundreds of business owners and prospective deals," VC Rick pauses and looks as if he's Atlas, carrying the weight of the world on his shoulders. "Many entrepreneurs think, 'I've got to give my pitch in fifteen minutes. If I speak very quickly, I can cram it all in.' Or they give me a lecture on the top 50 technology trends or get off business altogether. No one, except their pandering staff, wants to hear about their little dog that is as old as their business and comes to the office everyday. Know that the purpose of this meeting is to get the conversation to continue."

How VC Rick Will Judge You

Once you are in the door to VC Rick, his attention narrows. He will eye you with the suspicion of a father meeting his daughter's date. Above all else, Rick wants to respect you and your team. It is you and your management that Rick's fund buys.

Rick is wondering if he can partner with you and will use every single moment of truth in this first encounter to judge you and your management style. After all, VC Rick could potentially be in the foxhole with you over the next five years and he wants that experience to be positive. If you are not intense about your cash flow, if you are testy about probing questions, if you levitate when the marketing is criticized, if you argue about terms of the deal, you will be shown the door.

Before you present, keep in mind that there's always a Plan B and another fund. If you would run into a burning fireworks factory if you thought there was money being offered to you, investors will sense that. Slick or desperate are not the first two words VC Rick wants to use in describing you.

Equally, being a salesman and discussing the details of your products, rather than client needs, is what too many entrepreneurs do. Be a leader.

What the Investor Will Be Asking

Rest assured, all the questions you ask yourself, VC Rick will want to know and demand answers of you. Before you begin your PowerPoint presentation, get your head buzzing with VC questions.

- What is the product?
- Will they pay for it?
- Can I make it?
- Can I make it reliably?
- Can I make *lots* of it reliably?
- Who is the customer?
- Where are they?
- How will I get my product there?
- Is there an intermediary I can use to sell my product?
- Is more product development needed? At what cost?
- Who is going to fund this boondoggle and who will pay me?
- Who will do the work?

While you are going through this thought process, VC Rick at the other end of the boardroom table has his own thoughts to add. Will I get my money back? Will I make some returns? Will I make a barrel full of returns?

You see, it's all about the investment opportunity. VC Rick doesn't care about the beauty of your mousetrap, only if it is a better mousetrap. Is it better than the competitors'? Will customers actually get up off their comfy sofa to buy your mousetrap? And the grand finale—will that mousetrap make money?

VC Rick says, "Those who present on their technology, and not the future cash flows, will just not be successful. Unless you can demonstrate a credible plan on how you will turn your company into a profitable business within the five years, do not bother us. You will be wasting your breath and, worse, the investor market will know that your presentation is not worth a measly dime." Indeed, doors will slam shut faster than a mouse trap, and there goes your chance at getting the cheese.

Now let's look at each slide (see Figure 10.2) in more detail to help flesh out your presentation.

First Up: Front Slide

Figure 10.2 is a sketch of what your front slide, or slide 1, should look like.

Figure 10.2: Slide 1

Content	Purpose
Name of company, logo, and tag line describing your business. Your contact details.	First impressions and quick idea of what your company does and how they can reach you if they pick up the pack in a year's time.

Your Company name & logo

Your name

Your title

Elevator sentence

Contact information

The fund's logo, name, and date

Fifteen seconds, that's all you get. As your front slide comes up, it sets the bar. It must capture the imagination and grab the investor's attention. Keep to a tight script of company name, what you do, and move to the next slide.

What is important to establish with the front page of the presentation is exactly who you are and where you are coming from, nothing more. Extensive graphics or catchy colours may be appealing for the eyes, but they may also distract and confuse your audience who are deciding on your trustworthiness and integrity.

The best place to express that creative flare is in the elevator sentence, which is the "tag line." This is the sentence that you spent hours, even days or months pondering, to come up with that unforgettable phrase that no one can resist and that succinctly expresses the value of the business.

Elevator Sentences for Large Multinationals

The standard elevator pitch is a good idea but can also evolve into sounding dangerously like "my car is flashier than yours." Figure 10.3 gives some examples of highly effective tag lines. Keep it based on your customer need and the hand-on-heart promise to help your customers.

Figure 10.3: Tag Lines of the Famous

Company	Elevator sentence
Google	Organizing the world's information
Fedex	The world on time
Disney	Family entertainment
Alcan	Innovative aluminum and packaging solutions
Westjet	Because owners care
IMAX	You haven't seen it all until you've seen it in IMAX
Tim Hortons	Always Fresh
Pfizer	Working for a healthier world

Too many entrepreneurs are about the profits they can make first, with the customer shut out of the pitch. The Japanese have a word, "sesshin." It means to touch the mind, heart, spirit, and deep down in the private space of those souls around you. A truly great business reaches *sesshin* for the customer. We need to get beyond the brash, fast-talking MBA speak and back to quiet sincerity.

Interestingly, private equity does favour the quieter scientific geek over the loud promoter.

Executive Team

"I want to see who's going to run the company and [if] they have done it before." See Figure 10.4 for the second slide, your executive summary.

What is the business acumen, domain knowledge, operational expertise? Every company can do with more talent. Funds know they can fill your CFO role, strategic thinking, and coach. They see themselves as the "wealth plan" creators.

VCs will be looking for a number of things from Slide 2.

- *A Firm Grasp of Marketing.* VC Rick will be looking to see if you understand the customers. Is your team customer focused? You

Figure 10.4: Slide 2

Content	Purpose for Investor
Business acumen, domain knowledge, operational expertise. Quick bullet points focused on the connection to your company and past success. How did you get into what you do? How long have you been doing it?	To assess: What you have accomplished in your life If your skills match this opportunity If you have passion and expertise Are you running a lifestyle business or an investment business? Does management have a good track record? How long have you been in this industry? How complete are your skills?

might be surprised to learn that your receptionist is treating callers like an annoying part of the day. When VC Rick phones your office and gets a snarky reply from the receptionist, this signals a culture less than sensitive to clients and may cause VC Rick to pass on your proposal. Have customers that investors can contact. You validate the opportunity if there are key customers who will give testimonials, which can be tricky as customers are busy. If the investors need to go out and find their own validation, this will draw out the process.

- *A Solid Network.* No one expects you to hire all the talent you need. That's where your band of advisors comes in—they are your mentors and should open their Rolodex. VC Rick will be scoping out who are the key people involved—your board of directors, advisory board, and investors already in. Who are your friends?
- *Do You Think Big?* The big vision has to be expansive and you must plan to go far. It's a global world today and if you want to be the best in Scarborough, your city, or province, well, chances are you're not going to get that funding. You need to have a plan to take your business to the world. In 2003, 90% of revenue for Canadian companies operating in their first year came from outside of Canada. It used to be the U.S. market but now South America and Asia are popular.

The Need

Describe the burning need in the market place—get the investor's head nodding and thinking: "Oh yeah, my Uncle Ted was telling me about CIBC & Winners losing his credit card information. Security of online information is a big pain for banks." (See Figure 10.5.)

It's got to be a big enough pain. What is it exactly that your company does that gets customers to reach inside their wallets and give you their hard-earned cash? In other words, how does your company do something to make your customers' lives easier, happier, or just plain better?

Figure 10.5: Slide 3

Content	Purpose
What is happening in your clients' situation to cause them dissatisfaction?	To assess: Is there enough of a burning need for your clients to switch their buying habits and pay for your stuff?

- Is there a need for your product/service?
- If there is a need—why has it not been filled until now?
- Has it been done before and is there research to show the results?
- Are your customers buying your product for speed, efficiency, prestige, convenience, safety, or cost savings?
- Can you back up your claims with numbers and dollars?

The Proposition

What is the meaning or passion of your product or service? (See Figure 10.6.) No high tech diagrams here; just keep it simple, for example, IT security for your credit card online purchases. Our product sends you an e-mail whenever your credit card number is used.

Figure 10.6: Slide 4

Content	Purpose
What is it that you do and how are you different from what's out there already?	To assess: How can you fill the need? What are the key selling points of your business as they apply to the problems. Is there the WOW factor?

The approach taken to develop an elevator pitch is provided in Figure 10.7 and it will identify your passion succinctly.

Figure 10.7: Developing an Elevator Pitch

Elevator Pitch for Killing Mice	
Facts	Market need is for those homeowners needing to get rid of mice in the house.
Pain	Getting the dead mouse out of the mouse trap without touching it.
Proposition	Pellet Inc. creates poison pellets to kill rodents safely, and since the carcass dries up, it can be scooped into the garbage without having to touch a dead mouse.

By clearly defining the story of the "pain," how you can help your customers becomes evident. As you give the segment, you can show why you are picking it and why that customer group is of interest to you. Are there attractive groups that you are choosing not to chase and why? If you want your business plan to stand out, this is where to show your understanding of your customers and how passionate you are about them. Figure 10.8 outlines the basis of Disney's phenomenal success.

Steve Jobs, founder of Apple and also Pixar, did change the world by creating pain where there wasn't any. He said you can have

Figure 10.8: Disney's Elevator Pitch

Elevator Pitch for Disney Movies	
Facts	Market need is for those families watching movies together and wanting to enjoy the experience.
Pain	Age-appropriate entertainment that parents know they do not need to pre-screen.
Proposition	Disney movies only have content suitable for family viewing; no cringing and scrambling for the remote.

a computer in your kitchen and, at first, this seemed preposterous. Today, it is no longer a Jetsons' cartoon fantasy but reality for many households.

The Product

Describe your company's ability to help with the pain. Leave out the jargon. Show a simple diagram of your business model and explain, using an example of a real customer. Use arrows to point out where the money gets made and how much (see Figure 10.9).

Is it a one-trick pony or is it on a platform? Is it franchiseable? Having seen many owners get stalled by a simple finance question, I must repeat, *"Know your plan!"* Have at your fingertips the finance ratios and drivers. You are auditioning as a worthy CEO, not just a marketing hotshot or a technocrat. The fund managers will be watching carefully to see if you are capable of running a business, not just a product launch. Your ability to hold a knowledgeable discussion about your numbers is the critical test. If you turn your head to your investment advisor just once to get help, you are one more dead deal.

What is it that you sell and what is the value proposition or the solution? Obviously, you do not want to be seen as the crazy uncle in the garage with your latest invention, but the investors do want to know that you believe you are not just doing the same old thing as everyone else. If you are selling sporting goods, it is not good enough to say sportswear.

Figure 10.9: Slide 5

Content	Purpose
What is it that you do and how are you different from what's out there already?	To assess: How you will fill the need. Key Selling Points of your business to the problems. Where's the WOW?

Is it discount-priced, warehoused sportswear, children's sportswear, serious outdoor mountain climbing gear, or gold lamé jackets for the fashionable ski bunny?

Research In Motion (RIM) is a leading designer, manufacturer, and marketer of innovative wireless solutions for the worldwide mobile communications market. "Show me a picture," demands VC Rick, "of how the world was confused before and then afterwards. All need help to understand what it is you do. Paint me a picture." Show the impact of your product. In a diagram, show how your clients are dealing in the marketplace. Once they get your product, can you draw simpler flows of arrows?

On a second slide you can show a simple model that illustrates how your company stops the pain. It may be divided into two parts—the World Before Your Company on the left and the World Afterwards on the right.

The Revenue Model

VC Rick says, "Now you've got my attention. I want to see that you've built your business model bottom up. Applying percentage changes for forecasts is lazy and laughable." (See Figure 10.10.)

You don't have a business if you don't have revenue. Remember the revenue model is not a business model; the revenue model is one piece of the whole overall jigsaw puzzle. Illustrate the revenue

Figure 10.10: Slide 6

Content	Purpose
Cash flow projections You will make money—in this way…	To assess: Investors want to see projections of real income coming through. The earnings forecast shows if your model is realistic.

model because it will make it easy and quick to understand; include the method that money comes in and how that money reaches your pocket.

The Market

This is the place to bring out the statistics. (See Figure 10.11.)

- PEST (Political, Economic, Sociological, and Technological) threats and opportunities for your business
- Company SWOT Analysis (Strengths, Weaknesses, Opportunities, and Threats)
- Demographics of your target market (age, income, preferences, etc.)
- How big is the market and what percentage could you get?
- Dollar amount: show that people are making money in your area
- Revenues
- Success rates
- How big is the field you are playing on?
- Your market share
- What is the size and potential of your customer base?

Figure 10.11: Slide 7

Content	Purpose
What is the dollar value of the entire market? What are the company's historical and projected growth rates? What is the company's current and projected market share?	To assess: Can this business scale up? You had better be beyond a niche market. Are there many smaller guys doing well or a few big gorillas? Potential revenue streams? What are the barriers to entry by competitors? Should you take your product to a big company and license it instead?

Figure 10.12: Slide 8

Content	Purpose
Why are you better? Who can kill your business? How many competitors are there and how big are they?	Is there anyone out there you can buy or who could buy you? Why would clients pick you? What is your competitive advantage?

The Competition

"This is tricky," says VC Rick. "The reality is that the world is managing without you. Why can you do better?" Figure 10.12 shows what you'll need to convince a VC that you can stay ahead of the competition.

"No one else is doing this." Maybe no one you know is doing this, but if it is a good business, someone's coming up from the sidelines. The one hundred monkeys theory describes how when one monkey started washing the grit from his food, ninety-nine others were also starting to do this. Strange but true. There were loads of other Bill Gates out there, but most did not stay home prom night and order in pizza with his best buddy to work on their idea.

VC Rick says, "You must have a competitor because if you are smart, someone else is doing it. Why are you better and who can kill your business?" Better find out about other guys and don't name Google or Microsoft. If you dwell on the eight-hundred-pound gorilla who could take you out, you give VC Rick the exit strategy he needs.

Look at it this way, Van Gogh studied the Dutch masters and Japanese art and he copied their techniques before he broke through with his own brilliance. If you want to be a great painter, you do need to see what has been determined as great across the ages to bring depth to your own art.

In the same way, seeing Microsoft's business plan will guide you to create your own technology firm. If you are going for private money, no matter what size of revenues and clients, you need to instil a sense of confidence with investors. After all, you can cook the books so that an

Anderson auditor would not catch the deceit. To get peace of mind, investors need to set up a series of steps for you to follow. If you have done some market research to see the size of your potential market, some of this will have rubbed off on you, so that you now have an opinion of whether the research is right or not. Otherwise, you will lack depth in your own business thinking.

Barriers or Risks

How unique is your company? What makes you or your company so special? What's your brainy formula, magic, fairy dust, secret recipe, X-Men qualities? See Figure 10.13 for some advice.

The technology or product, which in early-stage investing is the keystone to the business, is understandably of prime concern. Is the technology incremental or transformational? In other words, is it just a better staircase or is it an elevator—a totally different technology that takes away from the current market leaders? How will you entice customers to switch from their habitual technology? When there is status quo competition, customers have to heave themselves off their current habit over to your elevator—changing loyalties takes work.

Is this technology coming out of left field? Can it be disintermediated? That is, can something come between it and the market and replace the technology? Can it be scaled? Can it be transferred out of the lab and commercialized? How easy is it to copy? Are there patents? Can the company protect their patents? VC Rick likes significant intellectual property. He likes patents rather than know-how embedded in your three engineers' brains. He wants to know if someone in your company

Figure 10.13: Slide 9

Content	Purpose
Industry analysis of the risks and how you plan to get over them. Your competitive advantage and why you are difficult to copy.	Are you savvy enough to know the problems and do you have specific strategy to face these, or does the fund manager have to raise them?

made a speech and disclosed patents, do you have the resources to defend your patents. Where is the tech team located? VC Rick prefers them to be close by as they want to talk eyeball-to-eyeball and probably on a regular timetable.

Despite the world being flat, India is a long way for VC Rick to go. If you can—add patents, white papers, proof of concepts, methodologies, etc. Do you know the value of partnerships? Strategic alliances are agreements between large and small companies to perform joint activities. These could be research, marketing, sales, or looking after one segment of the market. These arrangements have increased in past years. Small companies stand to gain a great deal, as they might be able to get financial, marketing, distribution, or other resources. Alliances have been bandied around for years. Research shows that strong market competitors are those with alliances or partnerships with players within their industry. For example, British Airways has the most alliances with other airlines. This translates into seamless travel experiences for travellers wanting to go from London to Prague.[1] Little guys can play with the big guys too.

The Risks

Investors want to know that you understand your industry, have taken the risks into consideration, and have planned to resolve them (see Figure 10.14). You must show that you have taken the appropriate steps to control the systematic risk; it will give the investor confidence

Figure 10.14: Slide 8

Content	Purpose
Industry analysis of the risks and how you plan to get over them. Why is your product difficult to copy?	Are you savvy enough to know the problems and do you have a specific strategy to face these, or does the fund manager have to raise them?

[1] Douglas Reid, Queen's University, Presentation to Strategic Leadership Forum, 2003.

in your management team. For unsystematic risk, it's best to show that you understand the threats and have contingency plans in place.

Ensure that any intellectual property rights that need to be protected are secured, if not water-tight. Your product or concept should be unique and difficult to replicate. Patents make investors excited because it shows you've done your homework. If you have secured any intellectual property rights, show that too.

Political activity will impact your future earnings. For example, a government that uses taxes to attract new industry can mean that the U.S. outsources call centres to Canada rather than India. The trend is for governments to use taxes to attract investment. Legal system changes can also close doors of opportunities but open them too. New driving laws can mean car seats are required by children and help drive up revenues. The environment can impact on future cash. West Nile disease scares boost the need for outdoor mosquito repellent devices. Technology is changing your clients' behaviour. Software to prevent spam flooding your e-mail would be very interesting to investors. You would barely have to explain the "pain" or the need for this product.

Society impacts your company and creates booms and busts. We are all familiar with how boomers are moving into retirement years, justifying the increase in retirement investment planning and lifestyle products and services. Travel packages for over-fifties are springing up all over the place. It's clear that knee and hip replacement joints are the growing trend, along with medical applications to serve this need.

Go-to-Market Strategy

No strategy will be a disaster. If you have partnerships with other companies, use their logos. Have at least five action steps with specifics and deadlines. Figure 10.15 will give you an idea of the answers for which VCs are looking.

VC Rick will look to see if you have any contracts with your customers and suppliers. As a businessperson, you will know that when big companies give contracts to smaller companies, they need a business

Figure 10.15: Slide 9

Content	Purpose
Will you sell directly or use a channel, such as a distributor or trade show? Partners?	How quickly can you reach the largest market? How will you get clients to switch to your product? Do you have a focused beachhead to hit first?

plan to know that your company will be able to scale up and produce the volume of product required. Also, the big customer will want to be reassured that you will be around for the long haul and are not a fly-by-night operation.

Investors want to see your team's track record of proven marketing acumen and financial management. Almost no one gets VC money without actually having demonstrated in the business community that she can really perform. You could be asked for last year's budget and strategy plans. Past plans indicate what level of milestones you set for yourself and whether you achieved them. Do you over-promise and under-deliver or, worst of all, not plan at all?

"A major weakness in presenting," says VC Rick, "is that management teams spend too much time on the product and they forget about their "Go-to-Market" plan. Investors will see you as a time-waster if you are stuck in that rut."

Milestones Met

Milestones met lists your accomplishments so far. What have you done with money in the past? (See Figure 10.16 below.)

Figure 10.16: Slide 10

Content	Purpose
What have you done with money in the past?	Are you someone who does what you say you can do? What's your track record?

As an entrepreneur and founder, you have sold your kidneys to get out of the Beta testing stage. Getting customers and listing your milestones achieved shows you can make money.

What are the big steps of your business? When did you start?

- 2001: Founded the business
- 2002: Signed the first deal over $1M
- 2003: Raised first $1M in angel investment
- Strategic Alliances: Distribution partnership; preferential arrangements
- Key Customers: put some logos on this page.

You want to show you've advanced the cause by hitting milestones and also that you've had customers or clients who have paid for your services or product.

Target Milestones

Milestones should be tangible. Things like "understand our customer better by March 2009" is useless. The items listed below are good examples of target milestones.

- Conduct planned research survey with 30 clients by June 2008
- Disseminate information and reach conclusions by January 2009
- Implement recommendations by March 2009

This is a planned strategy for growth that demonstrates disciplined focus in management. (See Figure 10.17.)

Figure 10.17: Slide 11

Content	Purpose
What will you do with the money?	You have forward planning capabilities with key checkpoints. You will spend strategically.

Figure 10.18: Slide 12

Content	Purpose
Provide historical data and forecast three- to five-year projections. Income statement and balance sheet. Cash flow analysis.	Is it a nice business but not a good investment? Investors want to see past performance and where you will be in the future. After three to five years, what will be their payback? What is the current revenue and EBITDA? What is the level of sophistication? How much money do you want?

Financial Information

Show the balance sheet and keep it simple (Figure 10.18). Add in your salary and time as part of the start-up costs. Have accounts receivable, if you sell a product or charge someone something. Show deferred revenue. Also show what you've spent so far—it shows that you are active.

Add a simple income statement that shows salaries and office costs and make sure EBITDA is highlighted. You may not have an income statement at this time, but use a projected income statement.

A cash flow statement is needed as well. Again, if you have no cash flow to build a cash flow statement, do not include one, but do add a projected cash flow statement. You will be expected to have at least a quarterly cash flow statement, possibly a monthly, and, in some cases, even a weekly projection will be necessary. It depends on the amount of risk the investor feels he is taking and how demanding he is.

Using these financial statements you need to build a model that shows the number of clients you expect to attract and the subsequent cost and profit implications. VC Rick can then play with this model to construct his own worst and best case scenario.

You are not a used car salesman telling investors how much they will make. The smart investor will figure out Internal Rate of Return

(IRR) themselves. Give them the tools to figure our how much they will make. Use examples of growth from your competition. When did they begin and where are their revenues now?

"Nothing pops the profit balloon quicker than lack of forward revenues." VC Rick gives that Grim Reaper smile of the VC and goes on to list his most frequent gripes. "Yes, that's incredible technology, but how many salespeople will you need? I'm glad to hear it's a killer technology, but how can you expect to expand your business and not pay for people? Wonderful, it's a disruptive business model but what are your projected revenues and not as extrapolations? Fantastic, you have a compelling service idea, but can you price how many new clients you need per month to meet your IRR?"

If you can't answer those questions, pack up, and head back down to base camp. You must give revenue, expenses, and EBITDA, but leave the spreadsheets back at the office.

Build budget for operations from the bottom up. Budgets should be in great detail, taking into consideration the industry and market within which you operate. The more precise you are about your budget, the more it shows that you are keen about details and that is what investors like to see.

Investors want to know that your return on sales is going to track upwards at an attractive angle. You need to show why the trend line is going to move upwards with the introduction of your product or service. Here is where to lay out the drivers in the market. What switched trends? What drives sales? What factors can play on the market purchasing power? What are new trends that change the whole landscape of the marketplace? Explain the opportunities set up by the changes in trends.

Investment Highlights

VC Rick rocks back on his chair. "On the final slide—please, please don't title the slide Summary. Everyone goes brain dead. You will give the nod for everyone to do their BlackBerry Prayer (bow their heads as they check for messages).

Figure 10.19: Slide 13

Content	Purpose
You can call these take-aways or something original.	Key points for investors to remember.

Always finish with the financials, as they are the key points you want the investor to remember about your company. You can call it The Road Ahead, Next Steps, Take-Aways or Challenges. Recap the highlights you want the investor to have stuck in his head." (See Figure 10.19.)

Three Presentation No-Nos

- **Talking about the Product.** Be the CEO that you want to be and that means focusing on the revenue and cash flow projections, not going on about the product.
- **Arguing.** It is human to be unhappy when the investor tells you your baby is ugly. All parents think their baby is the best. Plan to listen and be receptive to every comment. Write them down and go over the points again with your partner or advisor in a week's time. It will focus your action plan.
- **Presenting Weak Financial Information.** Immediate red flatline. Have the right statements available and understand the numbers.

Biggest Mistakes by Owners and CEOs

- **Monkey Business.** If your business is a little sapling—even if you cover it with tinsel, add flashing lights and hang candy canes— you will not convince the private equity investors that you have a mighty oak. Put away the special effects and disclose anything vaguely dodgy. These are the big boys of finance and they can not be fooled and will find your law suits or skeletons.
- **Letting Your Fears Rule.** Every owner before you believed that parting with equity would be a huge sacrifice and struggled to see the upside. Once owners get to this stage of giving ownership in exchange for money, they believe it's ownership forever. That's not

the case. The investors will want out of your business—within three to seven years. If you want to buy back your company, you can certainly build that into your plans. As you reach financial milestones, you can earn back your ownership. Venture capitalists are investors who supply additional mentorship services—that is, advice, contacts, additional resources. This input is difficult for the people who run the investee company to receive. Owners are not always welcoming and can sometimes be resistant. If you were to talk to owners who have gone through the private equity stage of investing, 99% of them would tell you this type of advice helped them more often than not.

- **Thinking You Are Diluting Your Power.** Don't behave as if the investor has you pinned down with a tractor beam. You have power too. You can say no to the deal and you could probably survive without their money. Keep it in perspective. Every investor knows that you are the one running the business, even if you only own 15%. Once negotiations end, it is back over to you. When you have been king of your sandpit for a while, you may not be used to having someone make suggestions; you may react poorly. These fund managers are at the top of the business food chain, most of them having been where you now stand—owner of a growing business. You would be lucky to find that calibre of finance skills mixed in with strategy experience. If you think the fund managers and VCs expect you to sit at the feet of the "wisemen" (them), that is just not true. They want to go shoulder-to-shoulder partnership with you because the answers to the business are within you. See private equity as an opportunity to have drive and a balanced perspective at your board room table—that is what these VCs will bring.
- **Balking at the Costs of Financing.** Think about what you would pay to have a top-notch CFO come in and do all the accounting measures to crank your business. What would you pay to have a solid business coach push you up the ladder of success? Do you have any idea what a financial consultant or a financial strategy from a high flying accounting firm would cost? All of a sudden, these VCs and fund managers are looking very cheap and very exciting. Keep

in mind, if you want to make your business grow and have a slice of that bigger business, get the finance partners that can help you do it. They've been in your spot many times before and have tried and true formulas to apply.

- **Not Being Prepared.** A young entrepreneur who raised millions credits his mom for teaching him, "Empty vessels make the most sound." Before he met with investors, he knew each concept he wanted the money guys to remember and, being a chatty type, he kept to his script. Go over this chapter on VC Rick and the killer questions until you can answer them in your sleep. Be able to answer in coherent sentences, even if you were as drunk as a middle-aged guy at a college reunion party. Visit the fund's Web site and be able to quote nuggets about their investment criteria to the investors. Most have their full resumes on display. Try to find something in common. Rehearse your presentation at least three times in front of a tough audience. I suggest a sixteen-year-old daughter or niece. She's sure to be meaner than any fund manager and point out that your suit has a stain on it or that you pick your teeth when nervous. *Remember, if you fail to prepare, then prepare to fail.*

- **Be Realistic.** Is the business concept one that can scale? Is the industry large and growing? Is the marketplace receptive? Can your business become the dominant force in a specific market segment? If not, there's not going to be sufficient returns to the investors. The investors will give their views on the value of your business. You need VC Rick more than they need you. Do not dictate terms as you will be quickly shown the door. It may not be the best deal, but it's today's deal.

- **Shop 'Til You Drop.** If you have mailed out your proposal for funds willy-nilly you may have a bad case of overexposure. The receptionist will send you a letter of thanks and your plan will now be in their database. Next time you come around, cap in hand, they will look you up on their database. It pays to focus and avoid the shotgun approach. It is a small industry and VCs talk to each other. No one likes to know they got into a marriage with a person who had their phone number written on the bathroom wall.

- **Leave the Hockey Sticks to the Stanley Cup Playoffs.** Steep upward revenue lines projecting unrealistically high growth years into the future will make the fund managers fall in a heap laughing. Investors want to see the hockey stick revenue growth, but let them come to that conclusion themselves. Be conservative, very conservative.
- **Not Enough Supporting Data.** Build a footnote binder: all those articles getting you pumped about your business—keep them. Have them in a binder with you. As the analysts begin their investigation, they will come to you and ask where you got certain facts and data. If you are able to hand over fat binders, neatly indexed, of all the documents used to hold up your plan, that will provide enormous goodwill. The analyst will be able to quickly access any document you used, and this is a huge boost of confidence. Beg, steal, or borrow any marketing data and research that backs up your views. Third-hand data gives credibility. If there is data that contradicts your views, make sure you are aware of it and have answers to overcome any discrepancies with your plans.
- **Time Dependent.** A shotgun marriage rarely has a happy ending with both partners believing they have a good deal. It can take months from the first meeting to the final handshake, which is why you will hear, "Get money when you do not need it."
- **Legality.** Selling shares in your company by yourself is illegal. Use a limited market dealer to sign off your contract and make sure there are no irregularities.
- **Not Tapping Your Advisors.** Your lawyer, accountant, and the corporate finance consultants are worth their fees, as they are working for you. Funds and VCs are working for themselves. Check with advisors; they all have a broad network of contacts. Make these people earn their fees. Ask them for leads. Most will be delighted to add value to your business in that way.
- **Valuation Fights.** Check around the market for valuations in your city and region, but at your stage of the food chain. Companies turn down private equity opportunities due to valuation differences.

Subsequently, their competitors pick up a good shot of capital to rocket ahead of their competition.

VC Rick shows me to the door and says with a smile, "Too many tips ruin a golf swing." Then he's gone.

TAKE AWAYS

The opportunity to present the business story is often wasted as business owners think the meeting is about the business, when the focus needs to be on why the business is a terrific investment.

CHAPTER 11

THE WIN/WIN DEAL

Entrepreneurship has become not only a tremendous engine of growth but also a critically important style of managing. I think we need people with that kind of courage and vision, and they need those of you who have capital to invest.

Harvard Business School Dean, Kim B. Clark

The Home Stretch!

The investor is interested. Now what? Sign papers, pop the champagne? Unfortunately, not. The term sheet is to be prepared and, after some negotiation, signed. The due diligence will commence. Hold on. Let's take a breather for a moment and recap on the path taken to obtaining private equity funding. The chart in Figure 11.1 provides a useful picture.

Let's be honest—selling shares in your business is infuriating when what you think is wonderful and valuable about your business often gets pushed aside and ignored.

The valuation process, as the fund runs a very critical eye over your company, is much like a house makeover show where potential buyers waltz around, making rude comments about the purple kitchen and Great-Aunt Susan's china hanging on the wall. Before the owners can splutter a word of protest, they are marched through the place with the bossy host who points out those piles of CDs that should have been

Figure 11.1: The Financing Process

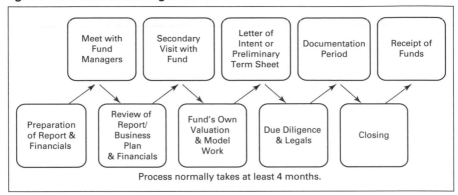

Process normally takes at least 4 months.

Source: Loewen & Partners

thrown away, the two rooms that could be one, the sooty fireplace, the sink stained with dripping taps, and the dingy paint. The owners are whisked away, the experts race in, and before you can say, "Bob's your uncle," they rip out that red carpet with stains from the dog's muddy walks, add a quick lick of paint, and new lights. A call to Got-Junk and a gang of helpers cart off old paperbacks and children's clothing piled in the garage. Finally, a scrub, tidy up of pots and pans and—presto—those same rude buyers are perking up in interest, particularly if they bump into another buyer admiring the fresh feel of the place. Then things get really hot.

You too, want to have your business looking its best and presenting itself in a shiny way to a few, select buyers. Auctions (showing your company to many buyers) are popular and may get you the highest price but *caveat-emptor*. You are seeking a long-term relationship, not offloading property, so pick who you want as a partner and make price a secondary priority.

How the Investor Values Your Business

Okay, by now you have satisfied all requests for investment proposals, presentations, strategy documents, and financial information from the investors. What's the next step? You now have got to be prepared for some discussion sessions around valuation.

The investors have to commit to how much money they are willing to invest, as well as how much of the company they will want to own. Stay calm. There will undoubtedly be a significant element of the rocket science stuff—hardcore math and accounting formulae. However, there is also a healthy dose of subjectivity. Issues such as the strength of the management team, market share of your products, threat of competition, technology risk, and the extent and nature of your capital requirements will arise. These issues will not only be reflected in the overall valuation of the company, but also influence how many board seats the investor will require. The end result of this leg of the process will be a tug-of-war debate as to how much of the company you are willing to give up to the investor and also what risk terms you are able to live with over the ensuing "partnership" period.

When buying a house, you want to know what features will ensure protection of value for the property. Likewise, if you understand the math for private equity investors, you will understand how they assign value to your business. How much will they help you in developing your business? Much like the example of buying a house, the bids vary depending on who is making an offer and what they judge to be of value. Investors have their reasons too. Imagine you have a house and now you are going to share that investment with a private equity investor. Do you and your partner want it to suit your owner-controlled goals or is it for investment and resale? Then, what return do you want?

The three variables for private equity in deciding valuation or how much to pay for a business can be explained using a house example.

- **Growth.** You rely on holding the house and getting a return because the neighbourhood went up in value. This is the "buy, fix, and sell" method.
- **Leverage.** You fix up the house and the neighbourhood rises in value. This is the "buy, add value while paying down the debt, and sell" method.
- **Multiple Arbitrage.** You buy by borrowing other people's money. You develop the house as well as wait for the value of the neighbourhood to rise. This is the "buy, arbitrage, and sell" method.

Growth occurs when the fund pays five times the earnings and a few years down the road it sells at seven times earnings; investors are happy with that as they have made some money. The fund may pay seven times earnings, knowing that there is the ability to grow the company at 10% over the next four years. Would you be satisfied if you bought a house, lived in it for five years, paid the bills, and the value of the neighbourhood went up by 10%? It would give you a reliably solid profit.

> Try not to overestimate the value of your business.

One CEO irritated by the use of earnings before interest, tax, depreciation, and amortization (EBITDA)—declared his company to be worth a multiple of thirteen times, thus assuming that he could grow his company at 23% a year. That is how valuation works—future earnings potential of the company. If you bring in partners and are confident that you can grow your business at 23% per year over the next five years, by all means expect such a steep multiple. Otherwise—now that you understand how debt is used as one of the key value levers much like buying a house—you can see how funds would be challenged to see future profits.

Valuation Methods

The valuation methods used depend on your company's stage of development. For example, seed and early-stage companies are valued upon the basis of how much hard capital you have injected into the business. Factors such as intellectual value, so-called sweat equity and opportunity cost, also come into play. Previous successful involvement in a private equity-supported venture will enhance your appeal to the investor.

Companies at the expansion stage will be valued differently. Investors may base their valuation on comparable company multiples of sales. Further down the spectrum late-stage companies will most likely be valued on the basis of comparable earnings multiples. At the end of the day, the key factor that the investor will focus on is predictable future growth culminating in predictable future earnings.

Company valuations may differ from industry to industry. Various valuation methods are highlighted in the table in Figure 11.2, but the details of each of these are beyond the scope of this book.

Figure 11.2: Different Industries Have Differing Valuation Methods

Adjusted Book Value	Industry Comparable
Asset Valuation	Multiple of Earnings
Capitalization of Income	Multiple of EBITDA
Capitalized Earnings	Multiple of Cash Flow
Cash Flow Method	Multiplier or Market Value
Replacement Cost	Rule of Thumb Methods
Discounted Cash Flow	Tangible Assets
Excess Earnings Method	Value of Intangible Assets

To give you an idea, here is a quick break down of two more popular valuation measures used that are used.

- Multiple of EBITDA
- Discounted Cash Flow (DCF)

You may have heard EBITDA being used as a valuation and worry that the value of your business should not come down to one number. Value does not, but there has to be a starting point. Figure 11.3 explains the EBITDA formula.

Figure 11.3: EBITDA Multiple Valuation

> ## FORMULA: NORMALIZED EBITDA TIMES MULTIPLE LESS NET DEBT
>
> 1. EBITDA → calculate EBITDA on a "normalized" basis, which means removing any abnormal items not directly related to the operation of your business. These include bonuses above market average, salaries paid to family, irregular costs such as equipment write-offs, adjustments due to corporate tax management.
> 2. Multiple → standard private equity EBITDA multiple is "six times." This multiple is often adjusted, however, for different industries. A quick analysis of recent deals usually provides an indication of multiples.
> 3. Net Debt = Total debt minus cash

The DCF method compares the discounted revenue multiple of your company to similar publicly traded companies. In other words, the fund will find a company in your industry that is already listed on the stock market to compare to your projections and check if your assumptions are fair. This method is used for a company with existing revenues and credible projections. The value of the company is then determined as a multiple of the current year's revenue. Your last full financial year is very important, as this is what will determine your value. So if you have had a lean year due to a death in the family or something unusual, put off valuation and get a full year with good revenues.

This multiple of your current year's revenues is then compared to similar publicly listed companies and is then discounted by around 30% to 40%. The discount applied is the lack of a track record and the lack of liquidity. The DCF analysis is used for a company with credible revenue projections. The value of the company is the cash it generates. However, the DCF method is only as good as its input assumptions, namely:

- free cash flow forecasts,
- discount rates, and
- perpetuity growth rates.

The debate on whether an investor will pay a premium or a discount for your business can be simplified as outlined below.

An investor will pay a premium if he sees:

- smooth growth in sales and earnings,
- proof of concept, and
- recurring revenues (predictability).

An investor will apply a discounted value if he sees:

- spotty or erratic financial results,
- "hiccups" that require explanation, or
- key business plan elements pending (customers, new products, key personnel).

Investors typically aim to earn between five to ten times their initial outlay within a five- to seven-year investment term. Investors are not hung up about piling on the fees. What they really want to see is capital growth, which is reflected in a handsome return upon exit, be it an initial public offering (IPO) or sale of the business to a strategic buyer.

Investors will be tough on valuation, but remember, they still want to ensure that the current owners have an incentive to get out of bed every morning to make the business successful. Enough said. Let us now look at the next stage in the financing process—the term sheet.

What Is the Term Sheet?

Receiving funding is great, but it has to be negotiated upon terms that are mutually satisfactory. This process begins with a term sheet.

Investors use a term sheet as a basis for drafting the investment documents. The term sheet is negotiated between the prospective investor and you, the entrepreneur. It outlines the key financial and other terms of the proposed investment. Although the provisions of a term sheet are not intended to be legally binding, certain clauses such as exclusivity, confidentiality, and costs may have some binding effect. A term sheet contains a whole host of provisions designed to protect the value of an investor's capital. These terms define the rights of the investor/fund manager and will typically include clauses defining the ownership position as well as the decision-making process over the duration of the investment. The exit strategy is sometimes clearly stipulated because there might not be an exit yet, or it is not written up in the term sheet. When bringing in investors, you are changing your rights, so the clearer these are detailed, the better.

Negotiating the Term Sheet

Warning: this is the hardest part of the deal. You may have investor fatigue and would accept a dead mackerel at this stage. The fund manager knows that. While the structure and detail of the term sheet are important, actually arriving at the term sheet stage is a major accomplishment in itself, as it is confirmation that the investor is really interested in investing in your enterprise.

Although it may seem that there is a whole lot to negotiate in a term sheet, it should be kept in mind that a term sheet is just a stepping stone towards an actual deal. Be alert to the fact that most investors will load term sheets with pre-conditions to financing as well as escape clauses in their favour.

Negotiating a term sheet need not necessarily be an adversarial exercise, but be prepared for a fair amount of negotiation, especially around the valuation of the company.

"The term sheet should cause momentum to finalize the deal," sums up Suzanne Dingwall Williams, founding partner of Venture Law Associates. "But the shared risk of not closing must be strong for the potential investor." In other words, there should not be a situation where the due diligence drags on and after six months the fund announces that they've changed their minds and, by the way, thanks for paying for the lawyer and accountant fees and good luck with your financing. This scenario suggests that your term sheet was very badly written.

In rushing to the finishing line you must be aware of the potential bear traps that could ensnare you.

Bear Trap 1: No-Shop Clause

Your investor will want to include the "no shop" clause, which means that you cannot show your business to other investors while this investor is humming and hawing whether to buy in as partners. "This is a little clause that the deal is subject to closing on terms the fund likes," says Dingwall. "The investor may justify keeping you on the hook, saying all of our partners need to see you." The only catch is that if they don't approve your business after three months, then there's no risk to the fund.

Do not go for this justification; find out the fund's approval process. Forty days of being exclusive to one fund is the longest you need. Sixty days is too long to be out of the market looking for investors. So if another deal comes along, their attention will go there and not to you. Meanwhile, you are not allowed to show your deal to others because of the "no shop" clause.

Bear Trap 2: Investor's Legal Expenses

Some investors say, "I want my legal fees paid, even if I don't get the deal closed." It's not the norm and you are right to push back against including this in the term sheet. Some costs are part of getting deal flow and investors should be kept motivated to close the deal if they know they have limited time to have sole rights to examine your business and that they must bear the costs of their own due diligence. This is all negotiated. Normally, there is a cap on legal expenses at a fixed amount. Do not leave the amount open-ended.

Bear Trap 3: Confidentiality Clause

The confidentiality clause protects the assets of your company. It must apply to both parties and must protect customer trade secrets. If your investor wants the clause inserted, and most do, understand it. Get the information in your term sheet, as it keeps your legal costs down and you are not negotiating back and forth. "Even if the deal falls apart there is no harm or foul to your business," says Rick Segal of J.A. Albright Venture Partners. You need to make sure that the results of due diligence are confidential. The investor cannot reveal the results to anyone as they could poison the market. It is also a good test to keep out investors with competing deals or competitive spaces.

Bear Trap 4: Giving It All Back

The investor says, "I bet on you and your team and if you leave, then I'm paralyzed. Your shares should be surrendered." You could have a shotgun clause that basically says either you buy or you sell and it is a two-way shotgun. I can put shares to you and you can buy me out. Clauses for founders to sell back their shares if they leave the company are critical to define upfront. The period for exercise of shares should be short, not an open-ended time, and it should be negotiated furiously.

Bear Trap 5: Non-Competition

Investors may try to put the non-compete clause into the term sheet, rather than in the employment contract because it adds more teeth. What this means is if you leave the company and the investor buys back the shares, you must stay out of the market for two years.

The non-compete does not apply to the investor due to their broad focus across different parts of the value chain in one market. In the business of speculative investment, you can't predict what the future "market" will be.

In other words, in investor dating, if you break up you are not allowed to date other people but the investor can.

Bear Trap 6: Security and Covenants

Asking for confidentiality at the first meeting, which should be warm and fuzzy, will chill the meeting. In the early meetings, be discreet and don't give out any product secrets or future plans that would compromise your business, but know that the non-disclosure agreement (NDA) in the term sheet is acceptable.

The onus is upon you to look at the investor's portfolio of companies and ask the fund managers if you think it is prudent for them to learn details of your strategy. Ask yourself if any of those portfolio companies could take your ideas and use them to your detriment. As you know, investors on boards of competitors have a fiduciary duty to report information that they learn about your company. Some investors may even meet you for an information gathering session to glean competitive information for their gain. If investors are using their Blackberry, then they are more likely to invest. If they are paying full attention—"Warning, Will Robinson, warning!" The meeting is more likely to be a fishing expedition to pick your brain and secrets and expand their knowledge of the market rather than invest in your company.

Bear Trap 7: Who Bears the Cost of Due Diligence?

Some cost is borne by the company and some by the investor. The legal costs relating to the contract and closing is performed by lawyers. It is necessary and costly. Know the legal rights of raising capital.

Due Diligence

The most disturbing part of investors checking for the full details on your company, isn't the process itself, but how the closeness to signing the deal causes huge stress for both parties.

An entrepreneur could be forgiven for feeling it is all too much, but do try approaching it positively, framing it as a chance to teach your new partners about you and your business. After all, as that wise philosopher Seneca said all those centuries before, "est ad astra mollis e terris via," which means there is no easy way from the earth to the stars. Keep whispering that to yourself.

Be Prepared!

Ensure that your company is ready for the financial, legal, business, and other corroboration required by the potential investor. Failure to do so will delay or even stop the deal. Be proactive—do not wait for the investor's checklist—start early in collecting the required information and preparing the necessary materials such as shareholder agreements, customer contracts, and patents. These are all the legal documents that your investment proposal has included to prove their existence. You will accelerate the process.

Remember that the due diligence exercise is not an attack on you or your business. The exercise is necessary, in that it gives the investor a deeper understanding of your business and ultimately a sense of comfort. Investors often go about conducting due diligence in their own particular style. However, there are certain areas that are almost always covered. The major due diligence areas of focus are illustrated in Figure 11.4.

Figure 11.4: Due Diligence Checklist

Employment contracts—what has been signed by employees, length of employment, non-competes?

Intellectual property—legal patents

Financial review—accountant reports

Marketing—all plans over the past five years

Technology—blueprints, special knowledge

Customers—signed five-year contracts

Reference check on management team

The Laws to Know

"Before raising money from investor clients," says the detail-obsessed Vipool Desai of ARA Compliance, "it is vital to understand the rules and regulations that govern this activity. Requirements may vary significantly, depending on the jurisdiction where the client is resident." The overriding purpose of securities regulation is to protect investor clients by:

- establishing standards for the people and firms that are in the business of marketing securities; and
- establishing disclosure standards regarding the securities being offered.

Private equity transactions are typically exempt from such requirements, as long as certain criteria are met. For example, within Canada securities may be offered without a qualified prospectus to accredited investors (i.e., investors who meet certain assets and/or income tests).

Nevertheless, where a firm is in the business of offering exempt securities to the public, regulators may establish a registration requirement. For example, in Ontario, any firm that is in the business of dealing in private securities must be registered as a Limited Market Dealer (LMD). Registration requirements are imposed to ensure the regulators have scrutinized the firms and that the Commission has jurisdiction if the dealer is engaged in improper activity.

Look up your Securities Commission and find out the law. In many states or provinces, it is illegal to invest or sell shares without using a LMD. The reason for this is to avoid fraud. For example, if a Mr. Wiggins puts $400,000 into your company and then shouts, "I was given misinformation; I want my money back!" it lays you wide open to a law suit. Government is far happier when you use an approved financial advisor on their list that is knowledgeable enough to point out a *caveat emptor*, verify the financial numbers to reduce any misunderstandings, and be there to clear up disputes.

There are a multitude of other laws that need to be followed. One of these is copyright or patent law. Apparently, according to David McIntyre, patent lawyer, "If RIM in its early days had done the correct patent applications early in its start-up years, they would have avoided the $30M and mounting lawyers' fees it is now paying to fight to protect their technology."

Check Out the Fund Too!

Return the favour and do a little diligence of your own. A few bad apples can ruin the whole bowl and in private equity, this applies too. You can call up any of the companies that are or have been in their portfolio and have a quiet meeting to chat off the record. Get your financial advisor to run a check on their legal suits, as these will also give you a strong sense of their style of business. There are sharks out there that will not care about your future. In one case, a fund was accused of buying the competitors of one of their portfolio companies. Part of the deal was requiring the competition not to sell to this one business. By effectively reducing opportunity for the growth strategy, this fund ensured bankruptcy. Wouldn't you know it—the private equity fund was "lucky enough" to be able to buy the failed company outright from the owner.

This is the dark side of private equity, but do understand that the majority of funds are honest and excited to work for you to grow your business.

Five Negotiation Tips for a Win/Win Outcome

You must understand that you will not be in the driver's seat. Come to terms with moving on from a lifestyle to a professionally lead business. You will have "value creation" plans listing milestones to achieve over the next year. As the saying goes, if you want to get bigger, you will have to grow up. Some negotiation tips are outlined here to assist you.

- *Treat the Investor and the Process of Due Diligence with Respect.* Some entrepreneurs treat due diligence as an annoyance led by a fund manager who they think is similar to a bumbling Elmer Fudd who does not understand the business.
- *First Offer Is Not the Last.* Be prepared not to like all the terms of the money deal but stick around; it's not over with one yes or no.

Expect the valuation to get you in the guts. Before the deal, set your highest price and lowest price using experts to guide you.

- *Take Your Time.* When handed the term sheet, go through it with your advisors. There is no need to give the nod straight away or agree over the phone.
- *Think Win/Win.* If there is something you do not like, have another plan of action to suggest. Your behaviour will be noticed and there will always be future deals closed with someone who thinks broadly.
- *Be a Deal Closer.* Know the timing can be three to seven months from first conversations to money in the bank. Just as a shot gun marriage is not a positive way to start off a life of bliss, neither is being caught in a crush for cash. Sow the seed before you need the cash.

Top Ways to Get the Relationship Off to a Great Start

Get the board meeting timetable agreed to and set up your team for the year and never break this schedule. Invite the investors to meet everyone on the team if they have not done so already. Also, get the first strategy session organized.

There are common questions the private equity investor will ask and, in fact, many public companies are asking their CEO and boards to behave as if they had a private equity investor digging into their company performance. Your board will appreciate it if you already are targeting these matters.

Take seriously these big priorities for private equity (see Figure 11.5). Respect your performance clauses, buy-back arrangements, decision making, monitoring, reporting requirements, board seat role and meetings, approval of plans, and spending. The investors use these tried and true methods because they work.

Your business plan is what you are contracted to do and your term sheet will be held against whatever you do achieve. When you miss milestones, your term sheet will lay out exactly the penalties, which may mean losing more equity. Most investors are realists; if you are falling behind, communicate these difficulties and see if you can renegotiate the plan. An investor in the know is easier to work with than a

Figure 11.5: Private Equity's Big Priorities

Operational Strategy
Do we have an operating plan that will raise shareholder value?
Do we have clear, objective metrics to monitor performance?
Are the compensation rewards for top management linked to increasing shareholder value?
Are there clear penalties for non-performance?
Board Incentive
Is the board committed to giving enough time and clarity regarding their role?
Does the board have a financial incentive to maximize shareholder wealth?
Financial Strategy
Is there too much cash on the balance sheet?
Do we have the best capital structure with the lowest weighted after-tax cost of total capital, including debt and equity?

surprised (shocked) investor. Use the board meetings to communicate bumps along the way and renegotiate your performance measures at the board of directors' level and with investors.

Once you've dropped the ball and missed targets, and you have not communicated problems, you will have angry investors. Don't expect to be able to renegotiate lower standards then. It will be all storm and drang!

Now that you have the cash to take your business up to the next level in the business cycle, take the time to revel in a job well done. Now it's time to do the next stage of work—spend that money well!

Make the Canadian Dream Come True

Entrepreneurial spirit begins with children and we need to ask what values we are passing along to the next generation. Is it a distrust of business and assertiveness, often labelled as "American?" What do we value and who do we celebrate? Do we give our Canadian version of Bill Gates a platform on which to speak to others or do we pull him down?

Private equity money is invested by entrepreneurs who take on an enormous risk, while highly aware that they could end up with zip for their efforts. Would you invest millions of your investment portfolio in a company developing an unknown power source or would you prefer to stash it in real estate?

Private equity people push past the timid and safe wallflowers in order to get up and dance, rather than wait to be asked. It is the visionaries like Michael Brown, co-founder of Ventures West Capital, who sink their money into emerging businesses with little track record of success. Brown invested seed capital into a start-up company working on a new power source and continued to assist in the growth capital. Today, this business, known as Ballard Power, is the world's first and most successful fuel cell development corporation. It exists because Michael Brown had the guts to finance those entrepreneurs who believed Ballard could be global right from the start.

Private equity's top funds have achieved terrific returns that some critics say are a result of manipulation or short-term tactics. These claims have been put through empirical testing with a few of the studies mentioned earlier that proved the contrary. "Instead, the conclusion to be drawn from consistently high returns of these funds," says Robert Pozen of Harvard Law School, "is that their managers have developed the strategies and processes needed to obtain superior performance."[1]

Moxy glows in the hearts of many Canadian business owners and through special partnership with private equity, it will thrive. "Entrepreneurs and the investors who finance them are cut from the same cloth," says Dean Carol Stephenson, Richard Ivey School of Business. "They share a unique talent for seeing business opportunities where most of us see insurmountable obstacles, and they have the passion and drive to risk the climb. Essential to each other, together they are vital to economic growth, productivity, and job creation in Canada."

---

[1] Robert Pozen, "If Private Equity Sized Up Your Business," *Harvard Business Review,* November, 2007, page 7.

Having now read *Money Magnet,* you are well set to meet the people with money, and I wish you all the best in attracting the top investors to your business.

TAKE AWAYS

The deal is only the beginning of the relationship. If you take the time to develop your business relationship thoroughly, with expectations well tabled, your working partnership with your investors will be far more profitable over the long run.

APPENDIX

SELECTED WEB LINKS TO GOVERNMENT-FUNDED PROGRAMS

We have chosen a selected list of Web links to government sponsored programs aimed primarily but not exclusively at *small to medium sized enterprises (SMEs)*. Brief extracts from the respective Web sites are also provided but readers are encouraged to view the actual Web sites for more specific detail as well as for updates on the various government-funded programs. Web page addresses may change over time.

Program	Brief Description
Government of Canada **www.ic.gc.ca/epic/site/ic1.nsf/en/ h_00156e.html**	This site provides a general *list of various government agencies* that offer assistance to business.
The Advanced Manufacturing Investment Strategy (AMIS) Program **www.ontariocanada.com/ontcan/en/ progserv_amis_en.jsp**	AMIS is administered by the Ontario Ministry of Economic Development and Trade. The AMIS program seeks to *encourage eligible companies operating in Ontario to transform processes and adopt leading-edge technologies* that will increase productivity and competitiveness.
Business Development Bank of Canada (BDC) **www.bdc.ca/en/business_solutions/ venture_capital/about_us/default.htm**	BDC is a financial institution wholly owned by the Government of Canada and plays a leadership role in delivering *financial and consulting services to Canadian small and medium-sized businesses, with a particular focus on the technology and export sectors of the economy.* BDC is also mandated to be a complementary lender in the market.
Export Development Canada (EDC) **www.edc.ca**	EDC is a Crown Corporation operating on commercial principles. *EDC provides innovative financing, insurance, and bonding solutions to Canadian companies that export goods and services, or invest in other countries.* Approximately 90% of EDC's customers are small and medium-sized businesses.
Industrial Research Assistance Program (IRAP) **http://irap-pari.nrc-cnrc.gc.ca**	IRAP *assists Canadian small and medium-sized enterprises (SMEs) meet technological challenges and build innovation capacity.* Canadian

	small or medium-sized incorporated businesses are eligible for support Applicants have to present a strong business case for a technology, demonstrate the technical, financial, and managerial capacity to take an idea from concept to commercialization and demonstrate a clear need for financial support.
Ontario Innovation Demonstration Fund (IDF) **www.mri.gov.on.ca/english/programs/ idf/guidelines.asp**	The IDF is administered by the Ontario Ministry of Research and Innovation. IDF is a discretionary, non-entitlement funding program to *help companies in their efforts to commercialize innovative technologies in Ontario.* The fund focuses on the commercialization and initial demonstration of innovative technologies, processes and/or products. The IDF places special *emphasis on bio-based, environmental, and alternative energy technologies.*
MaRS—Business Mentorship and Entrepreneurship Program (BMEP) **www.marsdd.com**	BMEP is managed by MaRS Discovery District on behalf of the Ministry of Research and Innovation. BMEP programs and services can be accessed through Ontario Commercialization Network (OCN) organizations. BMEP helps innovative science and technology companies bring new technologies to market by providing the necessary skills and services. BMEP is designed to meet the needs of *startup and early-stage science and technology companies as well as small and medium-sized enterprises in these sectors.*

(Continued)

The Office of Small and Medium Enterprises (OSME) **www.pwgsc.gc.ca/ontario/** **osme-bpme/whoweare-e.html**	The OSME *assists Small and Medium Enterprises (SMEs) as they navigate the procurement system.* The office engages SMEs to understand their concerns and encourages them to do business with the federal government. The OSME also provides regional input for solutions, through advice and policy development, to reduce barriers and increase opportunities for SMEs to do business with the government."
Ontario Centres of Excellence Inc. (OCE)—Investor Acceleration Fund (IAF) **www.oce-ontario.org**	OCE is a leading driver of the research to commercialization process, with a strategic focus on improving Ontario's competitiveness through innovation. OCE partners with industry, universities, colleges, research hospitals, investors, and governments to bridge the gap between academic research and the marketplace. *OCE accelerates innovation in Ontario through strategic investments in three program areas: research, commercialization, and talent.*
Ontario Scientific Research and Experimental Development Expenditures (SR&ED) **www.cra-arc.gc.ca/taxcredit/sred/** **regions-e.html**	SR&ED is administered by the Ontario Ministry of Revenue. The Ontario government provides a *deduction for scientific research and experimental development carried out in Ontario.* Rules used in the calculation of Ontario SR&ED are complex. See Web site for specific details.
The Canada Small Business Financing Program (CSBF) **www.ic.gc.ca/epic/site/** **csbfp-pfpec.nsf/en/Home**	The CSBF program *seeks to increase the availability of loans for establishing, expanding, modernizing, and improving small businesses.* It does this by

	encouraging financial institutions to make their financing available to small businesses. Under the Program, a small business must apply for a loan at a financial institution of its choice. If the loan is granted by the financial institution, the federal government will reimburse a specific percentage of the lender's losses in the event of default.
Sustainable Development Technology Canada www.sdtc.ca/en/funding/index.htm	SDTC program provides funding for development of clean technologies.
Technology Partnerships Canada (TPC) http://ito.ic.gc.ca/epic/site/ito-oti.nsf/en/h_00004e.html	TPC is a special operating agency of Industry Canada with a mandate to *provide funding support for strategic research and development, and demonstration projects* that will produce economic, social, and environmental benefits to Canadians. TPC's assist Canadian companies perform R&D that takes new technologies closer to the marketplace.
Ontario Fuel Cell Innovation Program www.mri.gov.on.ca/english/programs/ofcip/guidelines.asp	Fuel cells and fuel cell-related technologies funding by Ontario, Ministry of Research & Innovation.
Ontario Premier's Catalyst Award www.mri.gov.on.ca/english/programs/pca/program.asp	The Catalyst Awards provide five awards of $200,000 for developing a commercially successful new, or significantly improved, product or service based on a breakthrough technology.
Advanced Manufacturing Investment Strategy www.ontariocanada.com/ontcan/en/progserv_amis_cfp_en.jsp	The program is designed to encourage companies to transform processes and adopt leading-edge technologies that will increase their productivity and competitiveness.

(Continued)

North Job Creation Program www.mndm.gov.on.ca/nohfc/program_enjcp_e.asp	The program provides loans for Northern Ontario companies expanding their enterprises.
Northern Ontario Technology companies www.mndm.gov.on.ca/nohfc/program_enjcp_e.asp	The Emerging Technology Program is designed to encourage both the private and public sectors to develop exciting and viable new technologies that will contribute to future northern prosperity.
Business Advisory Services www.sbe.gov.on.ca/ontcan/sbe/en/st_busadvise_en.jsp	Business Advisors provide targeted business advisory services to Ontario businesses to help them compete and grow, both domestically and internationally.

If you enjoyed this book and would like to learn more, please visit: www.moneymagnetbook.ca

GLOSSARY OF COMMONLY USED TERMS

Advisory board
An advisory board typically consists of a group of individuals, chosen by the company founders, whose experience, business acumen, and network can positively influence the growth of the company. It is less formal than the board of directors and does not have any legal responsibilities with regard to the company.

Angel investor
Wealthy individuals who inject seed finance to entrepreneurs in return for an equity stake. They usually participate in the early stages of growth. Angel investors typically operate alone (or in very small groups) and may play an indirect advisory role. Angel investors also add value by providing entrepreneurs with knowledge and contacts. A participative Angel investor may decide to become a non-executive director in the investee company.

Bootstrapping
The process of strictly containing costs and expenses and building up cash flow, thereby reducing or obviating the need for outside investors.

Bridge finance

A short-term financing mechanism that enables a company to continue with its normal operations until it can arrange longer-term financing. Companies sometimes require this type of funding because they run out of cash prior to receiving long-term funding.

Burn rate

The rate at which a start-up company with low or no revenue utilizes available cash to cover expenses, usually expressed on a monthly or weekly basis.

Business plan

A business plan is a written document that is vital for raising finance. It describes the nature of the business, the sales and marketing strategy, and key selected financial data, including a projected profit and loss statement.

Buy-out/Management buy-out

This is the purchase of a company or a controlling interest of a corporation's shares. This often happens when a company's existing managers wish to take control of the company.

Capital pool

Unlisted securities may be sold directly to investors by a company (through a private offering) or to a private equity fund, which pools contributions from smaller investors to create a capital pool.

Comparative valuation analysis

Comparative valuation analysis compares the investee (private) company valuations against that of comparable listed companies. A discount is applied to compensate for a shorter track record and lack of liquidity on the share price.

Compound annual growth rate (CAGR)

The year-on-year growth rate applied to an investment or other part of a company's activities over a multiple-year period. The formula for calculating CAGR is:

$$(Current\ Value/Base\ Value)^{(1/number\ of\ years)} - 1$$

CAGR is a more accurate measure than simple arithmetic averaging. For example, if a company's sales rose from $100M in year one to $150M in year two and then fell back to $100m in year three, then there has been a 50% increase in year one, followed by a 33% decrease in year two. Simply adding the two periods (year one to year two and year two to year three) would give 17% and therefore an arithmetic average of 8.5% (that is, 17% divided by 2). However, using the CAGR formula (or geometric average) the average growth is equal to 0%, which is a more accurate reflection of the situation.

Cost of goods sold (COGS)

COGS is an income statement item that indicates the cost of obtaining raw materials and producing finished goods that are sold. Opening inventory plus net purchases of merchandise less ending merchandise inventory equals the cost of goods sold.

Debt financing

Debt financing is money that you borrow to run your business. Debt financing is essentially a loan. A creditor agrees to lend money to a debtor in exchange for repayment, normally with interest, upon agreed payment terms and dates. Certain loans may require security. The creditor does not obtain any ownership claim in the debtor's business.

Due diligence

The investigation exercise carried out by investors to assess the feasibility of a potential investment and the accuracy of the information and data provided by the target company.

Earnings before interest, taxes, depreciation, and amortization (EBITDA)

EBITDA is calculated by deducting expenses (excluding tax, interest, depreciation, and amortization) from revenue. In the private equity industry, "normalized" EBITDA is used (*see below*).

EBITDA Multiple Valuation

Formula: *Normalized EBITDA times Multiple less Net Debt*

Normalized EBITDA: This calculation is attained by removing any abnormal items not directly related to the operation of your business. Abnormal items may include matters such as bonuses that are above the industry average, salaries and bonuses paid to related parties (such as family members), irregular costs such as equipment write-off, bad debt expenses and transactions related to affiliated companies, and other adjustments for the purpose of corporate tax management.

Multiple: The standard private equity EBITDA multiple is "six times." This multiple is often adjusted, depending on the industry. A quick analysis of recent deals usually provides an indication of multiples.

Net Debt: Total debt minus cash.

Elevator pitch

A concise presentation, lasting only a few minutes (the length of an elevator ride), by an entrepreneur to a potential investor about an investment opportunity.

Equity financing

Companies looking to raise financing may use equity financing instead of or in addition to debt financing. To raise equity financing, a company creates new ordinary shares and sells them for cash. The new share owners become part owners of the company and share in the risks and rewards of the company's business.

Exit strategy

An exit strategy is the way in which a fund or investor is able to realize its investment in a company. There are several exit routes, including an initial public offering, acquisition, selling to another private equity firm, or a company buy-back.

Initial public offering (IPO)

An Initial Public Offering (IPO) is the first sale of shares by a private company to the public. IPOs are often issued by smaller, younger companies seeking capital to expand, but can also be done by large, privately-owned companies looking to become publicly traded. From a private equity perspective, IPOs are an exit route for private equity firms, assuming that a private equity company had a stake in the company.

Internal rate of return (IRR)

This is the most commonly used performance benchmark for private equity investments. IRR is a time-weighted return expressed as a percentage. IRR uses the present sum of cash draw downs (money invested), the present value of distributions (money returned from investments), and the current value of unrealized investments and applies a discount.

Mezzanine financing

This is a type of loan finance that sits between equity and secured debt. As the risk for mezzanine financing is higher than with senior debt, the interest charged by the provider will be higher than that charged by traditional lenders, such as banks. Sometimes an equity provision is incorporated into the deal through warrants or options.

Pre-money and post-money

Pre-money and post-money are valuation measures of companies. Pre-money refers to a company's value prior to receiving outside financing or capital injection. Post-money refers to a company's value after it gets outside financing or capital injection.

Return on investment (ROI)

The proceeds from an investment, during a specific time period, calculated as a percentage of the original investment. Also, net profit after taxes divided by average total assets.

Reverse takeover (RTO)

An RTO is a strategy by a private company for gaining access to public markets through takeover of a listed company, quite often a "shell" company.

Seed capital

Seed capital relates to the provision of very early stage financing to a company with a business venture or idea that has not yet been established.

Term sheet

A term sheet is a document confirming the intent of an investor to participate in a round of financing for a company. By signing this document, the company agrees to begin the legal and due diligence process prior to the closing of the transaction.

Venture capital

Venture capital is money provided by investors who typically invest in early stage but high growth companies. Venture capital is an important source of financing for start-up companies.

INDEX

Page numbers in italic indicate visuals.

Abatis Systems, 17
accomplishments, 170, 172, 209
　　(*See also* milestones)
accounting systems, *28,* 31
Ace Bakery, 31
acquisitions, 45–46, *47*
Advanced Manufacturing Investment
　　Strategy Program (AMIS), 238
advisors/advisory board, 7, 47, 51–52,
　　77, 84, 113, 125, 152, 172, 199, 216,
　　243
AIM, 15
Alcan, tag line, *197*
Alice program, 61
alumni phenomenon, 113–15
ambition, 9, 10, 27, 31, 37, 49, 108, 125
American Beauty (film), 50
American Idol (TV), 32, 34
AMEX, 74
angels, 6, 8, *11, 70,* 71, 72, *72,* 73, *76,* 88
　　attracting, 95–97
　　characteristics of, 91, 94–95
　　compared to venture capitalists,
　　　98–99
　　dealing with, 100

motivation of, 92
owner relationship, 92, 93, 94, 98–99
risk and, 92, 96
sector interest of, 96
angels—types
　　corporate, 93
　　family members, 93
　　old money, 94
　　retired executives, 93–94
Apple Inc., 14, 38,
　　39, 201
ARA Compliance, 230
Argosy Partners, 81
arrogance, 117, 215
Asia, 199
asset-backed loans, 75
attitude, 14, 18, 34, 61, 107, 117, 124,
　　133, 135
auctions, 220
auditors, 87
automobile industry, 9
autocratic leadership style, 29, 38, 135

Bain Capital, 8, 46, 136
baby boomers, 22–23, 159, 161, 208

balance sheets, 57, 149, 170, 176, 179–80, *179*, 211
Ballard Power, 234
Balsillie, Jim, 73
bankruptcy, *83*, 231
banks/bank financing, 4, 5, 12–13, 16, 17, 18, 27, 29, 45, 77
  compared with venture capitalists, 75, 83–84
  and corporate growth cycle, *70*
  and early operating companies, 74–75
  and mature companies, 81, 82–83, *83*
  owner relationship, 74, 81, 82–83
  pros/cons, *83*
  risk tolerance of, 83
  compared with private equity investors, 50, 53, 54, 56, 59, 83–85
BCE (Bell Canada Enterprises), 11, 78
BDC Venture Capital, 111
Beatles, The, 27
Bedford Capital, 127
Bell Helicopters, 133
Berke, Eric, 56
Berkshire Hathaway Inc., 16
Bermingham (construction equipment co.), 9
biotechnology sector, 94, 96, 101
BlackBerry, 73
Blackstone Group, The, 15, 51, 88
BMO (Bank of Montreal), 81
Body Shop, The, 128
bonuses, 135
Borealis Infrastructure, 75
Bosela, Sandra, 129, 134, 137
Boston College, 87
brand names/branding, 157
Branson, Richard, 33, 105, 108
Breslin, Adam, 119
Brickworks neighbourhood (Toronto), 94
bridge financing, *7*, 81 (*See also* mezzanine financing)
BridgePort (tech. co.), 9

British Airways, 207
Brown, Michael, 234
Buffet, Warren, 16, 49, 147–48
Building Private Equity Value (KPMG report), 16
Burgess, Andy, 19–21, 80
business
  appeal to private equity, elements. *See* private equity, attracting
  investor fit, 68–69, *69*, *70*, 71, 72
  transition readiness, 29, 30–31
  value of. *See* valuation
business—stages of growth, 6, 7, 26–27
  Stage 1—Product, *28*, 29–30, 33–34, 72
  Stage 2—owner-controlled, *28*, 31–32, 34, 37, 38, 52, *72*
  Stage 3—legacy, *28*, 32, 34, 35, 36, 37, 38, 50, 52, *72*
Business Development Bank of Canada (BDC), 73–74, 85, 238
business model, 9, 153, 157, 158, 167, 173, 202
business opportunity, 154–56
business plan, 10, 30, 34, 58–59, 68, 69, 73, 97, 117, 125, 153–54, 232
  cash requirements, 166–67
  components of, 98
  graphic material, 169–70
  levels of, *165*
  purpose of, 164, *165*
  writing, 164, 165–66
business schools, 10
buyout(s), 6, *7*, 8, 11–12, 46, 68, 69, *70*, 71, *72*, 81, 88, 114, 149

Canada
  dot.com bubble, 103
  privacy law, 120
  venture capital/seed start-ups, 101
Canada Small Business Financing Program (CSBF), 241
Canadian Venture Capital Association (CVCA), 6, 115, 122

Canterbury Park Management, 35, 53
Cao, Jerry, 87
capital
    cost of, 182
    development/growth, 7, 70, 71, 72–75, 72, 80–81
    requirements, investor question, 55
    sources of, 10–12, 11, 14, 76, 76, 86–87
    start-up, 6, 7, 8, 10, 33–34, 57, 69, 70, 72
    structure, 180
Carlezon, Jan, 123
Carlyle Group, The, 6, 136
Carnegie Mellon University, 61
Carrefour, 87–88
Carrescia, Peter, 59, 111, 116
cash flow, 30, 31, 52, 57, 82, 125, 149, 163, 174, 176, 178, 180–82, 181, 211
CBC, 34, 97, 99
Celtic House, 17, 111, 114
CEOs
    challenges to, 14–16
    communications skills, 133–34, 153–54, 232–33
    effective, 128, 149
    leadership style. See management styles
    mature, 57
    positive, 135
    and stages of business, 28
    strategic planning skills, 131–33, 132
    unsuccessful, 129
Chapters, 156
Cineplex, 22
China, 5, 22, 44
Cisco, 74, 79, 114
Club Penguin, 78
Cobalt Capital, 83
commitment, 27, 61 (See also passion; vision)
common shares, 84, 84

communication skills, 133–34, 153–54, 232–33
competition, 4, 21–22, 156, 205–6
competitive advantage, 55, 97, 98, 156–57
competitor positioning analysis, 174–75, 175
computers, 13, 157
confidentiality clause, term sheet, 227
construction industry, 9, 77
consultants, 172, 214, 216
contracts, 176, 208–9
control vs. wealth, 30, 31
copyright law, 157, 230–31
corporate angels, 93
corporate culture, 120–21
corporate funds, 85
Corporate Strategic Investors, 78
Cost of Goods Sold (COGS), 57
covenants, 11, 21, 80, 228
Covey, Stephen, 144, 161
Cowell, Simon, 32
credit cards, 74
critical success factors (CSF), 176
Crossing the Chasm (Moore), 23
current ratio, 180

Dancap, 75
"Deal of the Year" (CVCA), 111–12, 115
debt, 10, 20, 50, 52, 72, 81, 83, 92, 166, 180
debt-to-equity ratio, 180
Deluce, Robert, 75
Dennis, Sam, 120
Dent, Roger, 87
Desai, Vipool, 230
Desert Spring Products, 119
discounted cash flow (DCF), 160, 182–83, 223, 224–25
Disney, 78, 79, 79, 197, 201
diversification, 35, 36
Domino's, 8, 11, 135
dot.com bubble, 22, 103, 114, 156

Dow Jones, 14
Dow Venture Capital Fund, 85
Dragons' Den (TV show), 34, 97, 99
due diligence, 81, 116, 118, 174, 219, 226, 227, 228–29, 231
    checklist, *229*
Dunkin' Donuts, 11, 136

early-stage companies
    anticipated rate of return, 167
    investment match, 72–75
eBay, 79, 114, 144
EBITDA, 20, 57, 116, 178, 191, 211, 222, 245–46
    margin, 178
    multiple valuation, 223, *223*
Edgestone Capital, 75, 129, 134
ego, 29, 30, 31, 36, 37, 38, 73, 145, 152
Eichfuss, Rolf, 126
elevator pitch, 161, 197–98, 200–1, *201*
embryonic funds, 73 (*See also* seed funds)
Emerging Technology Program, 242
emotional intelligence, *28*, 32–33, 34, 107
emotions, 38–49, 100
empathy, 48
Empirical (co.), 29, 109
End of Work, The (Rifken), 54
endowments, 85
Enron, 14
entrepreneurs
    categories, 101
    courses, 10
    common mistakes of, 121–22
    female, 124–25
environmental investing, 94
Ernst & Young Entrepreneur of the the Year, 19
established capital, 71, *72*
ethics, 120–21, 231

Evergreen (co.), 94
executive summary, 167, 168–69, 170, 198–99, *198*
exercise of shares, term sheet, 227
exit strategy, 59–60, *60*, 77, 78, 97, 111, 125, 130–31, *132*, 157, 160–61, 169
expansion capital, *69*, 77–79 (*See also* growth capital)
expense model, 176
Export Development Corporation (EDC), 74, 238

Facebook, 109, 114
family, source of capital, 72, *76*, 93
family-owned business, 9, 47, 151
fear
    of challenge, 48–49
    of change, 49
    of failure, 43, 107
    of money loss, 126
    of rejection, 32, 33
    of success, 43
Fedex, tag line, *197*
feedback, *28*, 32–33, 34, 38, 49, 62, 135–36
finance industry model, changes to, 12–13, 18
financial choices, range of, *84*
financial disclosure, *55*, 63 (*See also* non-disclosure)
financial hierarchy, 69, *70*
financial information, presenting, 121–22, 211–13, *213*
financial model, 167, 176–77, 211
financing costs, 11, 214–15
financials summary—components
    balance sheet, 179–80, *179*
    capital structure, 180
    cash flow statement, 180, *181*
    cost of capital, 182
    income statement, 177–78, *178*
financing
    first stage, 77–79

mistakes, 56–60
profile, 184–86
types of, 166
financing—questions
business opportunity, 154–56
management team, 148–54
return for investment, 157–58
sustainability, 156–57
first impressions, 117, 128, 194
first-stage financing, 77–79
five-year projection, 8, 45, 47, 50, 51, 58
Flickr, 31
footnote binder, 216
Ford, 8, 11
forecast success, keys to, 176
Fortune 500 companies, 11, 36
fraud/embezzlement, 14, 15, 230
friends, source of capital, 73, 76, 93
fuel cell development industry, 234, 242
fund managers, 8
compared with venture capitalists, 106
expectations of, 107–8
future earnings, valuation by, 160 (See also potential future earnings)

Gates, Bill, 143, 205, 233
GE Asset Management, 75
global market, 22, 47, 49, 79, 163, 199
Godin, Seth, 173–74
going public. See IPO
Google, 55, 78, 79, 97, 114, 123, 156, 197
government-backed funding, 10, 73–74, 85, 126
Web sites, 237–42
Government of Canada, web site, 238
Granby Steel Tanks, 56
grants, 74
greed, 26, 56, 110, 126
Gross, Daniel, 106
gross margins, 177

growth capital, 7, 70, 71, 72, 80–81
(See also expansion capital)
growth curve, 21, 29, 68, 69
growth, steps to, 171
expansion plan, 175
management team, 171–72
market placement/position, 174–75
product/service, 172–74
growth potential
business plan, 98
investor question, 55
growth rate, 43, 58, 157, 158

Harvard Business School, 87, 147
Harvard Law School, 234
Headwater, 125
Hertz, 8, 11
high-growth company, investor fit, 75–77
high-performance focus, 28, 136
Hoang, Jack, 120
honesty, 54, 55, 62, 16, 123, 151, 191, 213, 231 (See also ethics)
Hospitals of Ontario Pension Plan (HOOPP), 85
Hotmail, 128
HSBC, 74, 81
humility, 170, 172
Hurley, Chad, 114

i3DVR (co.), 120
IMAX, tag line, 197
In Search of Excellence (Peters), 107
incentives, 43, 135
income statements, 176, 177–78, 178, 182–83, 211
India, 207, 208
Indigo, 156
Industrial Research Assistance Program (IRAP), 74, 239
industry associations, 94
Industry Canada, 10
industry events, 154

industry experts, 152
industry intensity risk, 110–11
information security risk, 120
inheritance, 93
innovation, 14, 15, 16, 35, 74 (*See also* government-backed programs)
Innovation Canada, 73
institutional funds, 6, 12, *76*, 77, 85, 87
integrative skills, 38 (*See also* teamwork)
Intel, 78, 157
intellectual property, 156, 157, 208
intellectual value, 222
Internal Rate of Return (IRR), 58, 211–12
Internet, 13, 41, 78 (*See also* Web companies)
inventions, 30
investment/investor
  checklist, 54, *55*
  fit, 68–69, *69*, 72–77
  and level of business, 9–10
investment proposal, 96–97, 161, 163–64, *165*
  balance sheet, 170
  common mistakes, 183
  elements of, 167–70
  executive summary, 167, 168–69, 170
  financial model, 176–77
  financials summary, 177–82
  first page, 169
  forecasted income statement, 170
  illustrations, graphics, 169–70, 177
  importance of, 164–66
  language, 168, 169
  length of, 168
  meeting, 184–86
  past accomplishments, 170
  projected income statements, 182–83
  sensitivity analysis, 183–84
  summary, 167
  use of proceeds, 170, *170*
  (*See also* presentations)
investors—types, 71, *72*
  angels, 6, *7*

  institutional, 6, *7*
  seed funds, 6, *7*
  start-up, 6, *7*
  venture capitalists, 6, *7*
  (*See also* specific investor types)
IPO (initial public offering), 5, *7, 11,* 14, 21, *70*, 76, 77, 78, 85–86, 88, 107, 149, 160, 225
  advantages/disadvantages of, 86–87, *86*
IT. *See* technology sector
iTunes, 14

jargon, 71, 164, 168, 202
J. A. Albright (co.), 78, 123, 205, 227
Jefferson Capital, 29, 78
Jobs, Steve, 38, 39, 157, 201–2

Kaputo, Dave, 114–15
Kensington Capital, 6
key ratios, 57, 58, 149, 165
Kids + Company, 61
Kitsch, Trent, 97–98, 99, 100
KKR (Kohlberg Kravis Robert & Co.), 11, 46
Knox, Elliot, 127–28, 129–30, 134, 137
Knox, Henry, 111–12
KPMG, 16, 17

labour funds, 85
lawsuits, *55*, 121, 123, 231
Lazaridis, Mike, 73
leadership style. *See* management style
Leflar, Kevin, 100
Legacy companies, 27, 28, 31–32, 34, 35, 50, 54, 60, 61, 62–63
legal risk, 120–21
lender/owner relationship. *See under* owner
Lerner, Josh, 87
life insurance, 74
lifestyle, 10, 17, 25, 27, 30, 38, 48
Limited Market Dealer (LMD), 230

Linkedin, 114
liquidity, 17, 21, 74, 80
liquidity event, 77, 130 (*See also* exit
    strategy)
listening skills, *28*, 33, 34, 38, 62
loans, 6, 8, 11, 17, 18, 74, 75, 81, 83, 84,
    92 (*See also* banks/bank financing;
    debt)
location, and angels, 95
love money, 72, *76*
luck, 154
Luft, Markus, 26, 125–26
Luther, Jon, 136

McDonald's, 31
McGregor Socks, 5
McIntyre, David, 230–31
McKinsey & Company, 12, 19, 149
McMillan, Alan, 29, 33, 78, 109
McQueen, Mark, 110, 121
management style, 32–33, 38, 133–36,
    150
management team, 31, *55*, 98, *102*,
    111–13, 114–15, 116, 125, 134, 148,
    149, 171–72
    audit of, 151–55
manufacturing sector, 9, 77, 96
Maple Leaf Angels, 92, 99
Mar, Suzanne, 83
market
    large, problems, 173–74
    opportunity, business plan, 98
    placement/position, 174–75
    size, 109–11, *109*, 149, 154–55, 204
MaRS Centre, The, 106
MaRS—Business Mentorship and
    Entrepreneurship Program
    (BMEP), 239
MasterCard, 74
mathematical fit. *See* investment/
    investor, fit
mature companies, 6, 9, *11*
    bank financing, 82–83, *83*

mezzanine financing, 8
    (*See also* Legacy companies)
medical devices industry, 94, 96, 101,
    120
medium-size businesses. *See* small and
    medium enterprises (SMEs)
meetings, 56–57, 71, 87, 117, 134, 152,
    184, 232, 233
Menawat, Arun, 120
Mendes, Sam, 50
mentorship, *47*, 62, 214
merchant banks, 81
Merchant, Ismail, 50
mezzanine financing, *7*, *70*, 71, *72*, 166,
    167, 183
MFS Investment Management, 19
Microsoft, 113, 156, 174, 205
Milavasky, Greg, 35–36, 53
milestones, 134–35, 153, 175, *194*, 209–
    10, *209*, 210, *210*, *211*, 214, 231
minority equity, 76
mission statement, 129–30, 133
Mohamed, Wael, 68
money laundering, 15
Moore, Geoffrey, 23
Morse, Eric, 148
Mothersill, Dan, 91
mortgages, 74, 75, 77
motivation, 7, 19, 20, 40, 43, 50, 74,
    135
Motorola, 78
music industry, 14, 19–21, 27, 32, 156
MySpace, 128

Nathan, Rick, 6
National Angel Organization, 91, 96
National Club (Toronto), 127
National Research Council of Canada,
    126
natural resource extraction sector, 75
negotiation tips, 231–32
net profit margin, 178
net worth, 35–36, 73, *109*

networks/networking, 44, *47,* 49, 62, 91,
    93, 95, 122, 124, 154, 199, 216
New York Stock Exchange, 15
niche services/markets, 74, 79, 155, 157
non-compete clause, term sheet, 227–28
non-disclosure, 100, 228
Nortel, *79*
North Job Creation Program, 242
Northrock Capital, 129
no-shop clause, term sheet, 226
Novadeq Technologies, 120

O'Leary, Kevin, 34
Office of Small and Medium Enterprises
    (OSME), 240
Official Community (Web site), 100
old money angels, 94
Oncap (equity firm), 12
Onex, 12, 22, 53, 88
Ontario Centres of Excellence Inc.
    (OCE), 240
Ontario Fuel Cell Innovation Program, 242
Ontario Innovation Demonstration
    Fund, 239
Ontario Premier's Catalyst Award, 241
Ontario Scientific Research and
    Experimental Development
    Expenditures (SR&ED), 240
Ontario Teachers' Pension Plan, 85
Open Text, 9
operating processes, *28,* 31, *47*
operational risk, 119–20
operations budgets, 212
opportunists, 26, 231
Orser, Barbara, 124
outsourcing, 208
    risk, 120
owner-angel relationship, 92, 93, 94,
    98–99
owner–banker relationship, 50, 74, 81,
    82–83
owner-controlled (business stage), *28,*
    31–32

owner–investor relationship, 18–19,
    29, 42, 48–49, 50, 53, 56, 213–14,
    232–33
and mutual respect, 62–64
    (*See also* owner and specific investor;
        personal control)
owner-venture capitalist relationship,
    98–99, 106–7, 110, 117

partnership percentages, 98–99
passion, 9, 19, 26, 27, 50, 56, 149, 150,
    200, 234
patents, 9, 30, 157, 207, 230–31
patient capital, 8, 45, 62, 75–76
Pausch, Randy, 61
PayPal, 79, 113–14
Pender Management, 119
pension funds, 77, 85
personal control, 36, 37–38, 49, 56
personal risk, lack of, 121
PEST threats, 204
Peters, Tom, 107
Peterson, Pete, 51
philanthropy, 94, 114
phone etiquette, 116–17
pitches. *See* elevator pitch; presentations;
    quick business pitch
Pixstream, 114
Pfizer, 78, *197*
Pixar, 201
planning, 117, 131–33, *132,* 143, 149
Plows, Peter, 83
political activity, 208
Porter Airlines, 9, 75, 76
positive leadership style, 135
post-money valuation, 99
potential future earnings, 45, 50,
    58–59
PowerPoint, *28,* 34, 161, 191, *191–94,*
    196, 197
Pozen, Robert, 19, 234
pre-money valuation, 92, 99
presentations, *28,* 34, 71, 121–22, 144–58

barriers/risks, 206–8, *206*
competition, 205–6
components of, 161–62
elevator pitch, 197–98, 200–1, *201*
executive summary, 198–99, *198*
financial statements, 211–13, *213*
and first impressions, 194
front page, *196*, 197
go-to-market strategy, 208–9, *209*
language, 202
and management style, 195
market, 204–5, *204, 205*
milestones, 209–10, *209, 210, 211*
mistakes, 213–17
need for product/service, 199–200
preparing for, 215
product, 202–203, *202*
proposition, 200–2
questions, 148–62, 195–96
recapping highlights, 212–13, *213*
revenue model, 203–4, *203*
supporting data, 216
tag lines, *197*
(*See also* investment proposal;
  PowerPoint)
Primaxis Technology Ventures Inc., 106
privacy legislation, 120
private equity
  attracting, 9, 23–27, 29, 31, 33–34,
    67–68, 95–97, 108–13, 116–19
  vs. bank loans, 45, 50, 54, 56, 59,
    83–85
  benefits of, 8–9, 19–21, 25, 27, 35, *47*,
    49–50, 51, 52–53
  boom, 22
  case study, 41–46
  choosing, 36–39
  defined, 5
  firms, 12, 16, 18
  negotiations, 56–57 (*See also*
    presentations)
  priorities, 232–33, *233*
  process, 7–8

profile, *11*
vs. public money, 14, 86–87
readiness for, 47–50
risk and. *See* risk
role of, 17 18, 59–60
and taking public to private, 87–88
types of investment, 6–7, *7, 69*
and unscrupulous investors, 231
value-add list, 46, *47*
vs. venture capital, 68
Private Equity Canada 2006 survey, 12
private equity investors—issues, 50–51
  checklist, *55*
  motivated board, 51–52
  risk recognition, 53–54
  skills recognition, 52–43
private equity investors, profile of, 48–49
private financing vs. public financing,
  86–87, *86*
product (business stage), *28*, 29–31,
  33–34
product-focused leadership, 57
products/services
  compensation for, 30, 31
  investor question, *55*
professional funds/investors, 18
  expectations of, 107–8
profiteers, 26
projected income statements,
  182 83
proof of the concept, 161–62, 167, 173
prospectus, 86, 230
Purple Cow (Godin), 173

quarterly earnings focus, 13–14, 15–16,
  17, 26, 52
quarterly reports, 87
quasi-equity participation, 76
quick business pitch (15 minutes),
  192–94

R&D, 14, 15, 108
ratios, 177, 180, 182

readiness for funding, 102–4, *103*
    questions, 184–86
real estate, 75
recapitalization, 17, *72*
receipts, 179
Red Hat, 94
Redback, *79*
rejection, 32, 33, 34, 36, 60–61, 68, 126, 145, 166
relative prices, 174
replacement/replenishment capital, *7, 69*
reporting capabilities, 51, 83
reputation, *11*, 121, 123, 150
Research in Motion (RIM), 9, 73, 113, 175, 203, 230–31
reserve takeover (RTO), 86
resumes, 116, 117, 151, 172, 215
retail sector, 19–20, 75
retired executives, angels, 93–94
retirement, 22, 23, 35, 42, 208
Return on Investment (ROI), 58–59, 62, 97, 157–58, 174
revenue model, 176–77, 203–4, *203*
Richard Ivey School of Business, 148, 234
Rieckleman, Ed, 12, 37
Rifkin, Jeremy, 54
risk
    angels and, 93, 96
    banks and, 82, 83
    company owner and, 61
    and financial options, *11*
    industry intensity, 110–11
    and market size, 110–11
    personal, lack of, 120
    and presentation, 206–8, *207*
    and private equity investor, 37, 38–39, 48, 53–54, 62, 63, 71, *72*
    security, 120
    strategic, 119
    venture capitalists and, 106, 119–21, 126
risk management, 17, 35, 119–21

risk-return ratio, 167
RJR Nabisco, 11
Roddick, Anita, 33, 128
Rogers, 78, 156
Room with a View (film), 50
Roy, Tom, 51
Royal Bank Technology Banking Group, 83
Roynat Capital, 26, 51, 81, 125
RRSPs, 74
Rubenstein, David, 6
Rydium Canada, 120

sales-focused entrepreneurship, 36
Sandvine (co.), 111–12, 114, 115
Sarbanes-Oxley, 15, 137
SARS, 119–20
Saxx Apparel Ltd., 97–98, 99
Schwartz, Jerry, 12, 22, 53
Schwarzman, Stephen, 15
search engine industry, 97
Seattle Coffee Company, 160–61
Securities Commissions, 230
security risk, 120
seed funds, 6, *7*, 68, *69, 70*, 71, 72, *72*, 73–75
    types, 100–1
Segal, Rick, 78–79, 105, 123, 227
self-knowledge, 48, 125–26
Seminerio, John, 17–18, 22
sensitivity analysis, *165*, 183–84
Sequoia (firm), 114
7 Habits of Highly Effective People, The (Covey), 144
Shopping Channel, The, *79*
Shore, Penny, 119, 121
Shore Publishing, 119
Silicon Valley, 149, 154
Simon Fraser University, 113
Skype, 128
Slate (magazine), 106
Sleeman Breweries, 9, 75

Sleeman, John, 75
Sleep Country, 9
small and medium enterprises, (SMEs),
    10, 12, 53, 126, 174
Smith, Adam, 48, 63
Social Capital, 94
software industry, 12–13, 101, 157, 173
Somerset Entertainment, 19–21, 80
Sony Music, 156
Sopik, Victoria, 61
South America, 44, 199
specialist knowledge, 29–30
Spintex, 9
spreadsheets, 13, 183, 212
SRED (Scientific Research &
    Experimental Development Tax
    Credit), 77, 241
Starbucks, 160–61
Stephenson, Carol, 234
stock market, 4, 5, 8, 12, 14, 18, 27, 76,
    81
    scrutiny of, 14–15, 21
    short-term outlook of, 15–16
    (See also IPO)
strategic alliances, 207
strategic depth, 134 (See also vision)
strategic risk, 119
stress, 53, 72, 115, 144–45
subordinated debt, 166
succession planning, 28, 29, 46, 47, 171
supply chains, 45–46, 47, 49, 163
Sustainable Development Technology
    Canada, 241
sustainability, 96, 156–57
SWOT analysis, 204

tag lines, 197, 197
talent recruitment, 43, 44, 47, 53
tax credit programs, 74, 241
Teacher's Pension Fund, 11
teamwork, 35, 37, 38, 43–44, 58, 59, 61
    (See also management team)
tech boom, 12

Tech Capital Partners, 111
Technology Industries Association, 77
Technology Partnership Canada, 241
technology sector, 176–18, 77, 78, 94, 96,
    116, 137, 154
telecommunications sector, 9, 128, 203
Telus, 79, 156
tenacity, 112, 113
term sheet, 232
    negotiating, 225–28
terrorists, 15
Third Brigade, 68
Thomas Lee Partners, 136
Thomson Financial, 56
Tim Hortons, 158, 197
Toronto Stock Exchange (TSE), 75,
    85–86
Torquest Partners, 56
Torstar, 11
Townsend, Nathalie, 129
Toys-R-Us, 11
Treurnicht, Ilse, 107, 117, 124
True North Investors, 37
Trump, Donald, 29

United States
    dot.com bubble, 104
    privacy law, 120
    venture capital/seed start-up, 102
University of Waterloo, 17
unsystematic risk, 208
Upper Canada beer, 9
use of proceeds, 55, 98, 170, 170

valuation, 129–39, 216–17, 219–20
    EBITDA multiple, 223, 223
    by future earnings, 39–40, 40, 47, 59,
        99, 104, 115–16, 160
    methods, 222–25, 223
    strategic vs. financial, 158–60, 159
value
    defined, 129, 158
    destroyer of, 129, 134

value (*continued*)
  intellectual, 222
  investor, 220–25
  and timing, 159
value-creation plans, 129, 231
VanderPlaat, Peter, 119–20
Vantrix, 9
VenGrowth Capital Management Inc.,
    59, 111, 113, 116,
    136–37
venture capitalists (VCs), 6, 8, *11*, 27, 32,
    33, 69, *70*, 71, *72*
  and alumni phenomena, 113–15
  and business valuation, 115–16
  approach to investing, *118*
  attracting, 116–19
  challenges to, 108–13
  characteristics of, 106–7
  compared with angels, 98–99
  compared with banks, 75, 83–84
  expectations of, 107–8
  and female entrepreneurs, 124–25
  and first-stage financing, 77–79, *79*,
    101
  and high-growth companies, 75–76
  owner relationship, 98–99, 106–7,
    110, 117
  and private equity, 68
  and readiness for funding, 101–3, *102*
  researching, 122
  and risk, 106, 119–21, 126
  screening process, 117

and sources of capital, 85
Venture Law Associates, 226
Ventures West Capital, 234
VISA, 74
vision, 4, 18, 22, 38, 39, 50, 52, 59, 63, 96,
    107, 112, 113, 117, 128, 133, 134,
    149, 153, 199, 233–34
Volker, Mike, 113

Waitman, Michael, 111–12, 114–15
Wall Street (film), 71
warrants, *84*
Washington, George, 111–12
Wasserman, Noam, 33, 110
Watson, Brian, 96
Wealth of Nations, The (Smith), 48
Web companies, 96, 100
Wellington Capital, 81
Wellington Financial, 121
Westjet, tag line, *197*
Williams, Suzanne Dingwall, 226
wisdom, 49, 144, 147
women entrepreneurs, 124–25
Women's Angel Club (Texas), 94
Woodbridge (co.), 11
WUTIF Capital, 113

Yahoo! Inc., 31, 79, *79*
Yaletown and Magellan Angel Partners,
    17–18
Young, Bob, 94
YouTube, 114